RECONSTRUCTING MULTIETHNIC SOCIETIES:
THE CASE OF BOSNIA-HERZEGOVINA

Institute for Strengthening Democracy
Konjic (Bosnia-Herzegovina)

Reconstructing Multiethnic Societies: The Case of Bosnia-Herzegovina

Edited by

DŽEMAL SOKOLOVIĆ
University of Bergen, Norway

FLORIAN BIEBER
Central European University, Hungary

LONDON AND NEW YORK

First published 2001 by Ashgate Publishing

Reissued 2018 by Routledge
2 Park Square, Milton Park, Abingdon, Oxon OX14 4RN
711 Third Avenue, New York, NY 10017, USA

Routledge is an imprint of the Taylor & Francis Group, an informa business

Copyright © Džemal Sokolović and Florian Bieber 2001
Ch.　Two　© Daniel Kofman
　　　Three © Fionnuala Ni Aolain

All rights reserved. No part of this book may be reprinted or reproduced or utilised in any form or by any electronic, mechanical, or other means, now known or hereafter invented, including photocopying and recording, or in any information storage or retrieval system, without permission in writing from the publishers.

Notice:
Product or corporate names may be trademarks or registered trademarks, and are used only for identification and explanation without intent to infringe.

Publisher's Note
The publisher has gone to great lengths to ensure the quality of this reprint but points out that some imperfections in the original copies may be apparent.

Disclaimer
The publisher has made every effort to trace copyright holders and welcomes correspondence from those they have been unable to contact.

A Library of Congress record exists under LC control number: 00135338

ISBN 13: 978-1-138-63648-4 (hbk)
ISBN 13: 978-1-138-63649-1 (pbk)
ISBN 13: 978-1-315-20381-2 (ebk)

Contents

List of Contributors vii
Acknowledgments ix

Introduction
Florian Bieber 1

PART I: CHALLENGES FOR MULTIETHNIC STATES

1. The Injustice of Procedural Democracy
   Thomas William Simon 11

2. Self-determination in a Multiethnic State:
   Bosnians, Bosniaks, Croats and Serbs
   Daniel Kofman 31

3. The Fractured Soul of the Dayton Peace Agreement:
   A Legal Analysis
   Fionnuala Ni Aolain 63

4. Social Reconstruction and Moral Restoration
   Džemal Sokolović 95

5. The Challenge of Democracy in Divided Societies:
   Lessons from Bosnia—Challenges for Kosovo
   Florian Bieber 109

6. Lessons from the Belgian Constitution
   for Multiethnic Societies
   Richard Lewis 123

7   The Building of Civil Society by "Core" Europe?
    Ariyoshi Ogawa   135

PART II: RECONSTRUCTING MULTIETHNIC BOSNIA

8   How a Quota Borda System of Elections
    may Facilitate Reconciliation
    Peter Emerson   147

9   Journalism in Post-Dayton Bosnia:
    How to Make the Media More Responsible
    Dušan Babić   157

10 Reclaiming Kozarac: Accompanying Returning Refugees
    Margaret Vandiver   167

11 Women in Between: "Where do I belong?"
    Enida Delalić   185

12 Restructuring Regions: The Case of Croatia
    Slobodan Bjelajac   197

Bibliography   209

List of Contributors

Dušan Babić is a Human Rights lawyer, media researcher and analyst, mostly focusing on press freedom abuses and their investigation and reporting. He is currently head of the Independent Media Commission's Regional Office in Mostar.

Florian Bieber is an instructor at the Department for International Relations and European Studies at the Central European University in Budapest and co-editor of *Southeast European Politics*. His publications include *Bosnien-Herzegowina und Libanon im Vergleich, Historische Entwicklung und Politisches System vor dem Bürgerkrieg* [Bosnia-Herzegovina and Lebanon in Comparison. Historical Development and the Political System Before the Civil War], Sinzheim: Pro Universitate Verlag, 1999.

Slobodan Bjelajac is an assistant professor at the University of Split in the Faculty of Natural Sciences and Education. His publications include "Što se slućuva vo prvite godini na tranzicijata?" [What is Happening in the First Years of Transition?], in *Socijalnata politika vo periodot na tranzicija* [Social Policy in the Period of Transition], Skopje: Dialogue, 1995.

Enida Delalić is a Ph.D. candidate at the Johann Wolfgang Goethe University Frankfurt, Germany. She has been working with refugee women in Germany and directed the film *Jenseits der Flucht oder Disseits der Hoffnung* [Beyond the escape or on this side of hope].

Peter Emerson is the director of the de Borda Institute, Belfast, Northern Ireland. He is the author of two books on electoral systems.

Daniel Kofman is Stipendiary Lecturer in Philosophy at Balliol College, Oxford University. He has also taught at many other colleges at Oxford University, and has published articles on self-determination, nationalism, as well as the break up of Yugoslavia.

Richard Lewis is Principal Administrator at Directorate General for Justice and Home Affairs of the European Commission. He has been a Visiting Fellow in Human Rights, University of Essex. He is the author of "What is European security?" in *Aspects of Statehood and Institutionalism in Contemporary Europe*, (ed.) Malcolm D. Evans, Aldershot & Brookfield:

Dartmouth, 1997 and "The Example of Belgium," *Occasional Paper*, Duke University, 1996.

Fionnuala Ni Aolain is Professor of Law at the University of Ulster, Northern Ireland and Visiting-Professor at Columbia University in New York. Previously she was an Assistant-Professor of Law at the Hebrew University of Jerusalem, Associate-in-Law at Columbia Law School in New York and Visiting Scholar at Harvard Law School. In 1996, she was a Special Representative of the Prosecutor of the International Criminal Tribunal for the Former Yugoslavia (ICTY), observing domestic war crimes trials in Bosnia. She has recently published *The Politics of Force – Conflict Management and State Violence in Northern Ireland*, Dublin: Blackstaff Press, 2000.

Ariyoshi Ogawa is Associate Professor of European Politics, Department of Law, Chiba University, Japan. He has been a Visiting Research Fellow at Department of Comparative Politics, University of Bergen. His publications include *EU Shokoku* [The Politics and the History of the EU Countries], Tokyo: Jiyu Kokuminsha, 1999.

Thomas William Simon is Professor at Illinois State University in the Department of Philosophy. He has been a Fellow at the Harvard Law School. His publications include *Laws and Philosophies: An Introduction*. New York: McGraw Hill, (forthcoming); "Groups: Rights, Wrongs, and Culture," *Groups and Group Rights*. (ed.) Christine Sistare, Larry May, Leslie Francis, Lawrence: University of Kansas Press, 2000; "Minorities in International Law," *Canadian Journal of Law & Jurisprudence* (July 1997), pp. 1-13.

Džemal Sokolović is a Visiting Professor at the Institute for Comparative Politics at the University of Bergen, Norway. He previously taught at the Universities of Ljubljana, Heidelberg, Graz, and before the war in Bosnia at the University of Sarajevo. He has published numerous articles and books in English, Bosnian and Norwegian on Bosnia and the problems of multiethnic states, among them *Nacija protiv Naroda* [Nation vs. People], Oslo: Sypress Forlag, 1997.

Margaret Vandiver is an Associate Professor at the Department of Criminology and Criminal Justice, University of Memphis. She is also a research associate on *The Genocide Research Project*. She is the guest editor with L.E. Day and J. McIllwain for the special 2000 issue of *Crime, Law and Social Change: An International Journal*.

Acknowledgments

This book, like many others, is the product of a group of people. Unlike many others, it has resulted from the work of many more people than those listed as contributors and, most likely, it is more their product than our own. Moreover, this book is an outcome of the tragic circumstances from which Bosnia and the Balkans are only slowly emerging. For this reason our acknowledgments are also unusual.

The articles in this volume were originally presented at the international seminar "Democracy and Human Rights in Multi-ethnic Societies," organized by the Institute for Strengthening Democracy Konjic, Bosnia and Herzegovina, in 1998 and 1999. The Institute was established three years ago in Konjic, a symbolic and controversial city in many respects. It was the site of crimes committed by Bosniaks against Serbs, but it was also the first place in Bosnia recognized by the international community as an 'open city,' that is, a town open to all returnees regardless of their ethnic or religious background. Konjic still boasts all three religions: Catholicism, Islam and the Orthodox Church. The last Bogumil (adherent of the heretical medieval Bosnian Christian Church) family in Bosnia lived here and converted to Islam in 1875, just three years before the Habsburgs replaced the Ottomans.

Within this context, the Institute undertook to organize a seminar in Konjic on democracy and human rights in multi-ethnic societies. In 1998 the seminar gathered participants from seven countries; in 1999 scholars from 16 countries took part; and representatives of more than 30 countries have announced their participation in the 2000 seminar. We would like to acknowledge all the contributors as well as the many other academics, journalists, practitioners and citizens of Konjic and Bosnia who brought their talks and discussions to our gatherings.

This book contains a selection of the presentations from the first and second seminars. It offers both theoretical and practical discussions on the challenges of reconstructing a multi-ethnic state destroyed by war. These challenges are enormous. The complexities of institutionalizing diversity in a democracy are augmented by the difficulties involved in the return of refugees and the creation of diverse and open media. Authors from Bosnia-

Herzegovina, the rest of Europe and North America demonstrate in these essays that there is no easy strategy for these issues—and that complexity, like diversity, should be recognized as a challenge, not as a weakness.

The Institute would not have been able to organize this annual event without the support of our sponsors: the Ministry of Foreign Affairs of Norway, Oslo; Institusjonen Fritt Ord, Oslo; the Norwegian Helsinki Committee, Oslo; the University of Bergen, Bergen; the Open Society Fund, Sarajevo; the OSCE Mission to Bosnia, Sarajevo; Sund kommune, Sund, Norway and Konjic municipality, Bosnia. Without their help we would not be able to carry on our devotion to democracy and human rights in multi-ethnic societies. Finally, we would like to thank Samantha Chaitkin for her thorough editorial work on this publication.

Džemal Sokolović　　　　　　　　　　　　　　　　　Florian Bieber
Bergen – Konjic　　　　　　　　　　　　　　　　　　Budapest

Introduction
FLORIAN BIEBER

Bosnia-Herzegovina's three and a half year war dominated global headlines in the first half of the 1990s. Since the Dayton Peace Accords and the presence of international peacekeepers in the country, Bosnia has disappeared from the headlines—with the exception of occasional reports on the arrests of war criminals and the ongoing tenure of nationalist political leaders, reaffirmed by elections. However, Bosnia has been the site of a paradigmatic experiment in reconstructing a multiethnic society with the financial and logistical support of the 'international community.' The war and the mixed record of reconstruction have triggered further scholarly debate on the viability of multiethnic states in general. This volume examines this undertaking at a variety of angles and seeks to highlight challenges to the endeavor.

In his theoretical discussion, Thomas Simon highlights a basic dichotomy that renders democratization in multiethnic states difficult: procedural vs. substantive democracy. The formal institutions of democracy can cause a system of minority oppression: "As a matter of fact, much of what passes for the usual democratic rules either does nothing about ethnic exclusion or actually fosters it."[1] In multiethnic states where the internal ethnic divisions are relatively stable (yet not static) and minorities have little chance of becoming a majority, unless they destroy the state as such, a more complex understanding of democracy is required. As Simon elucidates, this more substantive approach to democracy is not only necessary in multiethnic states, but in democracies in general, for securing the existence of democratic institutions when they come under threat.

The war in Bosnia, like most ethnic conflicts, has been closely intertwined with the question of self-determination. Daniel Kofman explores different interpretations of self-determination with regard to Bosnia and its national groups. Kofman compares the disintegration of Yugoslavia and the right to self-determination of the republics with the right to self-determination claimed by the Bosnian Serb and Croat political leadership. As there is a strong asymmetry between both claims, the author concludes that the central state in Bosnia should be strengthened in relationship to its entities.[2]

The ambiguities in terms of multiethnic democracy and self-determination have never been embodied more clearly than in the Dayton Peace Accords. The accords, which include the current Bosnian constitution, were primarily a compromise negotiated by the international community to end the war. However, they have influenced the post-war development and in many ways delayed the success of Bosnian reconstruction. Fionnuala Ni Aolain offers a comprehensive legal analysis of the treaty and its implementation since 1995. She maintains that despite its flaws, Dayton provides a framework for reintegrating Bosnia-Herzegovina. As such, however, the document should not be perceived as static, but must instead display greater flexibility if long-term integration and democracy are to be achieved.

In chapter four, Džemal Sokolović makes a case for the transformation of Bosnia-Herzegovina into an outright protectorate which would allow for a clearer break with the wartime past. The prominence of some members of the Bosnian Serb elite who participated, by word and/or by deed, in 'ethnic cleansing,' serves to illustrate this point. A similar proposal has also been made recently by the influential International Crisis Group, which argued that "a protectorate could implement rapid refugee returns, remove obstructionist officials, institute the rule of law, restructure communist-era economic and political structures, and prepare Bosnia and Herzegovina for entry into the Council of Europe and the European Union."[3] While this kind of mechanism reminds one not only of colonial rule, but also of the Austro-Hungarian administration of Bosnia-Herzegovina between 1878 and 1914/18, the failure of several principal ambitions of the Dayton Peace Accord five years after its signing has nonetheless made this alternative more attractive. In recent years, the international administration has already been playing a more assertive role, culminating in the ouster of Republika Srpska president Nikola Poplašen in March 1999.[4] On the other hand, the current High Representative Wolfgang Petritsch has emphasized the need to empower the population of Bosnia, because "our presence here has inadvertently absolved them [politicians] of their responsibilities as democratically elected leaders."[5] Including the population in the decision-making process, while insuring that this process is constructive and democratic, has become a lasting challenge to which no clear answer has yet been found.[6]

Unlike in Bosnia, the war in Kosovo came to an end in June 1999 with the complete occupation of the province by NATO and the establishment of a full-fledged protectorate. While the international community has learned some lessons from Bosnia, Florian Bieber argues that the peace proposals forwarded in Bosnia and Kosovo—the Dayton and Rambouillet agreements, respectively—nonetheless amount to hodgepodges with weak democratic credentials. Despite the fact that these peace agreements[7] initially emerged to end ethnic conflict (at least in the perceptions of their authors), the entire political systems they establish are framed in 'ethnic' terms, and pay insufficient attention to democratization and individual rights.[8] The dangers reach far beyond Bosnia and Kosovo, as Will Kymlicka points out:

> ...[T]he failure to develop a consistent and principled approach to minority rights may have even greater costs in the newly emerging democracies. At present, the fate of ethnic and national groups around the world is in the hand of xenophobic nationalists, religious extremists, and military dictators. If liberalism is to have any chance of taking hold in these countries, it must explicitly address the needs and aspirations of ethnic and national minorities.[9]

In an attempt to contextualize Bosnia in the framework of other multiethnic democracies, in chapter six Richard Lewis explores the applicability of the 'Belgian model' for Bosnia. Although Belgium has often been viewed as one of the less successful states of Western Europe, it has successfully negotiated differences between the two large national groups—Walloons and Flemings—and created a political system that remains inclusive and flexible. To apply the Belgium system to Bosnia, one would have to separate institutional features of this system from informal Belgian agreements and traditions, an equivalent of which would also need to be fostered in Bosnia contemporaneously with building new institutions. The key institutional element of the Belgian system is a combination of cultural and territorial autonomy. Units of cultural autonomy are based on the national groups, while the federal units are purely regional and not exclusive to a single group. At the same time, the Federal government is required to incorporate the groups' interests. This system of checks and balances prohibits any single group from imposing its program on others. How to establish such a complex system without creating political institutions incapable of taking joint decisions remains unresolved given that political elites in Bosnia have often been unwilling to cooperate.[10]

Ariyoshi Ogawa shifts the focus from institutions and the political system itself to civil society as a mediator between the political sphere and the general population. The concept of civil society, since receiving popular coinage in the past two decades, has come to assign descriptive and normative dimensions to societies or subgroups within the larger society. Cohen and Arato have defined civil society as "a sphere of social interaction between the economy and the state, composed above all of the intimate sphere..., the sphere of associations..., social movements, and forms of public communication. [It] is created through forms of self-constitution and self-mobilization. It is institutionalized and generalized through laws, especially subjective rights, that stabilize social differentiation."[11] As such, it is of great significance in mitigating ethnic divides and allowing for inter-ethnic communication beyond the political elite. In Bosnia, as elsewhere in Southeastern Europe, however, the non-governmental sectors have emerged largely with the support and under the guidance of Western Europe and the United States. It thus frequently reflects more the desires and ideals of financial donors and experts outside the country than the needs of the population.[12] Ogawa alerts us to this gap, which needs to be bridged in order to effect long-term peace building in multiethnic societies.[13]

The reconstruction of a multiethnic state such as Bosnia-Herzegovina poses a number of practical challenges, especially when this reconstruction coincides with the establishment of democratic institutions where they were previously lacking, and with reforms of a formerly socialist economy. In Bosnia the post-war years have so far brought only slow and hesitant progress in all major spheres, and the success of the experiment of reconstructing Bosnia as a multiethnic society has not yet been secured. Besides the difficulties associated with the nature of the political institutions established (or rather confirmed) by the Dayton Peace Accords, a number of formidable challenges remain, including the return of refugees, the role of the media and the electoral process.

The war in Bosnia was started by parties that had been democratically elected to parliament and claimed to represent their respective national communities. While it would be simplistic to claim that the war was started or caused by the 1990 elections, they provided the necessary legitimacy and power to wage war between 1992 and 1995. In the post-war period, the international community has made nearly annual attempts to organize free and fair elections in order to lend the peace-building process the necessary democratic legitimacy, while at the same time making no secret of its dislike for the nationalists who have continued to win most elections since 1995.[14] Some observers have argued that this contradiction undermines democracy in Bosnia and leads the international administration to assume quasi-dictatorial powers.[15] Peter Emerson, on the other hand, argues that the electoral systems used before and after the war have marginalized popular non-nationalist political forces and prevented the emergence of moderate political parties. He argues for an alternative electoral system based on a method first proposed by Jean-Charles de Borda in 1770 for the election of members into the French Academy of Sciences. This system allows voters to rank candidates with points, establishing as the winner the candidate who receives the greatest number of points. This system, though somewhat more complicated than conventional voting systems, allows voters not only to vote for, but actually to rank the candidates of an election, encouraging the election of more broadly acceptable politicians.[16]

Next to elections and the political parties they have legitimized, the media has played a very problematic role in both pre- and post-war Bosnia. The principle of complete freedom of speech has sometimes lead to the misuse of hate speech and the propagation of extreme nationalism and racism in the media.[17] In his article, Dušan Babić discusses the difficulties of developing a viable media scene in Bosnia, which must shed its Communist-era restraints, while refraining from inciting ethnic violence, as many news outlets did during the war. Babić also examines other limitations to the media in Bosnia, including the inadequate reach of the print media and the challenge to meet overall professional standards.

One group of Bosnian citizens has been particularly hard hit by the war and continues to feel its effects: refugees. Despite the proclaimed objective in the Dayton Accords of returning refugees to their homes, success has been meager so far. Over a million Bosnians are still displaced within the country or outside (mostly in Yugoslavia, Croatia and Western Europe) with only slim prospects of returning.[18] Margaret Vandiver and Enida Delalić offer two different perspectives on the status of Bosnian refugees.

Margaret Vandiver examines the general obstacles for refugee returns to areas where the refugees would constitute a national minority. She then turns to the particular case of Kozarac, in Northwestern Bosnia, and explores the attempts of refugees to return. The town was the scene of violent 'ethnic cleansing' in an early phase of the war and today remains within the Republika Srpska. Notwithstanding the initial hostilities toward returning refugees in the immediate post-war years, since 1998 a significant number have returned to Kozarac to begin reconstructing their community, still an exception in Bosnia.

As the return to newly homogenized areas has been the exception rather than the rule in Bosnia, Enida Delalić focuses on the experiences of refugees, especially women, abroad. Women have been particularly victimized by the war in Bosnia and by their fate as refugees.[19] Delalić describes the different phases of the experience, emphasizing hope as a resource for overcoming the trauma of being a refugee.

The final contribution, by Slobodan Bjelajac, shifts our attention from Bosnia to neighboring Croatia to highlight the gerrymandering that authoritarian and nationalist regimes engage in to accommodate their political objectives. While political and scholarly attention most commonly focuses on the central authorities, the regions remain neglected. The contrast between the creation of a highly decentralized Bosnian-Croat Federation, with its ten cantons, alongside the strictly centralized Republika

Srpska, is a stark reminder of how regional organization reflects ethnic politics. Bjelajac draws our attention, furthermore, to the lasting effects that nationalist governments can have on state structures, sometimes surpassing even their own terms in power. While the change of regime in Croatia has considerably altered Croat-Bosnian relations, some of the structures imposed by the previous regime may continue to prove obstructive, both for the reintegration of Bosnia and for the cooperation of its regions with Croatia.

Beyond the challenges described in this volume, others remain of great significance if Bosnia as a country and as a society is to become a success. Many of these are problems that also affect other countries in Southeastern Europe in their processes of transition from socialist to democratic, market-oriented societies. They include economic development and privatization, both of which have been of limited success so far. Furthermore, education, social protection and poverty remain pressing issues which will need to be addressed in order for long-term stabilization to be achieved in Bosnia-Herzegovina.

The reconstruction of a war-ravaged society like Bosnia is an enormous endeavor that so far lacks a blueprint for success. This book does not seek to offer the impossible. It does, however, make a case for a multiethnic Bosnia and for the reconstruction of multiethnic states in general. It does so by addressing both theoretical and practical challenges and opportunities. In a world where the vast majority of states are multiethnic, we have to (re)conceptualize interethnic relations and the possibilities for establishing thriving democracies within multiethnic realities.

Notes

1. Donald Horowitz, "Democracy in Divided Societies," in *Journal of Democracy* 4, no. 4 (October 1993), p. 28 (18–38).
2. On this topic see Omer Ibrahimbegić, *Supremacy of Bosnia and Herzegovina over its Entities*, 2nd revised edition (Sarajevo: Vijeće Kongresa bošnjačkih intelekualaca, 1999).
3. International Crisis Group, "Is Dayton Failing? Bosnia Four Years After the Peace Agreement," (October 28, 1999), available at: http://www.crisisweb.org/projects/bosnia/reports/bh51main.htm.
4. As early as 1996, Heinrich Schneider remarked that Bosnia is not a truly sovereign state, since it is not based on the will of the constituent peoples, but on the will of the international community and 'moderate' forces within. Heinrich Schneider, "*Friede für Bosnien-Herzegowina? Das Vertragswerk von Dayton als Herausforderung für Europa*," in *Integration* 19, no. 1 (1996), p. 11.
5. Wolfgang Petritsch, "The Future of Bosnia lies with its People," in *Wall Street Journal (Europe)*, September 17, 1999.

6   See for example the controversies surrounding the suggestion by Haris Silajdžić (one of the 'authors' of Dayton and president of the Party for Bosnia-Herzegovina, which oscillates between government and opposition) to rewrite the Dayton agreement, see the interview with Silajdžić in *Dani*, April 14, 2000. See also Jos de la Haye, *"Les élections municipales peuvent-elles rompre le pouvoir informel des partis nationalistes?"* Rapport 1/2000, University of Leuven, Belgium. Center for Peace Research, Department of Political Sciences.
7   While Dayton has been legally in effect since 1995, Rambouillet is only referred to in UN Security Council Resolution 1244 (Article 11), which established the international administration of the province: It is the goal of the UN to promote "the establishment, pending a final settlement, of substantial autonomy and self-government in Kosovo, taking full account... of the Rambouillet accords".
8   David Chandler has made a similar comparison between Bosnia and Kosovo, emphasizing the lack of democracy as a result of the international administration. David Chandler, "The Bosnia Protectorate and the Implications for Kosovo," in *New Left Review*, no. 235 (May/June 1999), pp. 124–134.
9   Will Kymlicka, *Multicultural Citizenship* (Oxford: Oxford University Press, 1995), p. 195.
10 See Florian Bieber, "Consociationalism: Prerequisite or Hurdle for Democratisation in Bosnia? The Case of Belgium as a Possible Example," in *South-East Europe Review* 2, no. 3 (October 1999), pp. 79–94.
11 Jean L. Cohen and Andrew Arato, *Civil Society and Political Theory* (Cambridge, Mass.: MIT Press, 1992), p. ix.
12 See "Sins of the Secular Missionaries," in *The Economist*, January 29, 2000.
13 See Andreas Klinke and Ortwin Renn, "Ethnic Cooperation and Coexistence: International Mediation, International Governance, and Civil Society for Ethnically Plural States," in *Ethnic Conflicts and Civil Society: Proposals for a New Era in Eastern Europe*, eds. Andreas Klinke, Ortwin Renn, and Jean-Paul Lehners (Aldershot: Ashgate, 1997), pp. 269–276; Julie Mertus, "The Liberal State vs. the Nation Soul: Mapping Civil Society Transplants," in *Social & Legal Studies* 8, no. 1 (1999), pp. 121–146.
14 See Paul Shoup, "The Elections in Bosnia and Herzegovina: The End of an Illusion," in *Problems of Post-Communism* 44, no. 1 (January/February 1997), pp. 3–15; Nicholas Wyte, "Bosnian Municipal Election 2000: No Need for Despondency," *CEPS Europa South-East Monitor* 10 (April 2000).
15 See for example Robert Hayden, *Blueprints for a House Divided: The Constitutional Logic of the Yugoslav Conflicts* (Ann Arbor: University of Michigan Press, 1999), pp. 134–139.
16 This alternative electoral system has gained some broader attention recently and is similar to the Australian voting system. See "Democratic Symmetry," *The Economist*, March 4, 2000, p. 97.
17 Jack Snyder and Karen Ballentine, "Nationalism in the Marketplace of Ideas," in *Nationalism and Ethnic Conflict*, ed. Michael E. Brown (Cambridge, Mass. and London: MIT Press, 1997), pp. 61–96.
18 International Crisis Group, "The Balkan Refugee Crisis: Regional and Long-term Perspectives," (June 1, 1999), available at: http://www.crisisweb.org/projects/sbalkans/reports/ba02rep.htm.
19 See Libby Tata Arcel, et al. (eds.), *Psycho-Social Help to War Victims: Women Refugees and Their Families from Bosnia and Herzegovina and Croatia* (Zagreb and Copenhagen: IRCT, 1995).

PART I

CHALLENGES FOR MULTIETHNIC STATES

1 The Injustice of Procedural Democracy*
THOMAS WILLIAM SIMON

In his Gettysburg Address of 1863, Lincoln characterized democracy as "government of the people, by the people, and for the people."[1] The old adage reveals a great deal. Democracy certainly has something to do with the people ruling in some form or another. People favor democracy, but after a general and vague form of agreement comes a perplexing series of questions that generate little consensus in their answers. What constitutes government? Who is to rule whom and for what purpose? Who are the people? What is the relationship between rule of, rule by, and rule for the people?

Of the three components in Lincoln's formulation, "government by" (Rule By) has received the most attention. Democratic theorists focus primarily on procedures. Further, the theorists offer little in the way of prescription or even indictment of the economic or social and political disparity among groups. The following serve as typical examples of the proceduralist position:[2]

> I follow...those who insist that "democracy" is to be understood in procedural terms. That is to say, I reject the notion that one should build into "democracy" any constraints on the content of the outcomes produced, such as substantive equality, respect for human rights, concern for the general welfare, personal liberty or the rule of law.[3]
>
> I regard democracy as a system for making governmental decisions. "Democracy" is to be defined in terms of procedures, not in terms of substantive policy....While there are many legitimate questions to be answered in political philosophy, one good question, certainly, is how the various institutions affecting governmental decision making should be structured.[4]

Giovanni Sartori, a contemporary democratic theorist, speculated that Lincoln thought that "for the people" (Rule For) was a consequence of democracy and not a defining characteristic.[5] In contrast, I take "for the people" as the most important aspect of democracy, as a central concern underlying any definition of democracy, more important than its close counterpart, "rule by the people" (Rule By). "Rule By" refers to a set of procedures that governs political decision making. "Rule For" serves as a shorthand for the substantive value judgments made about justice and injustice. The first represents Procedural Democracy; the second, Substantive Democracy. A global campaign has succeeded in presenting Procedural Democracy as the only version of democracy. It is an injustice that the dominant Procedural Democracy has managed to sever questions of democracy from questions of justice. Democracy must make a commitment to social and economic justice. Democracy only makes sense as a mythology if, in places like Bosnia, it is allowed to operate uncontested in the midst of widespread inequality or massive economic malaise.

It would border on insanity, for example, to insist that the Tutsi minority government in Rwanda institute majority rule after a genocide led by factions of the Hutu majority. The insanity of a majoritarian rule requirement for Rwanda does not make news because few political analysts pay any attention to Rwanda. The absurdities of Procedural Democracy do not fully rise to the surface in the Balkans because it serves as a useful tool for Western policy makers. Procedural democracy provides the international players in the Balkans with an ideal cover. They use it to justify their external inaction and to indict indigenous internal action (or inaction). Foreign economic aid is made contingent on progress on democratic reforms. The outcomes of democratic reforms, in turn, hinge on the implausibility of imposed procedures and the unlikelihood of effective implementation of democratic outcomes. Procedural democracy, then, does not offer one more way to measure success or failure of a nation to develop. Rather, an undue reliance on procedural democracy accomplishes a great deal. It almost guarantees failure; it produces a continuing range of options for Western powers to operate; and it assures a weakened state.

Looking at the social, economic, and political conditions in a society may seem like an obvious consideration in evaluating the democratic character of a country, but the effects of economic well being on democracy, while acknowledged, seldom play a central role in democratic theory or in policy making. Many democratic theorists do not pay sufficient attention to the problems of social and economic injustices. Western policy makers follow suit by treating such matters as economic conditions as secondary to democratic procedures.[6] The U.S. not only separated the democratic from the socio-economic aspects of reconstruction in Bosnia following the Dayton Accords, it also considered elections as primary. Substantive economic considerations continue to take a back seat to procedural concerns.

The critique of procedural democracy undertaken here does not imply the abandonment of the proceduralists' cause and promoting only economic improvement. Many examples, ranging from movements like Jim Jones's People's Temple to states like China, illustrate the harmful consequences that follow when visions of social and economic justice swamp concerns for internal democratic procedures. I include Jonestown along side China to underscore another point. Democratic theory and policy should not only address state-level organizational structures. The democratic character of meta state-level structures is a critical issue. How democratic were the Dayton Accords, which have framed and continue to frame every major change undertaken in Bosnia? In addition, the organizational parts within a state are also important. While the nation-state encompasses and conditions the other forms of organization within it, the democratic nature of the parts also can positively infect the democratic character of the whole. The democratic character of civic groups, social associations, and political organizations influence the democratic character of larger structures. Minimally, questions regarding democracy should not be automatically excluded from discussions about any level, meta or local, of organization.

Procedural Democracy: The Indeterminacy Problem

If procedural democracy contains serious conceptual problems, then a foundational critique should become a key item on the contestation-of-democracy agenda. The phrase "procedural democracy" generally is shorthand for certain kinds of procedures and institutional structures, which typically include voting, majority rule, representation, a constitution, separation of powers, and checks and balances. Appealing to one or more of these items characterizes a proceduralist approach to democracy. Procedural democracy confronts three major conceptual problems: consent to the procedures, indeterminacy among the acceptable democratic procedures, and justifications for specific procedures. Let us address the last two difficulties. Analysts regard democracy in the United States as consisting of a set of procedures that includes the following: voting in elections, majority rule limited by minority rights, representative government, constitutional guarantees of individual and civil liberties, and separation of powers with judicial review.[7] Disagreements over what qualifies as a member of this set of procedures are widespread. Should judicial review make up one of the elements of a democratic regime or does judicial review hinder the development of a democracy? Should the separation of powers be deleted from the list or does it constitute an essential ingredient of democracy? Should other devices, such as proportional representation, take their place on the list?

Let us call the difficulties associated with the changeability of the elements on the procedure list "the indeterminacy problem." Proceduralists need a standard for choosing one set of procedures over another. Otherwise, the democratic devices employed by proceduralists function without any fixed moorings. In other words, the choice of mechanisms remains in flux. No one set of procedures qualifies as necessary or sufficient (or some combination of these) for democracy. The democratic user or consumer can expand or contract the list of procedures almost at will. No theoretical argument about the procedures themselves will provide compelling reasons for choosing one procedure or one set of procedures over any others. To choose from the array of candidate procedures, proceduralists must make substantive value judgments about justice. However, proceduralists want to keep out substantive judgments.[8] In the proceduralist's world, procedures trump considerations of substantive results. Procedures operate on the neutral ground of fairness. Above all, proceduralists would refuse to evaluate procedures according to how well they measured up to substantive goals, such as promoting the welfare of the least advantaged. Supposedly, promoting substantive values under the guise of democracy subverts democracy by imposing a value system not chosen by democratic means.

One way to undermine the proceduralist argument is to conjure up a picture of democracy, that meets proceduralist's intuitions but ultimately violates moral intuitions. Even the proceduralist would admit that procedures do not serve as guarantees and that some procedures can yield very troubling results. Even if the proceduralist admits that abhorrent consequences can flow from democratic procedures, he or she would maintain that some set of procedures could patch up the disastrous consequences from another set of procedures.

The transition from the Weimar Republic to the Third Reich in Germany serves as a good test for the proceduralist's position. The Nazi party had considerable electoral success. Hitler attained absolute power through democratic means. The 1933 Enabling Act passed the legislature, the Reichstag, by an overwhelming majority (444 to 84). The "Law for Removing the Distress of People and Reich," the Enabling Act's formal name, granted Hitler's cabinet legislative power for four years. William Shirer drew the following conclusion from the passage of the Enabling Act: "Thus was parliamentary democracy finally interred in Germany. Except for the arrests of the Communists and some of the Social Democratic deputies, it was all done quite legally, though accompanied by terror. Parliament had [democratically?] turned over its constitutional authority to Hitler and thereby committed suicide."[9] Democratic procedures can yield one of the worst results imaginable: democratic suicide. A democracy can democratically abdicate its democratic responsibilities. Proceduralists would not admit defeat so readily. The Nazis violated many democratic procedures on their way to power. The procedural violations seemed endless: the Nazi party never achieved a majority; a decree, "For the Protection of the People and the State," suspended seven sections of the constitution that guaranteed individual and civil liberties; the storm troopers terrorized the electorate; the Enabling Act permitted Hitler to violate the separation of powers. However, even granting that Hitler's rise to power could scarcely serve as a model of how to follow democratic procedures, would the successful implementation of one or more democratic procedures have prevented Hitler's ascension?

Although answering the question would initiate some fascinating speculative historical reconstruction, some more general points emerge from the inquiry so far. Proceduralists have a considerable number of elements in the democratic grab bag. These elements prove useful in plugging any leaks in the democratic ship. The challenge, however, lies not in an *ad hoc* repair job but in first building the ship. What proceduralist planks would keep the democratic ship afloat at the outset of the ship's construction? To answer that question the proceduralists face the following claims about any given set of democratic procedures or elements:

1. There is no complete set of democratic procedures. No one proposed set has all the necessary and sufficient elements for a democracy.
2. There is no set of necessary elements for democracy. The absence of one element or of any combination of elements will not destroy the set, in the sense that the set no longer qualifies as democratic. If we

remove one or more of the elements from the set, the remainder could still qualify as democratic. So, a system without one or more of the proposed necessary elements could still qualify as a democracy.
3. There is no set of sufficient elements for a democracy. A system can have all the proposed sufficient elements of the set and still not qualify as a democracy.
4. No consensus exists as to the elements of the set.
5. Conflicting elements have equally strong justifications for inclusion in the set.
6. The set remains intact even with considerable modification of the elements.
7. Nothing justifiably blocks total abandonment of the set.

Each one of these makes a claim about the set of procedures. Proceduralists face considerable obstacles in their attempts to extricate themselves from any one of the claims. Alternatively, substantive normative claims about social justice avoid these claims.

At this stage, suffice it to say that the claims contain a great deal of plausibility. Their plausibility becomes apparent through even a cursory examination of the problems involved in forming almost any organization. In trying to make an organization democratic, the designers have a wide array of procedures available to them: consensus, committees, committee of the whole, majority rule, plurality voting, etc. All of these, and many, many more, qualify as candidates for inclusion in the set of democratic procedures. An organization operating by consensus can make as strong a case for its democratic character as can one run by majority rule. Although each type of organization operates according to radically different procedures, the procedures themselves do not provide grounds for denying the honorific title of democratic to the organizations. Generally, for every element or combination of elements of the set, there exists an alternative element or combination. Proceduralists need a substantive means for choosing among the alternative formulations.[10]

Social justice provides a framework for formulating a standard that picks out a certain set of procedures over alternative sets. Democracy presupposes at least some degree of a level playing field. No matter how broadly or how narrowly we define democracy, the definition only makes sense against a set of background conditions. Democracy does not make sense under conditions of social and economic injustice. One way to effect the leveling presupposition of democracy is to adopt rules of procedure that promote the leveling.

Consider a conception of democracy that explicitly acknowledges that democratic progress must accompany economic development. On this view of democracy, the institution of democratic reforms makes little sense against a backdrop of economic impoverishment. It is nothing short of an injustice to the people of Bosnia to treat democratic and economic development as separate and distinct policies as Western policy makers do. Next to Macedonia, Bosnia ranks as the poorest country of the Former Yugoslavia's republics. Prior to the 1992-1995 war, Bosnia had a fairly diversified economic structure.[11] In 1990, for example, Unis, producing over 50,000 cars a year, employed 9,000. In 1995, the Unis plant employed 200. Although many national statistics are unavailable and economic studies do not account for a burgeoning and powerful black market, it is safe to conclude that unemployment in Bosnia has reached outrageous level, approaching 80% according to some guestimates made in 1996. Bosnia's economic impoverishment makes its democratic prospects dim.

Further, the socio-economic rebuilding of Bosnia has been a failure largely because of the lack of resources devoted to and effectively targeted at rebuilding. According to a recent assessment, "on a rating scale of one-low, ten high, NATO's [post Dayton] military role would receive an eight; the political process, four; and the socio-economic process, one."[12] In 1996, the World Bank estimated that it would take $5 billion over a three-year period to rebuild Bosnia. The pledges never reached that level, and they have dropped sharply since the first relatively generous infusion of funds. To see how the failures of the rebuilding program seriously impede implementing democracy let us turn to specific procedural recommendations.

Specific Procedures

The indeterminacy problem does not get left entirely behind when discussing specific procedures. Some procedures gain higher status over others when measured against substantive standards. Let us now turn to an examination of some of the procedures themselves. "Procedures" can be divided into Citizen Activities (voting), Decision Procedures (majority rule, rule by minorities, consensus) and Institutional Structures (representation, separation of powers). Proceduralists disagree about which procedures they regard as essential to democracy. None of their arguments succeed, thereby reinforcing the indeterminacy problem. No procedure qualifies as necessary or sufficient for democracy. A way to justify a combination of procedures as necessary or sufficient for democracy is to adopt a substantive criterion. Let us go through each type of procedure, taking the most prominent example from each.

Citizen Activities: Voting

Proceduralists see voting as critical to democracy. "The more widespread the right to vote, the more democratic the system."[13] Despite its importance, voting does not hold the essential relationship to democracy that many democratic theorists have thought. Voting constitutes neither a necessary nor a sufficient condition for democracy. Voting itself is not sufficient for democracy either because the organization does not offer any real choices, as was true in the former Soviet Union, or because the conditions under which the election took place are highly questionable. Concerning the latter, consider the 1982 elections in El Salvador. As peasants voted with numbered ballots in transparent boxes, they had their identity cards marked and their thumbs stamped with ink—all in the name of eliminating voter fraud.[14] Given these and other conditions, such as the threats from death squads, voting in El Salvador could hardly serve as a determinant of democracy. One could consistently maintain that El Salvador held elections but that El Salvador does not qualify as a democracy.[15]

Bosnia serves as a recent illustration of the serious problems that arise when democracy becomes closely entangled with elections. The Organization for Security and Co-operation in Europe (OSCE), whose primary mission in Bosnia is to promote democratization, has to determine whether elections in Bosnia were "free and fair." American election monitors gave conflicting evaluations of the national elections.[16] Robert Frowick, a former U.S. diplomat, and others found that "free and fair" conditions existed based on before-and-after comparisons of various cities. Another American, William Stuebner found that continuing disputes among ethnic communities precluded "fair and free" elections. The OSCE Commission accepted Frowick's analysis. It proceeded with the election process until President Izetbegovic's demands halted the process. After considerable negotiations, Bosnia held national elections on September 14, 1996. Allegations of widespread fraud became the dominant feature of the election. Scores of voters were turned away from the polls, and the turnout consisted of 105% of the eligible electorate.[17] Despite findings of the Election Appeals Sub-Commission, the OSCE certified the election.

Aside from outrageous breeches of electoral rules, it would be difficult to devise neutral criteria for determining whether an election was "free and fair." Generally, assessments of "free and fair" elections will contain substantive value judgments. In Bosnia, the OSCE determines who votes and where they vote. During the 1997 municipal elections, the OSCE allowed non resident refugees to vote in their home districts. NATO troops went so far as to protect refugees only insofar as they went to their districts to cast ballots and immediately returned to their residence outside the district.[18] The OSCE used, in part, a value judgment, namely, a desired outcome (mixed ethnic voting) to evaluate the fairness of elections. For the Western powers, the elections in Bosnia were portrayed as a means to achieve a unified, multi-ethnic, pluralist state. Election officials continually express dissatisfaction with elections held in Bosnia because voters continued to cast their ballots along ethnic lines. The 1996 national elections replicated ethnic divisions, which seemed to confirm Stuebner's assessment. There are a number of ironies in the democratic posturing of the Western powers. The foreign powers operating in Bosnia drew ethnic boundaries to maintain peace. Since the outsiders helped to retain and to construct the ethnic boundaries that frame the elections, they cannot complain if election results somehow reflect the boundaries. Further, theoretically, nothing in the tenants of proceduralist democracy would rule out voting according to ethnic interests. After the cessation of hostilities, militarily, it made good sense to downplay ethnic divides. The military's temporary devaluation of ethnic grouping should not carry over permanently to democratic politics. Ethnicity constitutes one of many interests that individuals might democratically promote.

We could easily find other cases where voting did not take place under free and fair conditions. However, a more critical issue of how to define "free and fair" poses more serious objections to proceduralist democracy than examples of corrupt elections. For granting that an election took place under free conditions does not help the proceduralist's case. A free election does not entail free conditions before the election. Critics of United States foreign policy might concede, reluctantly, the free conditions under which the 1989 election took place in Nicaragua, and yet they still might contest the legitimacy of the election because of the highly unstable conditions, including the Contra War and the economic boycott, that preceded the election. War-torn and economically devastated Bosnia presents a case similar to the Nicaraguan one. Precedent conditions could so alter the quality of the election that no amount of freedom and fairness during the election could offset them. To dramatize the point consider a demand in 1994 that starving, seriously ill, and former gernocidaires Hutus in UN refugee camps outside Rwanda vote immediately in Rwandan elections. I would assume that the background conditions under which the election took place would offset any claims to a free and fair election. Although the conditions faced by Bosnians following the cessation of hostilities were not as desperate as the diaspora Hutus, their conditions were analogous.

Proceduralists need to extend the bounds of free conditions to include not only the election itself but also the related historical developments that preceded the election and, one might further argue, the circumstances that followed it. Precedent conditions could so alter the quality of the election that no amount of fairness during the election could offset them. Regarding the subsequent conditions, one could maintain that the authoritarian action taken by a Hitler or a Marcos after the election undermined the democratic character of the elections that put them into power. On the flip side of too much authority, the lack of effective authority given to democratically elected officials seriously undermines any pretense to democracy in Bosnia.

So, voting, even in a free election, does not provide a sufficient condition for democracy, since the conditions of the election itself or the conditions before and after the election could undermine the democratic character of the election. Proceduralists have difficulty keeping within proceduralist bounds, especially when conditions surrounding the election begin to enter the picture. Free elections entail more than following a certain procedure. Once proceduralists extend the boundaries beyond the specific election to determine the free conditions of the election, procedures themselves no longer make the case. Instead, proceduralists have replaced a singular focus on procedures out of a concern for historical conditions and outcomes.

Since we cannot infer the democratic character of an organization from the fact that elections took place within the organization, voting cannot serve as a sufficient condition of democracy. Voting also fails as a necessary condition for democracy since associations recognized as democratic might operate by alternative means that do not include voting.[19] An organization that makes choices by lot or that employs extensive deliberations with its members without any formal voting ever taking place could qualify as a democratic organization because of the commitment made to participation. In the case of Bosnia, I would push this analysis one step further by arguing for a version of democracy that intertwined civic duty (voting, etc.) with economic well being and participation. The war devastated Bosnia's infrastructure: "its gross domestic product had dwindled by 80 percent since 1990, its industrial production had declined by 95 percent, its electrical generating capacity declined 70 percent, 80 percent of its housing units were destroyed or damaged, repairs needed for 1,500 miles of roads."[20] It is still feasible to couple elections to the implementation of massive public works programs, employing Bosnians of all ethnic backgrounds and funded (at first) by foreign powers.

A rejection of voting as a sufficient and necessary condition for democracy does not entail a wholesale rejection of voting nor does it demean the importance of voting in particular situations. The critique only means that voting cannot legitimately rise to the high status of a sufficient and necessary condition.

Democratic theorists cannot underestimate the importance of extending voting privileges to citizens not previously enfranchised. Rejecting voting as a sufficient or as a necessary condition of democratic procedures does not imply dismissing the importance of voting altogether.[21] As Philip Green warned, "the struggle over equal political participation cannot and should not be a struggle against the vote."[22] The struggle for voting rights certainly plays an important role in the struggle for democracy. Universal suffrage in the United States became a reality relatively recently. For some time, property served as a major qualification for voting in the United States. In 1700, property holders voted in as many counties as they held property. At the time of the Revolutionary War, twelve of the thirteen colonies had property qualifications.[23] Voters did not popularly elect the Senate until 1913, and women only gained the vote in 1920. Electoral advances in formerly state socialist countries serve as easy examples. Less well-known examples come from within the United States. From 1933 to 1988, three hundred black residents were denied the vote for municipal councilors in Keysville, Georgia, where whites abolished a town government, originally incorporated in 1890.[24] Procuring the vote for the three hundred marked a victory for democracy. The struggle for democracy should include the fight for voting rights. Nevertheless, democratic theory and policy should include a set of priorities. It makes sense to feed the starving before ever introducing the prospects of elections to them.

Decision Procedures: Majority Rule

Decision procedures, such as majority rule, fare no better than voting in establishing necessary and sufficient conditions for democracy.[25] Majority rule is not necessary to democracy since alternatives to majority rule do exist.[26] Two procedures, especially when they operate in tandem, serve, theoretically and practically, as alternatives to majority rule. Surprisingly, lot and consensus have a long history of democratic use, going back to ancient Athens.

An organization could choose its "representatives," its decision makers, by lot instead of by vote.[27] Demarchy, as its proponents call this system, has received a significant amount of attention from a wide range of theorists.[28] Organizations operating according to lot selection rather than majority rule can qualify as democratic. Choosing representatives by lot avoids one of the most intractable problems of majority rule, namely, tyranny of the majority. While lot selection does not preclude the majority from attaining power, it does give the minority a better chance to share in that power. Majority rule could foreclose any rule by the minority, whereas lot selection provides, at least, some chance for the minority to win.

Consensus requires unanimity; all members of the decision-making unit must agree (or, at least, agree not to disagree) in order for a proposal to go forward. Organizations ranging from Quaker meetings to the United Nations' Security Council operate according to consensus.[29] A single member can block a decision by the group until convinced otherwise. Even a minority of one holds a great deal of power within an organization operating by consensus.

Lot and consensus nicely complement each other, as each offsets some drawbacks of the other. Instead of a legislature electorally chosen by majority rule, we could choose representatives to policy and planning juries by lot.[30] These juries would then make their policy and planning decisions according to consensus. This would overcome the absurdity of choosing policies and plans by lot and the difficulty of applying consensus to large-scale decision units. The lot-consensus system still leaves some questions unanswered. For example, who chooses the range of policy issues considered by the juries? Are the issues chosen by referendum? In the case of Bosnia, a good case can be made for the foreign powers that already have power internally to require policy and planning juries to give priority to economic development. This suggestion does not concede to proceduralists' tinkering. Instead, the suggestion is meant to at least raise the specter of democracy without either voting or majority rule. More importantly, if we analyze the proposal one step further, we will find that justifying the choice of a specific set of decision-making procedures for Bosnia depends upon justifying substantive value judgments about, for example, the high priority that economic development should take.

Questioning the sufficiency of majority rule for democracy also raises the well-known specter of the tyranny of the majority. The solidification of a permanent majority undermines democracy by bringing rule by some people (the majority) and not rule by all people. Many theorists try to save majority rule by appending protective devices for the minority. Minority rights allow the minority to defend itself against the tyranny of the majority. However, the safeguards do not work unless they take social justice into account. The very terms "majority" and "minority" reflect quantitative considerations.[31] Majority and minority designate how many votes fall on one side as opposed to the other. Majority rule assumes an indeterminacy between majority and minority whereby individuals can shift, depending on the issue, from one to another. Problems emerge once we give the terms a qualitative interpretation. What if the majority, consistently across time, includes certain social classes and the minority includes others, resulting in a permanent minority? What if the society breaks down into a few distinct divisions that make certain groups almost permanent majorities in some situations and others permanent minorities in other circumstances? The last question addresses the situation in Bosnia. Democratic theorists and policy makers have responded to it largely by tinkering with the institutional structures that support democracy in Bosnia.

Institutional Structures: Representation

A wide array of structures and features falls under the banner of democracy: representation, separation of powers, constitutionalism, balance of powers, and so on. Let us focus on one of these, namely, representation, to help support the thesis that no single institutional practice or feature is necessary or sufficient for democracy. Representative governance seems synonymous with democratic governance. Yet, representation is not a necessary condition for democracy since alternatives such as delegate and participatory systems are also feasible. Members of an organization may choose a delegate who is subject to instant recall and who will rotate her or his position with other delegates. If this seems like only a watered-down version of representation, consider a participatory system, where the delegates would know the preferences of all members of the political unit. In an age of instantaneous communication, in which teledemes could well become the reality, more direct electoral participation through a delegate may differ substantially from a system of representation. So, a democracy can still flourish without representation.

Representation also fails as a candidate for a sufficient condition for democracy. The origins of representation in England should give some pause:

> The king summoned representatives from counties and boroughs to come to his Parliament armed with powers of attorney to bind their constituents to whatever taxes or laws they agreed to. The power of attorney had to be complete (*plena potestas*), so that a representative could not plead that he must go back and consult his constituents. His consent, given in Parliament, must be as much theirs as if they had come in person. "As if". Representation from the beginning was itself a fiction. If the representative consented, his constituents had to make believe that they had done so.[32]

Here, representation as an obligation imposed from above could hardly qualify as democratic. So, representation does not hold as a sufficient condition for democracy. If early England seems too remote, we need only reflect on the remoteness of modern day representatives from their constituents. With good justification someone might refuse to label a system democratic if its representative represented only the elite and the wealthy. Although representation may not serve as the foundation of democracy, perhaps we can find a more palatable type of representation. Let us explore the democratic promise of proportional representation.

Voting may seem like a straightforward procedural device. However, voting comes in many different varieties. Plurality voting, where the winner takes all, includes at-large and single-member district mechanisms. At-large plurality voting gives the majority an inordinate amount of power. Single-member districts can stem the power of the majority somewhat by allowing for the election of minority groups, given their concentration in geographic areas. The choice of voting methods depends upon the goals. Some proceduralists aim to diffuse ethnic aspirations. Donald Horowitz, for example, has argued that, in certain circumstances, vote-pooling systems (such as, requiring candidates of one ethnic group to obtain votes from members of the other ethnic group) help diffuse interethnic tensions.[33] The new draft Permanent Election Law in Bosnia make a gesture in this direction by candidates for the BiH Presidency to collect signatures from one's own ethnic group in the other group's entity.[34] The goal of these proceduralist analyses is to devise mechanisms that diminish group aspirations.[35]

Other theorists aim to enhance rather than to diminish the political status of groups. They contend that some system of proportional representation offers the best protection for groups, especially disadvantaged ones. Some political scientists have urged the adoption of general schemes of proportional representation, with legislators elected in proportion to their party's share of the vote, because they have a greater likelihood of increasing the representation of women, racial minorities, and *non-majority* groups.[36] Women, for example, have a greater share of representatives in the many countries that have adopted proportional representational schemes than in those with plurality ones.[37] The data on racial minorities are not quite as clear-cut.[38] While a general proportional representation device has a great deal of merit, it has some drawbacks as well. First, proportional representation alone does not always increase the representation of, for example, women. In Iceland, women have made a rather poor showing even with proportional representation.[39] Second, proportional representation could just as well increase the representational power of non-disadvantaged groups as that of disadvantaged groups.[40] Proportional representation increases the representation of the non-majority, and not necessarily the representation of those who might need representation the most.[41]

One case over the past decade in Eastern Europe might prove instructive for Bosnia. Events over the past decade in Eastern Europe, particularly in those countries with heterogeneous populations, have dramatized the importance of the complex interplay that exists between Procedural and Substantive Democracy.[42] In Czechoslovakia, the minority Slovaks, through a number of structural devices, held an "absolute veto power over important legislation and constitutional amendments."[43] The Slovaks had equal representation in the Chamber of Nations. A majority of the Slovaks in the upper chamber had to approve important legislation in order for it to become law. The Slovaks attained this structural form of proportional representation through the constitutional amendments of 1968. However, the 1968 structural reform brought little actual power to the Slovaks. During the regime of Gustav Husak, Slovakia received special privileges, "including disproportionate investment and jobs in the state and Party administration."[44] The Slovaks received these advantages by executive decree and not through proportional representation. So, during the Husak regime, the Slovaks may have received more advantage from the programs than from the procedures. The Slovaks could have effectively destroyed any important legislation "such as citizenship, budget, taxes, votes of confidence, and domestic and foreign economic matters."[45] Although the Slovaks were fewer in number and generally poorer than their Czech counterparts in Czechoslovakia, historically the oppression of the Slovaks took place at the hands of the Hungarians and not at the behest of the Czechs. Whatever lessons one might care to draw for Bosnia from this case, one should keep some critical differences between the two cases. Unlike the people in Bosnia, the participants in the Czech versus Slovak procedural maneuverings did not just emerge from a devastating conflict, complete with ethnic cleansing. Second, the Czechs and Slovaks each had their own histories of operating as political units. Third, the Czechs and Slovaks engage in politics from a far stronger economic position than any of the groups engaged politically in Bosnia today.

Conclusion

Democratic procedures come in a wide variety of types. Whatever set of procedures are proposed, the choice of procedures in the case of Bosnia should be made according to how the elements of the set dovetail with and promote economic justice. In Bosnia, the choices among citizen activities, decision procedures, and institutional structures should be made according to how well the mechanisms would succeed in achieving a level of economic well being conducive to democratic politics. To accept the separation of democracy from economics is, minimally, to fail to recognize the contestability of democracy. To treat democracy as if it operated in a vacuum ignores reality. Democracy operates within economic constraints. To indict Bosnia for democratic failures without fully addressing its economic impoverishment, which prevents democratic development, is an injustice. To allow democratic initiatives to foster ethnic strife and thereby excuse the ineptitude of foreign powers is morally reprehensible. Those outside forces with their hands already deeply into the mix in Bosnia have the wherewithal to set a new example of global humanitarian politics. In the words of one astute former candidate, "it's the economy, stupid."

Notes

*   This analysis includes an expansion and revision of a discussion in *Democracy and Social Injustice* (Lanham: Rowman & Littlefield, 1995), Chapter 6.

1. "Sober thought may tell us that all governments are of the people, that all profess to be for the people, and that none can literally be by the people" (Edmund S. Morgan, *Inventing the People* (New York: Norton, 1988), p. 38). "And if elected I promise government by the people, of the people, for the people, in the people, over, around, through, above, behind, below, after, with and without the people" (From a cartoon appearing in a pamphlet entitled "Demarchy: A Democratic Alternative to Electoral Politics" By Lot, PO Box 492, Wollongong East NSW 2520, Australia).

2. The proceduralists' positions are far more complicated than the presentation in the text suggests. For a recent collection of diverse proceduralist positions see *Democracy, Theory and Practice*, ed. John Arthur (Belmont: Wadsworth Publishing Company, 1992). None of the proceduralists, however, frame their position in terms of rule for the disadvantaged, although some positions might be compatible with that view.

3. Brian Barry, "Is Democracy Special?" in *Philosophy, Politics and Society* (Fifth Series) ed. P. Laslett and J. Fishkin (New Haven, Conn.: Yale University Press, 1979), p. 156.

4. William Nelson, *On Justifying Democracy* (New York: Routledge, 1980), p. 3.

5. Giovanni Sartori, *The Theory of Democracy Revisited* (Chatham: Chatham House Publishers, 1987), p. 38, fn. 31.

6. See my "The Theoretical Marginalization of the Disadvantaged: A Liberal/Communitarian Failing," in *The Liberalism-Communitarian Debate*, ed., C. F. Delaney (Lanham: Rowman & Littlefield, 1994).

7. Robert Dahl lists the following conditions necessary for democracy: voting equality, effective participation, enlightened understanding, control of the agenda, and inclusion (*Democracy and Its Critics* (New Haven: Yale University Press, 1989), p. 222).

8. For an excellent critique of the proceduralist's position, see Charles R. Beitz, *Political Equality* (Princeton, N. J.: Princeton University Press, 1989), chapter 4.

9. William Shirer, *The Rise and Fall of the Third Reich* (New York: Simon and Schuster, 1981), p. 278.

10. Jane J. Mansbridge, *Beyond Adversary Democracy* (Chicago: University of Chicago Press, 1983). Mansbridge proposes a mix of unitary methods like consensus and adversary ones such as majority rule depending upon the size and the degree of conflicting interests among the members of the organization. Adversary democracy becomes more plausible the larger the size of the unit and the more the interests conflict (Mansbridge, p. 293). Mansbridge moves toward the thesis advocated in this chapter when she notes that "the interests of the poor are better protected in larger units" (Mansbridge, p. 281). However, Mansbridge's concerns are more with individual interests overall and not specifically with disadvantaged groups.

11. Lester H. Brune, *The United Sates and Post-Cold War Interventions*. (Claremont, CA: Regina Books, 1998), p. 135.

12. Ibid.

13. Felix Oppenheim, *Political Concepts* (Chicago: University of Chicago Press, 1981), p. 32. Likewise Riker takes voting to be "at the heart of both the method and ideal

of democracy" (William Riker, *Liberalism Against Populism* (New York: W. H. Freeman, 1982), p. 8).

14   Walter LaFeber, *Inevitable Revolutions* (New York: W. W. Norton, 1984), p. 287.
15   Edward S. Herman and Frank Brodhead, *Demonstration Elections: U.S. Staged Elections in the Dominican Republic, Vietnam, and El Salvador* (Boston: South End Press, 1984).
16   Brune, *The United Sates and Post-Cold War Interventions*, p. 129.
17   International Crisis Group, "Is Dayton Failing? Bosnia Four Years After the Peace Agreement," (October 28, 1999).
18   Brune, *The United Sates and Post-Cold War Interventions*, p. 135.
19   Philip Green, *Retrieving Democracy* (Lanham: Rowman & Littlefield, 1985) takes voting as a necessary condition for democracy: "the vote is properly believed by almost everyone to be a necessary condition of whatever we are going to call democracy" (p. 172).
20   Brune, *The United Sates and Post-Cold War Interventions*, pp. 136–137.
21   Burnheim dismisses voting when he proclaims that "electoral systems are inimical to rule by the people for the people" (Burnheim, *Is Democracy Possible?* (Berkeley: University of California Press, 1985), p. 82).
22   Green, *Retrieving Democracy*, p. 172.
23   Samuel Bowles and Herbert Gintis, *Democracy and Capitalism* (New York: Basic Books, 1986), pp. 45–46.
24   *Convergence*, Spring 1988, p. 2.
25   Elaine Spitz holds that democracy means majority rule. Elaine Spitz, *Majority Rule* (Chatham House, 1984). In contrast, according to Rawls, "the procedure of majority rule, however it is defined and circumscribed, has a subordinate place as a procedural device" (Rawls, p. 356).
26   Dahl explores a number of alternatives to majority rule, other than those discussed in the text, in *Democracy and Its Critics* (New Haven: Yale University Press, 1989), chapter 11, and finds the alternatives to majority rule equally wanting.
27   Burnheim, who coined the term "demarchy," dismisses voting as necessary for democracy when he proclaims that "electoral systems are inimical to rule by the people for the people" (Burnheim, p. 82).
28   Dahl, *Democracy and Its Critics*, and Fred Emery, *Toward Real Democracy* (Toronto: Ontario Ministry of Labour Occasional Paper, 1989).
29   Mansbridge, chapters 2 and 14.
30   James S. Fishkin, *Democracy and Deliberation: New Directions for Democratic Reform* (New Haven: Yale University Press, 1991), chapter 8.
31   It was not until 1937 that the Supreme Court began to give a qualitative, social interpretation of minority in the now famous Footnote number 4 of Carolene Products. For a fuller discussion, see my "Suspect Class Democracy," in *University of Miami Law Review* 45 (1990), pp. 107–58.
32   Morgan, *Inventing the People*, p. 39.
33   Donald L. Horowitz, *A Democratic South Africa? Constitutional Engineering in a Divided Society* (Berkeley, CA: University of California Press, 1991).
34   International Crisis Group, "Is Dayton Failing?"
35   Ian Shapiro, "Group Aspirations and Democratic Politics," in *Democracy's Edges*, Ian Shapiro and Casiano Hacker-Cordon, editors. New York: Cambridge University Press, 1999.

36 Douglas J. Amy, "Improving Representation for Women and Minorities: Is Proportional Representation the Key?" Paper delivered at the Annual Meeting of the American Political Science Association, Washington, D.C., September 1991

37 Will Rule, "Electoral Systems, Contextual Factors and Women's Opportunity for Election to Parliament in Twenty-Three Democracies," in *The Western Political Quarterly*, 40, no. 3 (September 1987), p. 487.

38 See for example, Robert J. Kolesar, "Proportional Representation in Cincinnati: From 'Good Government' to the Politics of Inclusion?" Paper delivered at the 1991 Annual Meeting of the American Political Science Association, Washington, D. C.

39 Anne Phillips, *Engendering Democracy* (University Park, Penn.: The Pennsylvania State University Press, 1991), p. 83.

40 "In weakening political parties, and permitting new minorities access to city hall, PR appears to have contributed to the growth of many groups, some of which were extreme and even undemocratic". Ronald J. Busch, "Proportional Representation and Religious and Ethnic Minorities," paper delivered at the Annual Meeting of the American Political Science Association, Washington, D. C., September 1991.

41 To take an extreme example of proportional representation, in his novel *Alpaca*, H. L. Hunt, the Texas oil billionaire, proposes that the more money a citizen has, the more votes he should have. On a more moderate scale, John Stuart Mill advocated a weighted voting scheme, wherein those with greater intelligence and education would have extra votes so that their opinions might have a greater influence. John Stuart Mill "Representative Government" in *John Stuart Mill, Three Essays* (Oxford: Oxford University Press, 1975), chapters 7 and 8. As an example of proportional representation according to education, in Great Britain until 1948 graduates of Oxford and Cambridge were each given two votes in the general elections.

42 See Cass Sunnstein, "Approaching Democracy: a new legal order for Eastern Europe – Constitutionalism and secession," in *Political Restructuring in Europe: Ethical Perspectives*, ed. Chris Brown (London and New York: Routledge, 1994), pp. 11–49.

43 Lloyd Cutler and Herman Schwartz, "Constitutional Reform in Czechoslovakia: E Duobus Unum?" in *University of Chicago Law Review* 58 (1991), p. 549.

44 Ibid, p. 520.

45 Ibid, p. 519.

2 Self-determination in a Multiethnic State: Bosnians, Bosniaks, Croats and Serbs*

DANIEL KOFMAN

Any serious treatment of the future of Bosnia-Herzegovina (BiH) must come to terms with the question of self-determination. It is indeed arguable that of the many shortcomings of the Dayton Peace Agreement (serving a quasi-constitutional role in BiH since its signing in 1995), a general defect underlying many others has been the failure to address the issue of self-determination directly. The reasons for this failure are not hard to guess. The Dayton Accords were an attempt to accommodate radically opposed visions of BiH and the incompatible claims of the different ethnic groups. The most charitable interpretation is that it engineered the best compromise available at the time, based on two overlapping lowest common denominators: one between Bosniaks and Croats, another between all three of the constituent ethnic groups (and the international community). A less kindly reading is that Dayton was the logical consequence of four years of international appeasement of ethnic aggression, genocide, and conquest primarily by Serbian and Bosnian Serb illegal forces, and on a somewhat more limited scale, by Herzegovinian Croats and their backers in Zagreb; an appeasement culminating in an accord the beleaguered Bosnian government had no realistic possibility of not signing, which granted the Bosnian Serbs quasi-independence on roughly half of BiH territory.

Whichever interpretation one inclines toward - and they are perhaps not mutually exclusive - the practical implications of the failure of the accord and surrounding pronouncements to speak clearly on self-determination are manifold. The powers allotted to Republika Srpska are incommensurate with membership in a larger federation, rendering that federation merely nominal, and it has used these powers to obstruct implementation of provisions of the Dayton Agreement constituting even this nominal unity, such as the provision that refugees have a right of return. Beyond these obvious points, members of each ethnic group continue to harbor aspirations incompatible with a unitary BiH state. The population of Republika Srpska in particular still overwhelmingly dreams of partition at the least, and beyond that of an *Anschluss* with Serbia. And these dreams receive ideological support in the West, as various diplomats and academics reiterate the reasoning they made notorious during the war: that a multiethnic Bosnia has no right of self-determination, and that even if one did grant that Bosnia had a right to secede from the former Yugoslavia, then the Bosnian Serbs would share an equal right to secede from Bosnia.

The motivation for this chapter, then, is the view that reconstruction, reconciliation, and a viable and independent democratic state of Bosnia-Herzegovina (that is, one not held together by external tutelage) are not possible unless the different ethnic constituents, as well as the international community, arrive at a clear and justified conception of who has a right of self-determination in the area, and whether that right entails a right of secession for each claimant. If this view is warranted, then while our chief concern is with the present and future, it will be necessary to examine the past. For the claim I wish to defend—that the Republic of Bosnia-Herzegovina enjoyed a right of secession from the Socialist Federated Republic of Yugoslavia (SFRY), but that none of the constituent ethnic groups had or have such a right with respect to BiH—needs to be established by examining the events, actions and claims of the concerned parties at the time of the breakup of the SFRY.

Re-examining the past to facilitate reconciliation in the future is not nearly as implausible as it might seem. The notion is encapsulated in the name of the famous South African commission established by the Promotion of National Unity and Reconciliation Act of 1995, and in the commission's slogan: "Truth: The Road To Reconciliation."[1] The same view has been expressed in the hopes of some that the public trials of the International Criminal Tribunal for the former Yugoslavia would ultimately have a reconciliatory effect. The contrast between the two cases, however, is instructive. In South Africa, the backbone of support for apartheid was already broken; by the time the Commission began, only marginal figures still harbored political aspirations opposed to an egalitarian (non-racist) republican ideal. In BiH, aspirations incompatible with a unitary state persist, and it is unlikely that exposure to the 'truth' of past war crimes, or even the removal from the scene of leading criminals, will diminish these aspirations in the eyes of those who believe that they are firmly grounded in *rights*. It is all the more vital, then, if meaningful reconciliation is to be achieved, that the *political* issues of the past be reconsidered if meaningful reconciliation is to be achieved.

In light of the above, I propose to do the following. I shall attempt, first, to sketch in brief form a theory of national self-determination and secession. This is necessary given the state of flux that international law is currently in with regard to self-determination and secession. Recent developments have been guided by normative views, and one can understand the former only if one grasps the latter. I shall then apply the theory to the former Yugoslavia, which will require a brief reconsideration of the events leading and subsequent to the breakup of the SFRY. I shall argue, against the views of certain writers, that the population of the Republic of Bosnia-Herzegovina had, and still has, a right to self-determination and secession, but that the entity known as Republika Srpska has lacked any such legitimate claim.

The Theory of Self-determination

We can begin by noting that international law has been notoriously ambiguous about the right of self-determination. Not that it has been silent about it; on the contrary, as one author put it, there has been a "veritable blizzard of General Assembly and Security Council resolutions [in favor of self-determination] over the years."[2] The UN Charter, in Articles 1 (2) and 55, asserts self-determination as a guiding "principle" of the organization. The "right" of self-determination is upheld by General Assembly Resolutions 1514, 1541, and 2625 (the 1970 Declaration on Principles of International Law Concerning Friendly Relations and Co-operation Among States), and the UN International Covenant on Civil and Political Rights, adopted Dec. 16, 1966, proclaims: "All peoples have the right of self-determination." The Helsinki Final Act proclaims as well (Article VIII) "the principle of equal rights and self-determination of peoples," that is, that "all peoples always have the right, in full freedom, to determine, when and as they wish, their internal and external political status, without external interference."

But in every case these declarations are accompanied by caveats to the effect that "nothing in the foregoing paragraphs shall be construed as authorizing or encouraging any action which would dismember or impair, totally or in part, the territorial integrity or political unity of sovereign and independent States."[3] For several decades the law of nations interpreted this ambiguity according to the "saltwater principle" upholding the right of colonies to acquire independence from the mother countries (with whom they were separated by saltwater), but disallowing secessions from these newly founded states in Africa, Asia, or elsewhere, if the central state opposed it. This interpretation has never lacked critics, including among international jurists.[4] But what does seem to have a broad consensus is the view that present statutes are themselves vague and open to widely conflicting interpretations.[5] It is arguably the case, therefore, that existing statutes on self-determination in international law are inadequate, and lag behind the customary practices of civilized nations.[6] For this reason one cannot simply read off of the aforementioned legal caveats and earlier "salt-water" interpretation a supposedly settled legal view of secession. The point is critical, yet frequently misunderstood, with regard to interpretations of the breakup of Yugoslavia (SFRY).[7] From human rights to secession, international law at the turn of the millennium has been *extended* by states and international organs in a novel post-Cold War setting, and it is misguided to protest in the name of older practices that recent decisions have been departures from international law.

This is as true for the case of Augusto Pinochet, the former Chilean dictator detained in Britain for months pending (ultimately failed) Spanish extradition attempts, as it is for the European Arbitration Commission's decisions on the breakup of the SFRY. In a trivial sense, of course, every development of customary law is a departure from hitherto-prevailing norms. The crucial determinant is whether the new practice follows a defensible interpretation of broad principles animating previous practice, where the defensibility will be based in part on the capability of the new practice to resolve previous conflicts of principles (for example between stability and self-determination) while possibly enabling a more rigorous implementation of other principles (such as securing human rights). In short, we need to come to some understanding of the normative justification of self-determination and secession before we can know whether recent developments are "violations," or rather, reasonable extensions of previous customary law.

I do not, of course, offer an extensive elaboration of a normative theory here. Elsewhere[8] I have rejected views either so conservative as to make secession permissible only in cases of restitution of previously conquered territory, or so permissive as to allow any territorial majority of any kind, anywhere, to secede from an existing state. The first view ignores the importance of states for national groups in the name of international stability, but ends up precipitating greater instability (as the case of Bosnia, I shall argue, demonstrates). The second view is indeterminate; attempts to institutionalize it would be destabilizing indeed (this is briefly elaborated below).

Inevitably, then, we must face the question of the value of sovereign statehood for ethnic groups. When considering what motivates ethnic groups to seek political independence, one finds that a territorial claim *per se* is generally not primary. Even when territorial resources are a factor—say, Northern Sea oil in Scottish nationalism—they are usually secondary to the primary quest for self-government.[9] What, then, motivates claims to self-determination based on ethnic distinctiveness? In our world, still dominated for better or worse by a system of sovereign states, statehood, or belonging to a state, confers benefits on groups with historical-cultural identities. We can understand what these benefits are by reminding ourselves of what a state is. In the first place, it is a locus of power with a unique degree of concentration both historically and with respect to other contemporary institutions. International jurists describe it as "the most extensive form of jurisdiction under international law. In general terms, it denotes full and unchallengeable power over a piece of territory and all the persons from time to time therein." Brownlie calls it "a jurisdiction, *prima facie* exclusive, over a territory and the permanent population living there."[10]

Sociologists equally focus on power. "Every state is founded on force," quotes Weber approvingly from Trotsky, and adds, "If no social institutions existed which knew the use of violence, then the concept of 'state' would be eliminated, and a condition would emerge that could be designated as 'anarchy.'"[11] Weber's famous formula of a "monopoly of legitimate force" has influenced many, including Anthony Giddens, who defines the nation-state as, "a set of institutional forms of governance maintaining an administrative monopoly over a territory with demarcated boundaries, its rule being sanctioned by law and direct control of the means of internal and external violence," or more succinctly, "a bounded power-container."[12] Boundedness, then, along with concentrated power, are the defining features.

Clearly much of the benefit to a group sharing a national identity derives from the control it acquires over the entire complement of jurisdictions comprising a state. This itself can be analyzed in terms of several benefits or interests: first, that a group can take control, to a much greater degree, of its own destiny. If a nation sees itself as part of a historical narrative, and continuing that narrative as freely or autonomously as possible is in its interest, then it has an interest in getting hold of the powers that shape that narrative in the future. Relatedly, by bringing all these jurisdictions—criminal and civil law, public construction, roads, rail, air and shipping routes, parks, gardens, historical sites, labor relations, fiscal policy, industrial incentives, gender, immigration and foreign policy—under its control, it can adapt them to the particular shared values, styles, tastes and beliefs of its members.

Another benefit, frequently overlooked, is that having a state at its disposal enables a group to represent its distinctiveness by the most powerful means available in the contemporary world, namely by the pervasive symbols of state, from coins, stamps, and flags on government buildings, to the singing of anthems at official and sporting events.[13]

Perhaps most important of all (though ironically least mentioned in philosophical literature), the fact that the entire cluster of jurisdictions shares the same boundary powerfully unites members by reinforcing their sense of community. Since state political decisions pervasively affect the lives of citizens, state boundaries naturally demarcate a field of significant common experience and communication. This explains how states consolidate and reinforce a common identity among their citizens by their mere existence; one cannot otherwise account for the phenomenal success of "nation building" in so many states that have inherited multiethnic colonial boundaries.

And last but not least, in obtaining independence a group acquires the highest and most prestigious external recognition available in the contemporary world—membership in the UN General Assembly, participation in international conferences, treaties, sporting events, and so forth—which stands to boost the self-esteem of the group and reinforce its perception of the distinction between group members and outsiders. All of these benefits of statehood together foster a sense of collective identity in a way scarcely available otherwise. Indeed, the crux of my argument is that even extensive political autonomy falls considerably short of the power of an independent state to foster collective identity, and that national groups lacking independence are and will no doubt remain fully cognizant of the difference.

Identities, of course, are often multiple and overlapping, and nearly always in flux. But a justification of self-determination need not falsely assume a world of discrete, separated and static group identities. On the contrary, part of the justification of self-determination is that if people are to be authors of their own lives, then it is up to each group to decide whether to reinforce its distinct identity with the most powerful means available—independent sovereign statehood—or whether it wishes to continue to nurture this identity within a wider one encompassing others. That is, it is up to Francophone Quebecers to decide whether they wish to be exclusive Quebecers, or Canadian Quebecers; it is up to Slovenes whether they wish to be Slovenian Yugoslavs or sovereign Slovenes.

Briefly, now, we must also consider some drawbacks to a general right of secession if we are to be in a position to suggest how the right should be qualified. First, as previously mentioned, a completely unrestricted right of secession for any territorial majority of any kind, as advocated by a handful of liberal philosophers, would be indeterminate, leaving no way of adjudicating between inevitable competing claims. It would also not rule out temporary claims of convenience or strategic expedience, such as the short-lived statelet of Fikret Abdić in Velika Kladuša, northern Bosnia. At its worst, it would be an invitation to armed conflict and ethnic cleansing, as every neighborhood becomes a potential claimant of statehood, even if only out of a desire to reunite with other statelets sharing its ethnicity.[14]

The above would be reason enough to restrict the right of secession to the sorts of groups capable of particularly benefiting from independent statehood, that is, groups with historical-cultural identities. Another important reason is that a more general right would be detrimental to democracy as it would threaten the minimum of commitment and loyalty necessary for a viable democratic process.[15] Other qualifications involve distributive justice: a group may not claim for itself a disproportionate share of state resources, at least not without offering fair compensation; similar considerations apply to sharing the national debt and other burdens. In addition, a seceding group must be respectful of human and minority rights—on some views at least as respectful of them as is the state from which it is breaking off.

But even with all these qualifications, the right of secession will still be indeterminate, as long as some national groups live intermingled with others. An institutionalized right of secession would not be justified if it provided an incentive to racism, xenophobia, and ethnic cleansing, nor if it created a permanent sense of instability as boundaries constantly became renegotiable. The right, then, needs to be restricted further, so that not every leftover minority group should think it may secede anew.

The basis of the right, as we saw, is that identity groups deprived of states of their own should have a matrix to foster and develop their identities. But it is not necessary, nor arguably even desirable, that all group members reside in that matrix, the independent state. It suffices that members living outside it—Hungarians in Transylvania, Anglophones in Quebec, Russians in the Baltic states—enjoy a full complement of individual and minority rights, including easy access to the cultural goods of their kin-state, and freedom to visit it and be visited by those from it; in short, freedom to participate in it. Stability requires the avoidance of pernicious incentives and indeterminacy, which in turn requires that when a national group secedes, the leftover minority of the remainder state does not itself have a right to secede, provided its own rights are respected by the new state.

International law recognizes something like this in the long-standing principle of *uti possidetis*[16] (literally: it may be possessed; that is, the frontiers of the seceding administrative unit should be kept intact). This principle establishes strict rules in secessions precisely to avoid recursive extravaganzas. Originally adopted with regard to the frontiers of colonies gaining independence, it has been extended by the European Arbitration Commission for the former Yugoslavia to the seceding republics of those states, and is now regarded by some as "a principle of customary law of general application."[17] It is useful to give it some, though not absolute, weight in a theory of national self-determination to prevent border rectifications by force of arms and ethnic cleansing. And clearly, administrative boundaries bear added significance when they define constituents of a federation, especially one whose constitution announces itself to be "proceeding from the right of every nation to self-determination, including the right to secession."[18] Roughly, the greater the autonomy and constitutional powers of the administrative unit, the firmer the application of *uti possidetis* should be, all else being equal.

The following general principles have now emerged.[19] Territorial groups with historical-cultural identities, especially if also regional minorities, have high priority. If they inhabit administrative units of long standing and with settled borders, and especially if these have constitutional significance, the principle of *uti possidetis* should apply. There are qualifications: the secessionists cannot be aiming to deprive the former state of its most important resource base, and they must respect the individual and cultural rights of their own minorities, which do not, however, necessarily include a recursive right to separate.[20]

Remainder minorities of regional majorities (Russians in the seceded former Soviet republics, Serbs in the seceded former Yugoslav republics, Anglophones in a potentially seceding Quebec) have particularly weak claims to partition the new states. If the seceding states are democratic and respectful of minority rights, the options available to remainder minorities—including dual citizenship—are robust and meaningful without recourse to destabilizing alternatives. The institutional matrixes of their identities are secure and based on the statehood of their nation, whether or not that state includes them. The claims of leftover minorities become stronger, however, if their concentration is very high, or if there is strong likelihood that their minority and individual rights will be violated (the Albanians of Kosovo and the Armenians of Ngorno Karabagh could make both claims convincingly). But that likelihood has to be shown with evidence; it is insufficient for the group merely to claim that it 'fears' attacks by the new majority.

These general considerations aim optimally to combine the principles of self-determination, stability, and territorial integrity long accepted as principles of international law. They also appear to be the rough direction in which the right of self-determination has developed in the previous decade, including in the decisions of the European Arbitration Commission (Badinter Commission) for the former Yugoslavia. As we shall see, those decisions fell short of endorsing the right of self-determination argued for here. They relied primarily on the view, reasonable under the circumstances, that the SFRY was in a state of dissolution. But they appear more cogent and consistent, I should like to suggest, against the background of the developing recognition of a qualified national right of self-determination, and it is in this light that an increasing number of jurists have interpreted them.[21]

The Break up of Yugoslavia

Let us turn, then, to the case of the former Yugoslavia, and see if we are not now in a better position to assess the claims and counterclaims that have been made. The history of the breakup of the SFRY has been recounted and analyzed in numerous works[22] and need not be repeated here. However, given that this history is sometimes related tendentiously,[23] it is worth drawing attention to a few salient facts. In the late eighties, a reform-minded nationalism was on the rise in Slovenia. Events came to a head in 1987 when the JNA (Yugoslav National Army) responded with a crackdown on the leading dissident organ, *Mladina*, the Socialist Youth weekly, and arrested the "Ljubljana Four." It is worth recalling the remarks of one of the four, Franci Zavrl, editor-in-chief of *Mladina*: "In early 1989, I and most others would still have opted for Yugoslavia. But then began Milošević's attacks in Kosovo, the attacks on Slovenes in the Army, and the whole irrational pressure from Serbia and Milošević. It drove us out much faster."[24]

The "attacks in Kosovo" referred to by Zavrl culminated in the March 1989 abrogation of Kosovo's status as an autonomous province. A clear violation of the 1974 Constitution of the SFRY,[25] it was carried off by surrounding the parliament in Priština with JNA tanks, and firing into crowds of protesters, killing scores.[26] This was followed by the imposition of a regime of repression, to last a decade, in which an entire administrative bureaucracy and police force of ethnic Serbs were imposed on the 85% majority Albanian population. At the end of the eighties these events were unfolding against the backdrop of a virulent Serbian nationalism, encapsulated in the famous Memorandum of the Serbian Academy of Sciences and Arts. Published in 1986, it described the 1974 autonomous status granted to Kosovo as an act of "treason" by Tito, implicitly equated the higher Albanian birth rate - and unsubstantiated allegations of crimes committed against Serbs - with "genocide" against the Serbian people, and called for the abrogation of Kosovo's status. Milošević was to oblige within three years.[27] By essentially taking over both provinces, Kosovo and Vojvodina, yet retaining their votes in the eight-man federal Presidency over the protests of Slovenia and Croatia, and with Montenegro already having been brought to heel as well, Milošević had in effect destroyed Yugoslavia as a federation and prepared the rise of secessionist sentiment in the remaining republics. As a final straw, Milošević prevented the Croat Stipe Mesić from assuming the head of the rotating presidency, a move which directly led to the Croatian independence referendum of May 19, 1991.[28]

A further point may be worth noting. It is sometimes claimed that Ante Markovic, the last Federal Prime Minister (1989-1991) before the disintegration and a Croat economic reformer who enjoyed wide popular support, might have succeeded somehow in "holding the country together" had the new "nationalists" in the breakaway republics been less recalcitrant and the West "done more" to support him.[29] These claims are oblivious to the fact that Milosevic had already plundered the Yugoslav federal reserves that year and redirected them to Serbia. As one writer put it, "In fact, Milošević's theft had already wrecked the economic plan for 1991, by making off with no less than half the entire primary emission of money set aside for all six Yugoslav republics for that year.... Indeed, the Marković plan was already a failure by the time it was touted in the West as Yugoslavia's salvation."[30]

Before returning to the question of the right of secession, it is necessary to outline the position of the international community at the time. A persistent myth in some Western circles is reflected in Donald Horowitz's assertion that while Western countries supported central governments against secessionists in Biafra and elsewhere in the past, "Barely a glimmer of such Western central-government bias was in evidence in the Yugoslav case."[31] In fact, considerably more than a glimmer of such bias was evident. On June 21, 1991, just four days before Slovenia and Croatia were set to declare their independence, American Secretary of State Baker arrived in Yugoslavia, declared staunch American opposition to the declarations of independence, threatened the Slovenian and Croatian leadership that the U.S. would also oppose recognition of any unilaterally declared states (citing the Helsinki Final Act), urged them to drop their UDI (unilateral declaration of independence) plans, declared U.S. support for the "territorial integrity of Yugoslavia," promised the Serbian leadership that the U.S. would refuse recognition of the breakaway republics, and urged Prime Minister Marković (however naively) to pressure the republics to abandon their plans.[32] Nor was the European Community, as a whole, saying anything essentially different at this point, despite later revisionist insinuations by some writers. EC President Jacques Delors, British Foreign Secretary Douglas Hurd, and Italian foreign minister Gianni De Michelis reiterated the EC's view that "the territorial integrity" of the SFRY must be preserved, and that the EC would not recognize the UDI's of Slovenia and Croatia. Its representatives continued to insist it was committed to the preservation of the Federation even as the JNA was planning attacks on both seceding republics. On June 19, 1991, The Conference on Security and Cooperation in Europe (CSCE) adopted a declaration in favor of "democratic development and [the] territorial integrity of Yugoslavia."[33] As Marc Weller, summing up the evidence, concluded:

> The support for maintaining the territorial integrity of the federation voiced by representatives of influential states and organizations, including the United States, the European Community (EC) and its members, and the Conference on Security and Cooperation in Europe (CSCE), undoubtedly strengthened Slobodan Milošević, the Serbian leader, in his perception that flexibility was not required in negotiations, since independence for Slovenia and Croatia was not supported internationally. Instead of offering to accept a looser confederation, the Serbian leadership had the central army declare martial law.[34]

At the same time that Baker and EC spokesmen were insisting on Yugoslavia's "territorial integrity," they also declared their opposition to Belgrade's use of force to repress the secessions.[35] But as with similar American declarations during Moscow's assaults on Chechnya, such admonitions against the use of force are bound to ring hollow when coupled with opposition to secession, since territorial integrity is constituted precisely by the display of a monopoly of force on the territory.[36] Once the international community declared itself committed to the territorial integrity of the federation, especially a leader like Milošević was bound to interpret the signals, while superficially mixed, as a green light to deploy force.

This interpretation would receive further confirmation after war did break out. Back in Washington after his failed final-hour trip to Yugoslavia, Baker uttered his famous "We have no dog in this fight."[37] Throughout the summer of war, Lawrence Eagelburger declaimed in like spirit.[38] As late as September 1, 1991, when Croatia was well awash in blood, the EC, while repeatedly condemning the use of force by all sides, called for Croatian forces "to be disbanded" and for the JNA (merely) to return to its barracks.[39] Indeed, it was Yugoslavia which, at the end of September, pushed for a UN Security Council meeting, the first to be held since the outbreak of war; and it was Yugoslavia again which requested, and received, the imposition of sanctions against all parties to the conflict,[40] thereby ensuring massive JNA military superiority for the next few years.

By October 1991 international acceptance that the dissolution of the Federation was a *fait accompli* was growing. (It would take yet another two months before Germany would recognize the two breakaway republics, that is, six months *after* the declarations of independence and the outbreak of war.) It was clear by this time that Serbia had itself accepted the dissolution and was aiming for the creation of a Greater Serbia out of chunks of Croatia and eventually Bosnia. It is neither possible nor necessary to pursue the narrative of diplomacy in detail here; we have covered enough to begin an assessment of the question of self-determination. After assessing the cases of Slovenia and Croatia, we will consider the more complex case of Bosnia.

The previous theoretical discussion argued that distinct national groups lacking states of their own in their region have a *prima facie* strong claim to be allowed to secede. When such groups form the primary residents of administrative boundaries of a federal structure, especially one whose constitution is predicated on the self-determination of the constituent units, then the boundaries of that unit should be kept, provided that the rights of leftover minorities are respected. The latter proviso, of course, is complex. On the one hand, the seceding group is likely to be ebulliently asserting its own identity, since the desire to have that identity flourish is the motivation and justification for the claim to independence. Such a situation is bound to make the leftover minority uneasy at the least. On the other hand, if the central state resorts to force and pursues irredentist claims using the leftover minority as its allies, the seceding group will more likely suspect the minority as a hostile fifth column abetting a foreign aggressor.

In the case of Slovenia, there was no significant leftover minority of Serbs to raise such questions. In Croatia there was. It is interesting to note the opinions of the Badinter-led Arbitration Commission, set up by the EC in October 1991 as it came increasingly to accept the fact of Yugoslav disintegration. The Commission did not concede the right of any republic (or far less, former province) of the federation to secession. That is, its opinions fell short of the more permissive view argued for above. It also made no explicit reference to a constitutional right to secede, perhaps on the grounds that the 1974 constitution left some ambiguity with regard to such a right.[41] It did, however, take the reasonable view, minimalist under the circumstances, that since this was a "case of a federal-type State, which embraces communities that possess a degree of autonomy and, moreover, participate in the exercise of political power within the framework of institutions common to the Federation," and since four of the Republics "have expressed their desire for independence," three of them by that time through popular referenda, therefore the SFRY "is in the process of dissolution" and the constituents could determine their own futures within the constraints of respect for minority and human rights.[42] One might expand the argument somewhat: when four of six republics have already indicated their wish to leave a federation, and when the fifth has already acted in violation of the constitution and declared it will no longer abide by it, the federation is in dissolution. This basis of the seceding republics' claims is critically enhanced, however—though the Commission did not take note of it—by the fact that each republic had a separate historical identity with a distinct national character.

To the question of whether the leftover Serb minorities in Croatia and BiH had the right of self-determination, the Commission replied in Opinion 2 that while "international law as it currently stands does not spell out all the implications of the right to self-determination," the principle of *uti possidetis* should apply. That is, the Serb minorities had a right to a full complement of minority rights and guarantees, but not a right of (recursive) secession from the new states. In Opinion 6, which deals with the possible recognition of Croatia by the EC, the Commission specified that the republic had not yet satisfied the provisions defending minorities in an earlier draft Convention of the Conference on Yugoslavia, and recommended that it do so; implicitly, it conditioned EC recognition on these changes.

Objections by some writers that even this grievously belated recognition by the EC went too far do not seem cogent. With an air of profundity, Woodward declares that "The idea that nations have a right to their own state thus turns...West European history on its head.... at the moment when the principle of national self-determination is used to create a modern state, it is reversing the West European process whereby states created nations, not nations states."[43] The historical claim that states created nations, familiar enough from the works of writers like Gellner, no doubt has some truth to it, though it of course cannot be the whole truth; otherwise there would never have been minority nations seeking national self-determination *against* existing states. But it also does not follow that if an earlier historical tendency was for states to create nations, that minority nations cannot have rights to states. It also "turns... West European history on its head" to abolish slavery and to decolonize; few today would consider this a weighty objection to abolition and decolonization.

More confusedly, Woodward goes on to analyze four "conflicting concepts of the nation" which can serve as the basis for a right to statehood: historicist, democratic, "the Helsinki (and United Nations) principle... that all existing, internationally recognized borders are 'inviolable' and define states," and the realist principle of physical control through military force. Since "there is no agreed-upon lexical priority among these principles" the departure from the "Helsinki principle" was an invitation to war; moreover, the European Community had applied the principles in an *ad hoc* and inconsistent way.[44]

In fact, the Badinter opinions prioritized the principles in an optimally reasonable way, despite falling short of an explicit endorsement of the republics' rights to secession (their rights to independence followed only from the dissolution of the Federation, a consequence of two-thirds of the republics wanting out). It held, quite consistently, that the republics could each have independence (thereby giving each primary identity group one state in which it formed a majority or plurality), but that leftover minorities required only minority and human rights guarantees, not further destabilizing partitions. Inasmuch as an "invitation to war" was broadcast to Belgrade, it consisted in the American and EC *adherence* to the

"Helsinki principle"[45] of preserving territorial integrity and the inviolability of Yugoslavia's borders, long into the summer of 1991.[46]

Contrary to persistent myths, this policy was pursued by Germany as well. As Alain Finkelkraut observed, the German decision to recognize Slovenia and Croatia, taken in December 1991 and implemented on January 15, 1992, came only "after the destruction of Vukovar, after the bombardment of the historic downtown of Dubrovnic, during the siege of Osijek. At that point, the war against Croatia had gone on for six months and had already inflicted about ten thousand deaths and made more than half a million Croats into refugees."[47] This was precisely the reason that German Foreign Minister Genscher gave for beginning to consider recognition: JNA escalation of violence in July 1991. Recognition, by internationalizing the conflict, would give the international community new levers to use against Serbia in an effort to stem the violence.[48]

Self-determination: The Case of Bosnia

Doubts about the soundness of Bosnia's claim to self-determination are well known. Indeed, they were rehearsed repeatedly in the media throughout the war not only by Bosnian Serb and Serbian officials, but also by Western diplomats and commentators intent on showing why the notion of a sovereign unified BiH was misconceived from the beginning. The arguments have since been taken up and elevated by writers like Susan Woodward and Robert Hayden to the level of attempts to explain the very cause of the war. There are actually a variety of claims, not always consistent with each other, but which generally run roughly as follows.

Bosnian Muslims, or Bosniaks, never formed a majority in the Republic of BiH. If self-determination is based on national belonging, clearly Bosniaks could not claim for themselves the independence of an entire republic in which they themselves were a minority. Either they wished to maintain a multiethnic republic, or they didn't. If they were indeed committed to a multiethnic republic, the SFRY was already one; what logic could there be in breaking away from it to set up a microcosm of it? If, on the other hand, the Bosniaks sought an ethnic Muslim state, either they would have to subjugate the other two main ethnic groups, which would of course altogether lack legitimacy, or else they would have to accept the partition of Bosnia, as Bosnian Serb nationalists demanded.

Sometimes the argument was put more simply. If the Socialist Federal Republic of Yugoslavia could be broken up, why not the Republic of

Bosnia-Herzegovina? Whatever arguments applied to the first applied with at least equal force—given their respective ethnic compositions—to the second. So any claim of a right to secession for a unified independent Bosnia was automatically self-defeating.

Robert Hayden[49] provides a Badinter-focused variation on this theme. If Badinter was correct that the SFRY was in dissolution, then so was BiH:

> The legal problem of the nature of the Bosnian conflict stems from the international recognition of Bosnia as an independent state in circumstances in which it did not meet the customary requirements for recognition in international law, because the putative Bosnian state had collapsed. While the international community recognized Bosnia as a state, a very large percentage of its putative population did not. The government that was recognized never controlled more than 30 percent of the territory, nor did it enjoy the allegiance of large, definable portions of the population...[50]

In short, "when it was recognized as an independent state and admitted to the United Nations" the Republic of BiH "was at least as advanced in a 'process of dissolution'[Badinter] as was the SFRY in January 1992."[51] (Actually, Badinter Opinion 1 was issued in November 1991).

These arguments have a certain persuasive appeal that accounts for their influence beyond the group of partisan pro-Serbian writers. But this appeal derives its force from the elision of several fundamental facts: First, a multiethnic society can have a supra-ethnic identity and a right of self-determination (e.g. Switzerland, Canada, and Belgium, to name a few). Secondly, not every homogeneously ethnic group enjoys a right of self-determination in the widest sense, which includes a right of secession. It was argued above that leftover minorities have relatively weak claims to secede (or to "partition" new states). The weakness stemmed from two essential facts: that their needs were different from the first secessionists (because they reside next door to their established kin-state), and that new states are particularly vulnerable, especially to irredentist claims from the remainder state.

That Badinter in Opinion 3 was thinking of the latter point is evident from his quotation of and comment on the 1986 judgment of the Burkina Faso vs. Republic of Mali dispute: The "obvious purpose [of the principle of *uti possidetis*] is to prevent the independence and stability of new States being endangered by fratricidal struggles..."[52] In other words, for good reasons, international law draws a *basic asymmetry* between primary and secondary secessions. Going beyond Badinter, however, it was argued above that strong evidence of likely discrimination, as well as high concentrations of a group's population in some single area, would increase the strength of a leftover minority's claims. But such evidence, of course, could only be available if the group did not first resort to force even before independence was declared.

Now let us reconsider the case of Bosnia. The largest ethnic group, the Bosniaks, could make a convincing case that in the rump-Yugoslavia available to them they could not hope to freely express and develop their distinct identity; this was evident from the briefest of glances in the direction of either Kosovo or the Sandžak. But as they were not a majority (in the 1991 census Bosniaks, Serbs, and Croats made up respectively 44, 31, and 17 percent of BiH), the only conceivably legitimate way Bosniaks could enjoy a right of self-determination was if they could carry a majority of the residents of the territory, and if they were committed to a multi-ethnic society in which their particular identity could flourish without subjugating the other groups. Herein lies the fundamental flaw in the microcosm argument. In a Serb-dominated (and Milošević-run) rump-Yugoslavia they stood to be a small and subjugated minority; in an independent multi-ethnic Bosnia they could flourish and promote their distinct identity as a plurality—the most important constituent group—while giving due recognition to the other main constituents, provided enough of those constituents were willing to go along.

It remains to consider what evidence there was that the BiH government met these conditions in fact, and consequently, what validity there was to the Bosnian Serb claim to partition. The evidence, in fact, is overwhelming that the BiH Presidency consistently announced its intentions to pursue a multi-ethnic policy, and acted accordingly. The Bosnian Serb leadership, on the other hand, declared its intentions from the spring of 1991 onward to refuse to comply with the BiH government if it sought independence. As early as July 1991 the SDS (Serbian Democratic Party, headed by Radovan Karadžić) mounted a boycott of Parliament, declaring that its constituents no longer considered themselves bound by its decisions.

Even before that, as early as May 1991, the SDS set up SAOs (Serb Autonomous Areas) manned by their own gunmen, and "began demanding the secession of large parts of northern and eastern Bosnia, which would then join up with the Croatian 'Krajina' to form a new republic.... More alarmingly, by July 1991 there was evidence that regular secret deliveries of arms to the Bosnian Serbs were being arranged by Milošević, the

Serbian Minister of the Interior, Mihalj Kertes, and the Bosnian SDS leader, Radovan Karadžić. Confirmation of this came in August, when outgoing federal Prime Minister, Ante Marković, released a tape recording of a telephone conversation in which Milošević could be heard informing Karadžić that his next delivery of arms would be supplied to him by General Nikola Uzelac, the federal army commander in Banja Luka."[53]

It is important to stress that all this was occurring well before the BiH government had even decided to seek independence (indeed, Croatian nationalists would repeatedly blame Bosnians for their understandably fearful dallying) and still several months before the EC had decided to instate a procedure for republics to apply for recognition. Moreover, many of the SAOs had no Serb majority, let alone majority support from all their residents (one cannot assume that all Serbs supported them). The entire Drina Valley lacked not only a Serb majority, not only a Serb plurality, nor was it even the case that no one had a majority; it had an absolute majority of Muslims. Other regions claimed by Serbs also had no Serb majority.

Only a brief chronology of events can be provided here. On October 14, 1991 Radovan Karadžić issued his notorious threat of annihilation of the Muslims in the event of war.[54] In January 1992, Milošević issued secret orders to transfer all JNA officers who had been born in Bosnia to Bosnian territory. Borisav Jović, Milošević's right-hand man, later explained: "We did not wait for international recognition of Bosnia to redeploy the troops in Bosnia. By the time of recognition, out of 90,000 troop in Bosnia... 85% of them were from Bosnia." On January 9, Bosnian Serb politicians proclaimed the Republika Srpska of BiH, and stated that it was part of the Yugoslav Federation. Again, the borders encompassed areas in which Serbs were a minority.[55]

On February 29 and March 1, the Bosnian Presidency held a referendum according to the recommendation of the Arbitration Commission (Opinion No. 4) that "a referendum of all the citizens of the SRBH *without distinction*" (emphasis added) be held under international supervision.[56] It was boycotted by nationalist Serbs, who had held their own referendum November 9–10. In the Bosnian referendum, 63.4% of eligible voters went to the polls; 99.7% of valid ballots voted for independence. Serbian paramilitary forces began ethnic cleansing at the beginning of April, as Arkan's "Tigers" seized control of Bijeljina and Zvornik with the support of JNA units.

By all accounts, the BiH government was completely unprepared for the savage war that befell it. Izetbegović had even hoped that the JNA would defend Bosnia. Even after the nature of the war had finally dawned on the

BiH leadership, its members for a long time resisted adopting a reciprocal policy of ethnic cleansing.[57]

As a potential leftover minority, did the Bosnian Serbs have any grievances against the Bosnian government which might have strengthened their case for partition? Journalist Blaine Harden summed up the situation on April 24, 1992 in the *Washington Post*:

> Independent observers in Bosnia agree that prior to the outbreak of fighting, the Serb minority there had no reason to fear ethnic discrimination, let alone ethnic violence. The Muslim-led government in Sarajevo had given the Serbs elaborate assurances of political and civil rights, and Milošević acknowledged as much to U.S. diplomats in private meetings.[58]

No evidence has been cited by critics discussed herein inconsistent with the conclusion of Lukic and Lynch that:

> the primary cause of the war in Bosnia and Herzegovina lay not in the relations between the various national groups but in Serbia's refusal to accept the sovereignty of the breakaway republic. Milošević was determined, independently of the attitude and conduct of the Bosnian Government, to establish a greater Serbian state encompassing all areas of ex-Yugoslavia where significant concentrations of Serbs lived.[59]

We can take stock here of the essential points relevant to assessing the legitimacy of SDS claims to partition:

1. The SDS resorted to force long before the BiH government's declared policy of multiethnicity could be tested, and indeed, even before the elected government sought independence.
2. The SDS demanded independence for territories on which Serbs had no majority, and which had no prior standing as political units of any kind.
3. While there was no evidence that Serbs faced discrimination, there was no hope that Serbs, under prevailing conditions, would respect the rights of minorities on territories in which they seized control; their primary aim in these territories was to "cleanse" them of non-Serbs.

Even had none of these facts obtained, the claims to partition of a leftover Serb minority would have been weak and highly questionable under the interpretation of self-determination offered above, as well as under the less permissive standard view of international law. Given that the facts *did* obtain, the conclusion is inescapable that Serbian nationalist claims to partition BiH lacked legitimacy, on any construal of self-determination in international law.

Hayden argues at length that the republican constitution of BiH had provisions granting veto power to any of its three main constituent groups on constitutional change, and that the BiH government "never controlled more than 30 percent of the territory."[60] But neither of these facts supports the conclusion he draws. On the first point, that constitution was in effect just so long as the SFRY was. It meant that constituent groups held vetoes over constitutional change in BiH *within* the SFRY. But the dissolution of the SFRY created a constitutional vacuum in which it was necessary to reconstitute BiH.

The means recommended by Badinter of assessing the self-determination of the Republic were the only legitimate, recognized means available: a referendum throughout the republic for all citizens *without distinction*. The alternative, to allow a Serbian veto to hold sway, would not have been self-determination but other-determination: rule by a minority over the majority. Once the will of a majority or supermajority (not demanded by Badinter, but provided by the populace) had been ascertained, it would have been possible further to assess Bosnian Serb claims to partition, had they not already resorted to force. As argued above, those claims carried virtually no substance because they were made by a leftover minority facing no threat of discrimination; nor did Serbs seek partition on lands on which they constituted a majority, prior to cleansing. Moreover, their chief aim was to partition an integral metropolis, Sarajevo, which violates the constraints of even the most permissive theories of self-determination.[61]

As for the lack of control of most of the territory by the BiH government, this again does not point to Hayden's conclusion. The Badinter opinion (No. 1) that the SFRY was in dissolution was based on the view that "in the case of a federal-type State," when four of six federal republics vote to leave (citing the referenda in three and the then BiH Parliamentary resolution, contested by the SDS), that federation is in dissolution. In BiH, there were no territorial units with analogous standing, the great majority of citizens (at the time including Croats) voted for independence, and the lack of control of the territory was accomplished with the military backing of Serbia proper, both by the JNA and by paramilitaries, and was maintained by a Security Council arms embargo imposed at the request of Yugoslavia itself. The lack of control of territory, then, merely underscored the violation by Serbia, in collusion with the SDS, of UN Charter Article 2 (4): "All Members shall refrain in their international relations from the threat or use of force against the territorial integrity or political independence of any State."

In 1940 the French government lacked control of most of its territory; who would have concluded that the French had thereby lost their right to self-determination under international law? As Brownlie points out, notwithstanding the stipulation of the 1933 Montevideo Convention On Rights and Duties of States that the possession of a government over a defined territory is a condition of statehood, effective government is neither necessary nor sufficient. "The principle of self-determination will today be set against the concept of effective government." If a state has been recognized on other grounds, "extensive civil strife or the breakdown of order through foreign invasion... are not considered to affect personality."[62]

Conclusion

In sum, there was both a factual and a normative asymmetry in the conditions of the SFRY and BiH. The factual asymmetry lay in the different respective reasons for the collapse of the SFRY, on the one hand, and the lack of control over most of BiH, on the other hand. The SFRY collapsed when most of the federal units, and most of the population, opted to leave (itself in response to the illegal hegemony imposed by Serbia). BiH, to the extent that it was in a state of "dissolution," was so because of armed aggression by a minority and its outside backers, in direct opposition to the expressed will of the majority of the population in an internationally supervised referendum. The normative asymmetry lay in the different requirements and rights in primary and secondary secessions, implicitly recognized in international law in the principle of *uti possidetis*, and defended in this paper in a previous section.

Bosnia, then, was one more case of a seceding republic, led by a group with a distinct identity that could not flourish in the repressive state it wanted to leave, and supported by the majority of its population due partly to its initial policy of multiethnicity, which fell victim to irredentist violence directed by the remainder state, compounded by lack of effective support from the international community for its independence and integrity.[63] The intervention that did take place was in response to the humanitarian consequences, which soon attained catastrophic dimensions.

Once it is recognised, as recent legal writing has increasingly done, that the decisions of the Badinter Commission were basically sound - in particular that there was a fundamental assymetry between the claims of BiH and those of the SDA-led RS - one will be able to assert with greater confidence and clarity the imperative of creating political institutions in Bosnia and Herzegovina unified at least to the minimum degree necessary for any functioning state. These institutions must eventually include a single overall enforcement agency: as long as each entity maintains its private near-monopoly of force (only the international presence necessitates the qualification "near-"), the most elementary rights and duties—from the right of return of refugees across and within entity borders to the obligation to pay taxes to the federal authority—will go unenforced; BiH will remain a paper state waiting to disintegrate the moment the Europeans and Americans no longer have the will to maintain the unitary facade. To create these common institutions it will be necessary to abrogate the relevant clauses of the Dayton Agreement, but that Agreement itself suggests the legal grounds for doing so, precisely because it also asserts the right of return of refugees. To the extent that one provision (the right of return) is unenforceable because of others (those endorsing entity-based enforcement agencies and administrations), it should be the latter provisions, not the former, which give way.

Once the various territories of BiH are integrated under a unified administration, it will be possible for the first time to address the thorny questions of how to enable all the minority identities to identify simultaneously with the common state. These questions are complex in any multiethnic state, and will no doubt be formidable in BiH, given its recent history. But they need not be insurmountable if the necessary first steps are taken. A clear understanding that BiH is the legitimate unit of statehood, and that the Republika Srpska, in particular, never had a right of secession, would help lay the groundwork for both integration and democratization. (Martin Raguz and other aspirants to a Croat 'Herzeg-Bosna' third entity would need to take this lesson on board as well.)

People's sense of who they are must be shaped and constrained by who and what they have a right to be and do. Once they are clear about that, once they grasp the constraints of fairness and feasibility in a world also peopled by groups other than their own, then their pursuit of the many facets of legitimate self-determination, from the most elementary civic freedoms, to representative government, to the expression of particular identities in private and public institutions, even to the maintenance of "special relations" with kin-states based on legitimate cultural associations and not irredentist dreams, will tend to reinforce rather than obstruct one another. It is then that both self-determination and democracy will have a chance in Bosnia-Herzegovina.

Notes

*   I would like to thank Andras Riedlmayer of the Fine Arts Library, Harvard University, for his excellent, expeditious, and generous bibliographical counsel.
1   See the web page of the Truth and Reconciliation Commission at http://www.truth.org.za.
2   Lee C. Buchheit, *Secession: The Legitimacy of Self-Determination* (New Haven and London: Yale University Press, 1978), p. 34.
3   This particular quotation is from the aforementioned Gen.Ass.Dec. 2625. See *Blackstone's International Law Documents*, 3rd Edition, ed. Malcolm D. Evans (London: Blackstone Press Limited, 1991), p. 211. Resolution 1514 (December 14, 1960), after asserting (in Article 2) that "All peoples have the right to self-determination," adds in Article 6: "Any attempt aimed at the partial or total disruption of the national unity and the territorial integrity of a country is incompatible with the purposes and principles of the Charter of the United Nations." See *Yearbook of the United Nations*, 1960, p. 49. The Helsinki Final Act stipulates that the principle must be pursued "in conformity" with the UN Charter and international legal norms, "including those relating to territorial integrity of States;" Articles III and IV respectively uphold the "inviolability of frontiers" and the "territorial integrity of states." See *International Legal Materials: Current Documents*, Bimonthly Publication of the American Society of International Law, Vol. XIV, No. 4, July 1975, pp. 1292 ff.
4   For a useful summary of juristic debate up to the mid-seventies, see Buchheit, *Secession*, pp. 127–137. The non-colonial interpretation, of course, predates the UN; its *locus classicus* is the pronouncements of Woodrow Wilson and his defenders. As an example of recent scholarship, Thomas Musgrave comments: "From the wording of various international instruments it appears that the legal right of self-determination extends beyond the colonial context." See his *Self-Determination and National Minorities* (Oxford: Clarendon Press, 1997), p. 90. Martin Dixon states that "Today self-determination is a well-established principle of customary international law and may well be a rule of *jus cogens*," in *Textbook on International Law*, 3rd Edition (London: Blackstone Press, 1996), p. 145. A rule of *jus cogens*, as stated in Article 53 of the Vienna Convention on the Law of Treaties, 1969, is "a peremptory norm of general international law" of such fundamental importance that "no derogation is permitted" and which cannot be modified by treaty, but only by another law "having the same character" (*Blackstone's International Law Documents*, 3rd Edition, p. 181). See also Dixon, *International Law*, 146–7, and endnote 5. For a recent attempt to *defend* the saltwater principle,

	see Lea Brilmayer, "Secession and Self-Determination: A Territorialist Reinterpretation," in *Yale Journal of International Law*, vol. 16, no. 1, January 1991.
5	Akehurst, for instance, observes that "Many people in the West have accused the United Nations of applying double standards, but these double standards are inherent in the Charter." The articles asserting the principle of self-determination "are so vague that it is doubtful whether they create any legal obligation at all." Michael Akehurst, *A Modern Introduction to International Law*, 1970, Sixth Edition (London: Routledge, 1986, 1995), p. 296. Ian Brownlie agrees with most contemporary commentators that "The present position is that self-determination is a legal principle," but that "Its precise ramifications... are not yet worked out." See his *Principles of Public International Law*, 4th Edition (Oxford: Clarendon Press, 1980, 1996), p. 597.
6	The term 'civilized' here implies nothing Kiplingesque. As previously indicated, peaceful secessions have taken place in the developing world (Senegal from Mali, 1960; Singapore from the Malaysian Federation, 1965; though these might more properly be called expulsions) and Eastern Europe (most of the former Soviet republics from the Soviet Union, 1991; Slovakia from Czechoslovakia, 1993) as well as in the West (Norway from Sweden, 1905; Iceland from Denmark, 1944). For the record, the Balkans, too, have had a so-far peaceful, if somewhat rocky, secession by Macedonia from the SFRY, though for reasons unlikely to earn the epithet of 'civilized' for the remainder state.
7	A common refrain of writers hostile to the secessionist republics is that "Led by Germany, European and American recognition of the former Yugoslav republics was accomplished in disregard of international-law doctrine forbidding recognition of secessionist units whose establishment is being resisted forcibly by a central government." See Donald Horowitz, "Self-Determination: Politics, Philosophy, and Law," in *National Self-Determination and Secession*, ed. Margaret Moore, Oxford University Press, 1998, p. 189. Horowitz's analysis of Yugoslavia relies mainly on two writers with pronounced pro-Serbian sympathies: Robert Hayden (see note 49) and Henry Huttenbach (he also mentions Hurst Hannum). Criticism by Hayden and Susan Woodward of the decisions of the Arbitration Commission is discussed in the next two sections of this chapter. In fact, since the breakup of the SFRY, many jurists have regarded the decisions of the organs of the international community as having *developed* customary international law by extending the principle of self-determination to the non-colonialist context. Thus Musgrave notes in *Self-Determination*, p. 125: "The response of the international community to the dissolution of the Soviet Union and of Yugoslavia therefore calls into question the extent to which self-determination based on ethnic criteria may now constitute an element of international law, and the circumstances in which it may apply." Likewise, Dixon, in his *International Law*, p. 146, observes that "state practice has re-shaped the principle of self-determination to meet the new circumstances of the post-colonial world. As the EC Arbitration Commission on Yugoslavia has indicated, the right of self-determination now certainly exists beyond the colonial situation." For the Arbitration (Badinter) Commission's application of *uti possidetis* beyond the colonial situation, see Dixon, p. 145, and below. See also Marc Weller, "Current Developments: The International Response to the Dissolution of the Socialist Federal Republic of Yugoslavia," in *The American Journal of International Law*, 1992, Vol. 86, p. 606: "The Yugoslav episode may reveal a core

of legally relevant practice on the substance of the right to secession. 1. Peoples are not legally precluded from secession, even outside the colonial context.... 2. Although the consent of the central authorities against which the secession is directed is encouraged, it is not constitutive of a claim to implement the right to self-determination.... 3. Once negotiations have been exhausted and a referendum has confirmed the popular desire for independence, the seceding entity enjoys elements of international personality, derived from the right to self-determination. In particular, the former central authorities are no longer permitted forcibly to assert authority within the seceding entity...."

8   I discuss this briefly in "Rights of Secession," in *Society* Vol. 35, No. 5, July/August 1998, and in a different version of the present essay, "Secession, Rights, Law: The Case of the Former Yugoslavia," in *Human Rights Review* 1:2, 2000. Sections of both articles are adapted here.

9   It is my contention that the primary value of territory is generally instrumental: it is a means of self-government. Governance has been territorial since the consolidation of the Westphalian system (1648); a group therefore requires the territory of its inhabitants in order to be self-governing. My approach is influenced by geographer Robert Sack's analysis of "territoriality" as "the attempt by an individual or group to affect, influence, or control people, phenomena, and relationships, by delimiting and asserting control over a geographic area." Robert David Sack, *Human Territoriality: Its Theory and History* (Cambridge: Cambridge University Press, 1986), p. 19. See also David J. Elkins, *Beyond Sovereignty: Territory and Political Economy in the Twenty-First Century* (Toronto: University of Toronto Press, 1995); and Alexander Murphy, "The Sovereign State as Political-Territorial Ideal," in *State Sovereignty as Social Construct*, eds. Cynthia Weber and Thomas Biersteker (Cambridge: Cambridge University Press, 1996). Some critics of secession question how a group right to self-government grounded in individual autonomy "quickly gives rise to territorial claims on behalf of such collectivities." See Donald Horowitz, "Self-Determination: Politics, Philosophy, and Law," in *National Self-Determination and Secession*, ed. Margaret Moore (Oxford University Press, 1998), p. 198. Recognizing the instrumental value of territory for governance is the first step toward dispelling the mystery. (Territories of course have other values: economic, military geo-political, and socio-symbolic.)

10 Dixon, *International Law*, p. 137. Brownlie, *Principles*, p. 287.

11 "Politics as a Vocation," in *From Max Weber*, eds. H.H. Gerth and C.W. Mills (London: Routledge and Kegan Paul, 1970, 1991), p. 78.

12 Antony Giddens, *The Nation-State and Violence* (Cambridge: Polity Press, 1985), p. 120.

13 Some American intellectuals voice disdain for "ethnic politics," viewing their own patriotism by contrast as merely "civic." But would they be willing to forgo the pervasive symbolization of their nation, perhaps replacing the symbols on coins, stamps and ubiquitous flags with some arbitrarily selected ones? On this, see Michael Billig, *Banal Nationalism* (London: Sage 1995).

14 One writer, Harry Beran, explicitly endorses "recursive secession" as the best way of ensuring that everyone gets what he legitimately wants. See his "A Liberal Theory of Secession," in *Political Studies* 32 (1984): pp. 21–31, and *The Consent Theory of Political Obligation* (Beckenham: Croom Helm, 1987). Needless to say, this proposal has not found many supporters in international relations or law.

15   The seminal text for an argument of this kind is Albert O. Hirschman's *Exit, Voice, and Loyalty* (Cambridge, Mass.: Harvard University Press, 1970). The argument has been directly applied against a permissive theory of secession by Allen Buchanan, "Democracy and Secession," in *National Self-Determination and Secession*, ed. Margaret Moore (Oxford: Oxford University Press, 1998), pp. 14–33, and against a constitutional right to secession by legal scholar Cass Sunnstein, "Approaching democracy: a new legal order for Eastern Europe – Constitutionalism and secession," in *Political Restructuring in Europe: Ethical Perspectives*, ed. Chris Brown (London and New York: Routledge, 1994).

16   Susan Woodward appears to believe, citing Serbian law professor Vojin Dimitrijević, that in invoking *uti possidetis* the Arbitration Commission "reached" to the Third World "to find a precedent" established "by the little-known border conflict between Burkina Faso and Mali," a tone conjuring up wily legal stratagems and contrived pleading. See Woodward, *Balkan Tragedy*, 213–214 and Dimitrijević, "The Yugoslav Precedent: Keep What You Have," in *Breakdown: war and reconstruction in Yugoslavia*, eds. Anthony Borden et. al (London: Institute for War and Peace Reporting, 1992). In fact, the principle can boast nearly as long and well-established a pedigree as any in modern international law. It was first applied in the early nineteenth century, with the dissolution of the Spanish Empire in Central (1810) and South (1821) America. The new states agreed that their titles should be coextensive with those held under the Spanish Empire. See Ian Brownlie, *Principles of Public International Law*, Fourth Edition (Oxford: Clarendon Press, 1990), pp. 134–5. The motive in adopting it at the time was clearly linked to the desire to avoid hostility. Hyde remarks, "When the common sovereign power was withdrawn, it became indispensably necessary to agree on a general principle of demarcation, since there was a universal desire to avoid resort to force, and the principle adopted was a colonial *uti possidetis*..." in his *International Law Chiefly as Interpreted and Applied by the United States*, 2nd edition, 1945, p. 499, n.3 (quoted in Brownlie, *Principles*, p. 134). The adoption of the saltwater principle by the United Nations and other international organizations, including the Organization of African Unity (OAU), during the heyday of decolonization in the sixties, was by implication an endorsement of the principle, as were several judgments of the time (the Temple v. Preah Vihear Case, 1962 ICJ Rep 6; Rann of Kutch Arbitration (India v. Pakistan, 1968); the principle was also invoked in 1985 in the Guinea–Guinea (Bissau) Maritime Delimitation Case (1985) 77 ILR 636.) According to jurists, including Badinter, the significance of the 1986 decision of the International Court of Justice (ICJ) on the dispute between Burkina Faso and the Republic of Mali, known as the *Frontier Dispute Case*, was that it "confirmed that *uti possidetis* was a principle of general application, not confined solely to South America."

17   Dixon, *International Law*, p. 145.

18   These words are taken from the opening sentence of "The Constitution of the Socialist Federal Republic of Yugoslavia" (Promulgated on February 21, 1974). In *Yugoslavia Through Documents: from Its Creation to Its Dissolution*, ed. Snezana Trifunovska (Dordrecht: Martinus Nijhoff Publishers), p. 224. For more on the rights of constituent republics and autonomous provinces, see below.

19   There is no suggestion here that these criteria could avoid all problems and conflicts. No set of criteria could accomplish that, certainly not the conservative and remedial ones still in vogue. But it is an unreasonable demand of any theory that it solve all problems. An adequate theory, to be workable, would require some sort of

20 permanent arbitration commission or court to adjudicate particular cases, to accumulate a body of precedents, and to interpret and adapt the general principles in light of the development of international law as a whole.

20 In extremely multiethnic states that have inherited boundaries from formerly colonial frontiers and are composed of dozens of ethnic minorities and no majority, the right of secession outlined here might not apply. Countries like Nigeria and India come to mind. Here, the critical factor in determining whether a right should be granted in a particular case will be the policy of the central state toward the group in question, rather than the group's aspiration to statehood alone.

21 For a few examples, see the second paragraph of note 7 above.

22 Reneo Lukic and Allen Lynch, *Europe from the Balkans to the Urals: The Disintegration of Yugoslavia and the Soviet Union* (Oxford: Oxford University Press, 1996); Laura Silber and Allan Little, *The Death of Yugoslavia* (London: Penguin, 1995); Marc Weller, "Current Developments: The International Response to the Dissolution of the Socialist Federal Republic of Yugoslavia," in *American Journal of International Law*, Vol. 86, 1992.

23 For example, Woodward introduces a discussion of the issue by alleging that "Western powers... sped up this process [of Yugoslav disintegration] by accepting the nationalists' definition of the conflict, undermining or ignoring the forces working against radical nationalists and acting in ways that fulfilled the expectations and reinforced the suspicions of nationalist extremists" (Woodward, *Balkan Tragedy*, p. 147). The "nationalist extremists" referred to are primarily the Slovenian and Croatian leadership, as the context makes clear.

24 Quoted in Laura Silber and Allan Little, *The Death of Yugoslavia*, p. 59.

25 Article 5 of the SFRY Constitution states: "The territory of a Republic may not be altered without the consent of that Republic, and the territory of an Autonomous Province—without the consent of that Autonomous Province" (Trifunovska (ed.), *Yugoslavia Through Documents*, p. 227). Of course, the outright abrogation of status of a republic or province and its forcible incorporation into another republic without its consent would be the most grievous breach of this provision.

26 *New York Times*, March 29, 1989.

27 For Milošević's refusal to condemn the Memorandum at the time, see Silber and Little, *The Death of Yugoslavia*, pp. 31–2. On the unsubstantiated allegations of crimes against Serbs, see Michael Sells, *The Bridge Betrayed: Religion and Genocide in Bosnia* (Berkeley: University of California Press, 1996), p. 56 ff. The novelist and ultranationalist Dobrica Ćosić is generally regarded as the principal inspiration behind the Memorandum, though Kosta Mihajlović, economist and later close adviser of Milošević, is thought to have been its main author.

28 "Croatian Leader Warns of Crisis," *International Herald Tribune*, May 15, 1991.

29 This was told to me by former British Foreign Secretary Douglas Hurd, in Lincoln College, Oxford, April 1996, but was a common refrain of British diplomacy in 1991–2.

30 Jonathan Eyal, *Europe and Yugoslavia: A Lesson From A Failure* (Royal United Services Institute for Defence Studies, 1993).

31 Horowitz, "Self-Determination," p. 191. Ironically, Horowitz is scathing toward recent philosophical literature sympathetic to a more permissive right of secession for having allegedly displayed "a thoroughgoing ignorance of the complexities of ethnic interactions" (p. 199). The claim cited in the text is intended as a corrective to this "thoroughgoing ignorance."

32	*New York Times*, June 25, 1991. Silber and Little, *The Death of Yugoslavia*, pp. 164–166. See also Warren Zimmermann (last U.S. ambassador to the SFRY), *Origins of a Catastrophe* (New York: Times Books, 1996).
33	Quoted in Marc Weller, "Current Developments: International Response," p. 570.
34	Ibid.
35	On Baker, see Silber and Little, *The Death of Yugoslavia*, p. 165. For Douglas Hurd, see the *Independent*, June 28, 1991, quoted in Weller, "Current Developments: International Response," p. 572: Hurd was "obliged significantly to qualify an early statement supporting the 'integrity of Yugoslavia' by adding that this should not include the use of force."
36	Weller seems to be one of the few commentators to see this clearly: "The source of this obligation to refrain from the use of force was not clear. If the right to self-determination protected an entity from the use of force by the central authorities from which it wished to secede, this would mean that there was no substance at all to the principle of territorial integrity and unity in its alleged internal application. For, without using force by way of 'internal police measures,' as is often claimed in such circumstances, the central authority would not be able to impose unity and a continuation of territorial integrity. On the other hand, the CSCE, the EC and individual states were still attempting to assert the existence of such a rule protecting states from the centrifugal forces of secession." See "Current Developments: International Response," p. 573.
37	Quoted in Mark Danner, "Endgame in Kosovo," *New York Review of Books*, May 6, 1999.
38	Some of his remarks are quoted in Danner, "Endgame."
39	Agreement on Cease-Fire, September 1, 1991. See Weller, "Current Developments: International Response," p. 576.
40	Weller, in "Current Developments: International Response," p. 578, notes that a state requesting sanctions against itself was unprecedented.
41	The preamble, cited earlier, refers to "The nations of Yugoslavia, proceeding from the right of every nation to self-determination, including the right to secession, on the basis of their will freely expressed in the common struggle of all nations and nationalities in the National Liberation War and Socialist Revolution...." Article 1 calls the SFRY "a federal state having the form of a state community of voluntarily united nations and their Socialist Republics, and of the Socialist Autonomous Provinces of Vojvodina and Kosovo." However, no article explicitly asserts a right of secession, and Article 4 holds that "The territory of the SFRY is a single unified whole," the frontiers of which "may not be altered without the consent of all Republics and Autonomous Provinces" ("The Constitution of the Socialist Federal Republic of Yugoslavia," in *Yugoslavia Through Documents*, ed. Trifunovska, pp. 224, 225, 226.)
42	"Opinion No. 1 of the Arbitration Commission of the Peace Conference on Yugoslavia, November 29, 1991," in Trifunovska (ed.), *Yugoslavia Through Documents*, pp. 415–417.
43	Woodward, *Balkan Tragedy*, p. 204.
44	Ibid., p. 212.
45	As we saw earlier, the Helsinki Final Act contained the same ambivalence about self-determination that other declarations had (see the discussion in the second section above and note 3). Contrary to Woodward, statesmen also invoked Helsinki when arguing *for* the self-determination of the republics and against Serbia's use of

	force. For an example of German Chancellor Kohl's reference to it in this light, see Lukic and Lynch, *Europe*, p. 270.
46	Woodward's muddle is most evident in the following passage: "By accepting the principle of national self-determination for the independence of states... Western powers were making war over territory inevitable. The struggle to create new states out of the Yugoslav federation was a struggle to get international recognition..." (*Balkan Tragedy*, p. 198). If the new states had to "struggle to get international recognition," it was because they hadn't received it, nor was any promise for them to do so forthcoming until the carnage had already shocked the European and world communities into *modifying* their policy.
47	Alain Finkelkraut, *Comment peut-on etre Croate?* (Gallimard: Paris, 1992). pp. 140–1. Also quoted in Lukic and Lynch, *Europe*, p. 274.
48	Genscher quoted in Lukic and Lynch, *Europe*, p. 270. For a detailed account of the legal obligations of the international community and its failure to meet them, see Marc Weller, "Peace-Keeping and Peace-Enforcement in the Republic of Bosnia and Herzegovina," in *Zeitschrift für ausländisches öffentliches Recht und Völkerrecht* (56/1–2: 1996).
49	Robert Hayden, along with his wife, Milica Bakić-Hayden, have been among the most vocal U.S. academics defending Serbia against alleged unfair attack. Hayden described the NATO bombing of Serbia over Kosovo as "textbook war crimes" and "committing the first unprovoked, opposed military aggression in Europe since Soviet troops invaded Hungary in 1956." That is, Serbia's attacks on Slovenia, Croatia, and Bosnia failed to qualify as "unprovoked"—after all, their populations had voted for independence—while the deployment of 40,000 paramilitary, police, and army in Kosovo *before* NATO bombing began, in breach of the pre-Rambouillet agreements, failed to qualify as provocation. Many of those same paramilitaries were reportedly previously responsible for war crimes in Croatia and Bosnia. The same article, "Humanitarian Hypocrisy," repeats Belgrade's line throughout the war that "Albanians were by then leaving mainly because of the NATO bombing". Robert Hayden, "Humanitarian Hypocrisy." *Pittsburgh Post-Gazette*, March 28, 1999.
	Other articles maintain that the war in Bosnia was a "civil war" because it was waged by local residents of Bosnia not controlled by Serbia, while the war between Serbia and Croatia was also a "civil war," this time apparently because it took place within the "civil" arena of the entire Yugoslavia. See "Bosnia's Internal War and the International Criminal Tribunal," *The Fletcher Forum*, Winter/Spring 1998, pp. 45–8, 50.) Also, "by classifying recent Yugoslav events as 'genocide,' the nature of the events is actually obscured rather than explained." See "Schindler's Fate: Genocide, Ethnic Cleansing and Population Transfers," *Slavic Review*, 55 (1996), p. 731. The "nature of events" that is "obscured" is the "inevitability" of the Serbian campaign of ethnic cleansing once the Bosnian government held a referendum and declared independence. (See also: Robert Hayden and Milica Bakic-Hayden, "Orientalist Variations on the Theme 'Balkans:' Symbolic Geography in Recent Yugoslav Cultural Politics," *Slavic Review* 51, and Bakic-Hayden, "Nesting Orientalisms: The Case of Former Yugoslavia," Slavic Review 54, no. 4 (1995), pp. 917–931.)
	I believe nevertheless that the space devoted herein to Hayden's argument about Bosnian self-determination is warranted by the influence such arguments have had beyond partisan pro-Serbian circles.

50	Hayden, "Bosnia's Internal War and the International Criminal Tribunal," *The Fletcher Forum of World Affairs*, Vol. 22:1, Winter/Spring 1998, p. 47.
51	Hayden, "Bosnia's Internal War," p. 51.
52	Trifunovska (ed.), *Yugoslavia through Documents*, p. 480.
53	Noel Malcolm, *Bosnia: A Short History* (London: Papermac, 1996), pp. 224–5. Malcolm adds, "There could be little doubt by now that Karadžić's actions were being directed, step by step, by the Serbian President: he even boasted to one British journalist in August that he and Milošević 'speak several times a week on the phone.'"
54	Silber and Little, *Death of Yugoslavia*, pp. 237–8.
55	Ibid., p. 240.
56	"Opinion No. 4, January 11, 1992," in Trifunovska (ed.), *Yugoslavia Through Documents*, p. 486.
57	Woodward grudgingly acknowledges this: "Claiming a unified Bosnia as its base instead of a separate national enclave, the SDA could not win with a policy of ethnic cleansing.... A referendum confirming the national sovereignty of Bosnia had to be supported by more voters than those who identified politically with the SDA as Muslims, and depended, therefore, on maintaining mixed communities." (Woodward, *Balkan Tragedy*, p. 243.)
58	Blaine Harden, "Fighting flares across Bosnia despite truce," *Washington Post*, April 24, 1992. Cited in Lukic and Lynch, *Europe*, p. 206. There was, of course, the infamous request by Bosnian President Izetbegovic in July 1991 to join the Organization of Islamic Countries (OIC), an act denounced by the SDS and Belgrade as abundant proof that Izetbegovic was bent on turning the republic into an Islamic state. But questions of the wisdom of Izetbegović's act aside, there is no more reason to object to BiH membership, then or now, in the OIC than to Canada's in the Organisation des pays francophones. Indeed, Francophones in Canada are only a minority, while Muslims in BiH were and are a plurality.
59	Lukic and Lynch, *Europe*, p. 206.
60	Hayden, "Bosnia's Internal War and the International Criminal Tribunal," p. 47 and passim.
61	SDS leader and indicted suspect of grave breaches of the Geneva Conventions on War, Radovan Karadžić, repeatedly stated throughout the war that he "wants to partition Sarajevo along ethnic lines," citing "Berlin, Jerusalem and Beirut" as models for his vision (this quote taken from Blaine Harden, "Bosnia's problems mount under Serbian siege," *Washington Post*, April 28, 1992, quoted in Lukic and Lynch, *Europe*, p. 207). For a voluntarist theory of secession stipulating the constraint that one not divide a metropolis, see David Gauthier, "Breaking Up: An Essay on Secession," in *Canadian Journal of Philosophy*, Vol. 24, No. 3, September 1994, p. 370: "To be sure, one can divide a single urban community if one is sufficiently determined; the example of Berlin is fresh in memory. But it is hardly an example to be emulated."
62	Brownlie, *Principles*, p. 73.
63	Some "realist" diplomats and academics continue to propose "solutions" aimed at achieving peace through the appeasement of irredentist Serb claims. For David Owen's views, see his *Balkan Odyssey* (London: Victor Gollancz, 1995), pp. 31–33. John Mearsheimer has published a steady stream of pieces favoring partition: "To entice the Serbs, NATO should offer a 'grand bargain' that partitions Bosnia as well as Kosovo, moving Serbia toward its dream of a homogeneous greater Serbia" (*New*

York Times op-ed, April 19, 1999); "There is still time to pursue the best alternative, a three-way partition of Bosnia. Large population transfers must be organized and assisted" (*New York Times* op-ed, October 7, 1997). See also *New York Times*, September 24, 1996: "Partition in Bosnia is unavoidable;" and *New York Times*, March 31, 1993: "...ethnically homogeneous states must be created..."

3 The Fractured Soul of the Dayton Peace Agreement: A Legal Analysis*

FIONNUALA NI AOLAIN

The Dayton Peace Agreement (DPA) was signed as a means to bring to an end the war in Bosnia-Herzegovina.[1] In the Western guarantor states the agreement was widely heralded as a triumph of diplomacy over chaos, reasoned agreement over crude warfare and as a multilateral agreement that forced confirmation of the legal existence and viability of the Bosnian state by all parties to the conflict. Despite the undeniable accomplishment of having ended mass fratricidal violence on Bosnian territory, the Agreement is a paradox of both substance and implementation. The DPA confirms the existence of the state yet contains ingredients that divide it into separate political and legal entities. The treaty pays homage to the language of self-reliance while ensuring that a long-term international presence remains a necessary element for the survival of the state. The Dayton Agreement fortifies the tripartite division of nation, community and individual in the new Bosnia where ethnic identity is all, and the body politic is a fractured soul.

The Dayton Agreement was negotiated in a purposefully created hot-house environment at the secluded Wright Patterson Air Force Base in Dayton, Ohio.[2] It was signed by the negotiating parties and a group of guarantor states, who were prepared to endorse and materially support a peace settlement for the Bosnian war, in Paris on December 14, 1995. The Agreement came after numerous failed diplomatic attempts by Western mediators to secure an end to war. It is a complex package of interrelated texts augmented by Security Council resolutions that establish the international forces and organs which support the Peace Agreement.[3] The DPA is the core of the compact between the belligerent parties. Its preamble acknowledges the need for a comprehensive settlement between all factions. The text of the Agreement makes broad commitments to military arrangements between the parties, demarcation lines, election programs, constitutional arrangements for Bosnia-Herzegovina, and the establishment of new commissions and institutions to support a peaceful transition and the observance of human rights.

In addition, the terse general text is supported by numerous detailed Annexes which spell out in greater depth the parties' commitments. Annex 1A concerns itself with the military aspects of the peace settlement, including the cessation of hostilities, the redeployment of forces and the deployment of the Implementation Force (IFOR). Annex 1B outlines the measures dealing with regional stabilization, including confidence and security measures and regional arms control principles. Annex 2 establishes the inter-entity boundaries. Annex 3 is concerned with the modalities of elections, guarantees for the protection of fundamental rights, democratic structures and inter-institutional relationships. Annex 4 contains the constitutional framework for Bosnia-Herzegovina. Annex 5 provides for the binding arbitration of disputes arising between the Bosnian Federation and the Republika Srpska. Annex 6 devises the domestic institutional structures designed to protect and enforce human rights in the post-war phase. These structures include a Human Rights Commission, an Ombudsperson, and a Human Rights Chamber. Annex 7 establishes the mechanisms intended to facilitate the return and protection of refugees, including a commission for displaced persons and refugees. Annexes 8–11 concern themselves respectively with the preservation of national monuments, public corporations, civilian implementation and the creation of an International Police Task Force (IPTF).

The DPA is an agreement with inherent limitations. Yet, despite these congenital defects, it is the sole framework that guides the new Bosnia in its post-war phase. This essay examines the prognosis for one element of Bosnia's institutional reconstruction following the Agreement, the Bosnian legal system. This essay also illustrates the inherent problems of the Dayton accords with respect to legal institutions and culture in Bosnia. By understanding the shortfalls of the international support structure and its domestic fledglings we may still have time to correct some of the deficiencies that have been imposed or agreed upon since December 1995.

In this corrective process there should also lie some deeper reflection. It leads me to deliberate on the wider issue of whether the international community should require any minimal thresholds in its facilitation of peace agreements between factious third parties. Is any agreement acceptable as a means to end mass violence? Or, are there minimal protections related to both the integrity of the individual and state that are non-negotiable in such processes? An agreement born out of the policies of ethnic cleansing and massive human rights violations must ensure that it does not become a vehicle to facilitate the continuation of the war by other means.

Restoring Legality—Some Principles

In the process of reviving Bosnian civil society, an indispensable element is the capacity and strength of the Bosnian legal system to regenerate and revitalize. Equally, regeneration on any level in Bosnia requires tackling some hard issues from the outset. Each institutional structure plays a part in the larger conflict of whether this state can be reborn as an ethnically mixed and inter-mixed one, or whether it will continue to perpetuate a fight over nation within territory.

Justice systems are among those institutions which suffer most during violent conflicts.[4] In a state born out of the breakdown of law and legality, law frequently has little currency for either the political leadership or the general populace. The descent into conflict is a rejection of law and legality in its most crude form. Rehabilitation of the legal system is not only about rebuilding courthouses and appointing unbiased court officials to interpret the reinvented rules. The rehabilitation process is far more fundamental than that. It requires no less than reestablishing the legitimacy of law itself.

My departure point for this discussion is a set of three principles which I use to inform the discussion of the interrelationship between the national and international in the reconstruction of a failed state entity, in this case, the Bosnian legal system. The first of these three is the principle of interdependence. The Bosnian legal system, as with most other aspects of life in a shattered state entity, is not yet and cannot expect to be independent for some considerable period of time. In its post-Dayton guise the legal system is not only dependent, it is also a construction of the international community. The international community is the guarantor and chief architect of the shape and structure of Bosnia as it exists today. This is a relationship of responsibility notwithstanding domestic political rhetoric in the endorsing states that seeks to undermine this obligation by advocating the unilateral withdrawal of international support pillars, be they military, civilian or financial in character. Inasmuch as the Bosnian legal system is in a situation of dependency on the international community, so, too, is the latter reliant on a strong and functioning system of law. No withdrawal or long-term solution to the political crises that have beset Bosnia can be envisaged without a legal structure to ease the way out for the international community. Dependency is a bilateral, symbiotic relationship.

The second principle is accountability. Just as it is paramount that restructuring take place, it must take place in an environment of openness and trust, both from the international community and the insider Bosnian communities. Accountability reflects the dual duties of the receiving state and the facilitators of reconstruction. Some have argued that accountability is achieved through "the requirement that a government's continuation in office depends on the active approval of the people as expressed in competitive elections."[5] As this essay will explore in greater depth later, periodic elections in a society fraught by multiethnic tensions and competing nationalisms are insufficient to protect accountability or even democracy itself. A wider vision of accountability includes respect for the rule of law and individual rights, popular participation, pluralism, fair competition and market development.[6] Accountability requirements also apply to states facilitating reconstruction with military and economic aid. Accountability means not only the translucence of financial investments, but also the transparency of agendas, and full knowledge as to the expectations and intentions on both sides.

The third principle is that of respect. Restructuring is not just another form of neocolonialism in legal guise. The international community has taken over the functions of the state in various ways (albeit with the rhetoric of temporariness). It consists of conflict mediators, police forces, rule makers, standard bearers, watchdogs and charity organizations. This must not impede or stifle the capacity of internal political communities to rebuild institutional capacity. According to this principle, real assistance to persons in Bosnia-Herzegovina means developing the capacity to solve problems for themselves. It means assisting and not hindering. To find lasting, stable solutions to the Bosnian crisis, outsiders have to think about really supporting the development of institutions and a political climate that would enable people to generate solutions. This is meaningful localization and not lip-service to subsidiarity. Such a simple principle stands in notable contradiction to much of the philosophy behind the institution-building and democratization efforts undertaken by many Western states in recent years.

At the root of these efforts has been the concept of *institutional modeling*,[7] the underlying idea being that if each major socio-political institution could become like counterpart institutions in Western democracies, the society as a whole would transform. This concept, in its rush to import foreign models, has a tendency to overlook existing domestic structures that function adequately. It suffers from the defect that its institutional components, presumed universalistic, have country specific, often American features. In short, institution-building programs are blithely unaware of the variety of political and legal forms that democracy and rule of law come in. Respect means that the mass importation of other legal systems' structures and principles must be avoided and that due consideration is given to the validity of cultural legal pedigree of the jurisdiction.

The Responsibility of the International Intervener

Some argue that the DPA was the best 'deal' that could be made under the particular circumstances of its birth. The realities of an ongoing armed conflict, the political marginalization of a number of key negotiators, the limited patience of the contact states, and the fragile consensus among them would inevitably hamstring any outcome. While all these empirical assessments are true, they overstate the limitations on the process.

It is easily conceded that the major task confronting the Western powers who convened the Dayton conference was the ending of violence. This was the primary goal, and a goal of immense rhetorical power. The Bosnian war was unique in modern terms because a slow genocide was visualized for worldwide television audiences on a nightly basis. Thus, ending violence had a significance not only for the civilians and combatants directly concerned with the hostilities, but also for a wider viewing public. The effect of this was clearly and correctly to focus attention on ending armed conflict. However, the danger of this concentration was that the ending of violence in itself was the goal, while the causal roots of the conflict and the means to create meaningful structures that would prevent its recurrence were left unaddressed.

Getting the balance right in such situations is difficult for the states facilitating resolution. There was no possibility that clashing communities in the midst of ongoing destruction were interested in or able to create common norms or institutions from the "bottom up." Indigenous solutions are impossible to cultivate while mass killings and expulsions continue. A heavier burden is instead placed on the interveners and facilitators. Peacemaking comes with obligations.[8] While a worthy endeavor, facilitating the transition from armed conflict to coexistence is not the end in itself. The intervener is judged on whether the transition to coexistence he facilitates is a durable one. Intervention is judged equally on the rhetoric used by the facilitating states in creating the process and its outcome.[9] When the components of a state are being created by international mediation, compromising high standards of accountability equates, in effect, to settling for the position that failed or weakened states and their citizenry are entitled to a lesser version of statehood.

When facilitating states are prepared to set low thresholds of conflict resolution from the outset, weak settlements are made.[10] The contact states and the fault lines between them which characterized the management of the Bosnian conflict are squarely at the root of a compromise on Bosnia that is flimsy on procedure and substance. The result is a weakened and compromised state, the very opposite of the stated rationale for negotiation. This resort to placing responsibility firmly on the shoulders of the international community may seem simplistic, finding an easy scapegoat for a complicated problem. Nonetheless, I would assert vigorously that negotiated settlements facilitated and prompted by the international community remain its responsibility. By setting the agenda of facilitation, the international sponsors also prophesy the outcomes that emerge. There should be no illusions about weak settlements solving complex problems. The opposite is true. The Dayton Agreement leaves open wide fissures that the international community has little choice but to constantly renegotiate, making detachment from Bosnia impossible in the short or medium term.[11]

What then are the options in the Bosnian context? Renegotiation of the peace agreement is both unlikely and undesirable in the short term. Ethnically-driven internal politics might view a reopening of negotiations as a means to limit positive and conciliatory commitments already made, rather than as a step towards deconstructing the ethnic monolith. However, as this article shall illustrate, to view Dayton as fixed is to eschew the possibility of recreating Bosnia as an ethnically mixed, multinational state. Thus, I propose a middle position. That is, that the international community, which bears much of the day-to-day responsibility for Bosnian societal activity, needs to view and execute Dayton as a transitionary structure, whose primary advantage has been to create a stable and secure environment. Thus, by encouraging civil society and emphasizing to the ethnic elites that the current ethnic hegemony and partisanship characterize only an intermediate stage, guarantor states may create a climate in which alternative structures are encouraged and fostered.[12] Alternatively, by fortifying Dayton's divisive structures, the international guarantors would further embolden those whose stock rises in such divided, ethnically-purified entities as those which currently comprise the nation of Bosnia.

The Challenges to Rebuilding

The Bosnian legal system descends directly from the legal system of the former Yugoslavia.[13] Each of the Yugoslav successor states did not instantly create new legal systems and institutions. The outward forms and courtroom symbols may have changed, but this is fundamentally the legal system of a socialist state with both a legal pedigree worthy of recognition and a notable number of built-in problems which need to be addressed.[14]

Further, while the new constitution of Bosnia-Herzegovina guarantees the democratic minimals of multiparty elections, free elections and an open media, there is no reservoir of tradition to support their normalization as part of ordinary political currency.

While admirable criticisms can be made of the pre-existing Yugoslav legal and political order, what should not escape notice for the purposes of this discussion is the extent to which the pre-war system sustained a complex web of constitutional checks and balances. In short, ethnic identity was central to political structures but identity and territory were not crudely matched pairs in pre-war constitutional arrangements. While it is also true that not all identities were equal (Albanians being a case in point),[15] the exceptions should not detract attention entirely from an ordered constitutional structure that sought to create a balance between group identity and national cohesion. The founding peoples of Yugoslavia were Croats, Macedonians, Montenegrins, Serbs and Slovenes, with Muslims being added after the 1963 constitution. Susan Woodward describes the arrangement as follows:

> The six republics of the federation recognized nations as historical-territorial communities. Individual members of the six constituent nations (not fully coincident with the territorial boundaries of the republics) had rights as members of those nations as ethnic peoples (defined by a common religion, language, and political consciousness).[16]

The DPA and its current epilogues make no attempt at either sophistication or intricacy. The territory-identity pair has been forged and its limitations are being clearly seen. The Bosnia that came into being after Dayton was the effective consolidation of division. Within the guise of unity, the *de facto* partition of the country between communities formed ever more homogenous ethnic zones.[17] The incompatibility of this duality with basic democratic principles illustrates the shortcomings in conceptualizing Bosnia's future stability.

In the pre-war context the privileged ethnic groups were regarded not as minorities but as "constituent peoples." There is a vast difference between the two concepts. A constituent people is equal in status with all other "peoples." Its rights are not the product of majority charity, but an entitlement on the basis of parity. Very likely, this terminology of "constituent peoples" gave rise to the language of self-determination and secession. This connection was made as a political matter, although the one does not necessarily lead to the other. But, without any doubt, to move from the status of a "constituent" people to that of a minority is a demotion and was collectively understood as such in the breakup of the Yugoslav

Federation. In the DPA framework, the protection of "entities" has hidden this demotion quite strategically.

The DPA does not address the problem of accommodating peoples accustomed to formal legal equality as a constitutional matter. It simply papers over the problem by entrenching the segregation of those same peoples. But this problem is not solved, as a pending case before the Bosnian Supreme Court attests, and moreover, because the international community also continues to insist in its rhetoric that the territory of Bosnia-Herzegovina must be rebuilt as an ethnically integrated state. Should that rhetoric move to practical action, internal and external actors will be faced with the conundrum that moving peoples towards integration requires a confrontation with their group status.[18] As yet, the international community has not learned the historical lesson from the former Yugoslavia that there must be a halfway house between complete apartheid and integration on the basis of demotion in status for one group. This halfway house is the missing link for stability and meaningful equality in a multiethnic state.

The Constitutional Conundrum

Deeply implicit in the Dayton Agreement is the overarching goal of the guarantor states to germinate democratic roots in the ashes of the successor states to the former Yugoslavia. At least, that is the theory. Elections, constitutions, constitutional courts, human rights protections and due process mechanisms play a rhetorical and public role in the political transformation that has been wrought by Dayton. The war is over and peace is brought by the carriage of democracy. Less overtly examined is the question of what form of democracy has been exported to Bosnia, a minimalist or maximalist version?

Arend Lijphart has made strong claims that the form of democratic structure most appropriate for a deeply divided society is that of consociationalism.[19] In his way of thinking, majoritarian structures undermine the project of remolding culturally fragmented societies. Consociational or consensus democracy requires a number of *a priori* schematic commitments: first, grand coalitions; second, stabilizing elite behavior;[20] third, segmental autonomy; fourth, proportionality; and finally, mutual veto. While some of these elements are present in the political legacy of Dayton, many are missing. Elite political behavior remains combative, and continues to aggravate mutual tensions and political instability.[21] Political cooperation is markedly absent in the common institutions, and extensive governmental coalitions are not on the horizon.

This leads to a more fundamental question: can the form of democracy envisaged by Dayton be properly termed "democracy" at all, or is it more aptly characterized as a form of liberalization with some democratic coating?[22] This question is highly significant. If the Dayton Agreement was content to set and endorse low democratic thresholds, arguably such a schema will serve to reinforce ethnic political partition, rather than to encourage an inclusive political spectrum. If we view the DPA as a commodity of intensely divided political elites, determined to maintain internal political hegemony in the physical space accorded to them, there is strong evidence of "low" and not "high" democracy in their product.[23] For the purpose of the legal analysis here, it is important to reflect on the fact that implicit in this "democratic export" by the mediating Western states is the legal system which supports and enforces it. Legality may not only fail on its own internal terms of reference; its failure may also be complicit in a much deeper wound on Bosnian society.

The new Constitution of Bosnia-Herzegovina, contained in Annex 4 of the DPA, spells out that the two entities, Republika Srpska and the Federation of Bosnia-Herzegovina, are to be regarded as members of a federal state, the Republic of Bosnia and Herzegovina.[24] It guarantees that Bosnia-Herzegovina "shall be a democratic state, one which shall operate under the rule of law and with free and democratic elections."[25] From the outset, we must understand that the Constitution of Bosnia-Herzegovina is a child of the international community. The Constitution was negotiated at Dayton and accepted by the internal parties concerned in three separate declarations. This is a Dayton constitution and not a Bosnian constitution, and this difference is quite substantial. The Constitution is not the product of a lengthy internal "consensus seeking." While not foisted upon the parties either, and thus not external to them, the Constitution is a document born of the reality of a compact made between an existing, internationally-recognized state and insurrectionist groups wielding *de facto* control over parts of the territory of that state.[26]

Entities and Citizens

The Constitution is not a document of one nation, but a document that recognizes three nations within its confines. Under the Constitution, the Republika Srpska is recognized as one "entity," a concession to the aspirations of nationhood demanded by its political leadership. Equally, the Federation of Bosnia-Herzegovina is acknowledged as an "entity." In fact, the term "entity" appears fifty-five times in the document, while the term "citizen" appears only seven times. The schizophrenia of the document is located in its attempts to reconcile multiple personalities. Thus, there is both the state of Bosnia-Herzegovina and the "entities;" there is citizenship for the individual located both in the state and in the "entities;"[27] and passports are issued both by the state and by the "entities."[28] This is not a constitution whose primary goal is navigating the relationship between the individual citizen and the state.[29] The Constitution is a document binding "entities," politically estranged territories forced into a marriage of convenience by the international community. It is not the product of political consensus between leaders and peoples. This is not a people's constitution, but an agreement of geographical coercion glued together by common institutions of which the Constitution is a part.

At Dayton, there was little hope that the parties negotiating settlement would avoid having a constitution imposed upon them.[30] The guarantor states, all democratic in orientation, would have seen the commitment to a constitution as proof of the parties' good will towards negotiation and peaceful resolution. For the parties themselves, a minimalist view of the obligations contained in a democratic constitution (regular open elections held periodically) would have allowed them to constitute the internal structural arrangements to their own nationalistic advantages.[31] This is precisely the outcome that has been achieved. The Constitution seals the tripartite division of the state, neatly concealing it in a package that glosses division with the illusion of rapprochement.

Sovereignty and Integrity

A constitution itself is capable of undermining the sovereignty that comprises the notion of the nation-state. State sovereignty is indisputably linked with territorial integrity. The integrity of the state is weakened when the state is divided into self-reliant entities, and cracked further by power-sharing formulas that encourage fissure. This is another paradox contained in the Bosnian Constitution. It bases Bosnia's claim to sovereignty and territorial integrity on international law, recognizing that the state exists within its internationally acknowledged borders. The creation of central government for the state goes along with that claim to sovereignty. However, the political reality is that "central government" is a misnomer in Bosnia. It is the entities which have the greater autonomy; the ceding of power has come from the center, from the state to the internal statelets. For example, while the central government conducts foreign policy, defense policy is the responsibility of the entities.[32] While the rhetoric of the DPA has concentrated on the international commitment to a united Bosnia, the reality is very different both politically and militarily. As Annika S. Hansen points out, "the distribution of power between national and federal levels illustrates a grave disjunction between the military and political sphere."[33]

The divisions of power within the state do not presuppose a unified Bosnia, but rather the opposite: two fragmented and polarized statelets.

Most problematic is the potential for the Constitution itself to endanger rights rather than protect them. For example, the very multiethnicity of the Federation may well be unconstitutional. The Constitution leaves little scope for protecting multiple rather than singular identities. It is not a document that seeks to carve out a middle ground of inclusiveness in order to protect rights. Instead, rights are the product of one's self and community definition, presumed to be based on exclusivity.

Multiplying Constitutions

The problem of fragmentation has been compounded by the creation of separate constitutions. Each entity has established its own constitution and been given wide powers under Annex 4 to proscribe and enforce laws in fields such as *inter alia* defense, police, citizenship, the issuing of passports, criminal matters, property law, finance and even external relations and cooperation with other states.[34] It would seem inconceivable to most states to create and endorse opposing centers of legal and political powers within their domestic confines. In short, it would be a form of sovereign suicide for a state. A natural consequence of allowing each entity enormous autonomy to make and enforce laws has been the strengthening of the ethnic partition of Bosnia-Herzegovina. In each entity, the institutional structures of the "semi-states" reflect a single group and are dominated by nationalist parties largely committed to their own communities and not to minorities.[35] The weakness of the common institutions serves only to make the entities more self-reliant and to create a situation in which they build up institutional and governance capacity premised on separation, while communitarian representation lags behind.[36] In this manner also, common institutions are perceived of as weak by their clients, the ordinary citizens of Bosnia-Herzegovina, while the localized "ethnic" structures deliver, and thus seem legitimate and credible statist structures.

The Republika Srpska has pursued its internal nationalistic agenda by writing a separate constitution that stands considerably at odds with the principle of a unitary state, and that rhetorically underpins Dayton. The Federation has also written a separate constitution that compounds the legal splintering of the jurisdiction. Recognizing the inherent problems of accommodating two competing and irreconcilable constitutional visions of the state, the Office of the High Representative (OHR) sought in the summer of 1997 to highlight these problems and suggest means for their resolution. The "entity" constitutions have sought to exacerbate the stranglehold of ethnicity politics through law. For example, the Republika Srpska Constitution recognizes only Serbs as citizens of the entity. Bosnians and Croats are legally constituted as lesser minorities.[37] Yugoslav political theorist Vladimir Gligorov has strongly and solidly observed, "Why should I be a minority in your state when you can be a minority in mine?"[38]

This policy is not only a demotion in status from the principle of equality the international community allegedly sought to inject into the peacemaking process, it is also a thorough reversal of the preexisting standing of peoples prior to the war. In the former Socialist Federal Republic of Yugoslavia, these peoples were defined as belonging to constituent nations, to whom equal rights between and within the nations accrued. The war and the state entities which emerged from it demoted these rights from the equal rights of nationhood to minority rights. Thus, while the national structure of enforced constitutionalism has not addressed the gap between minority and constituent nationality head-on, the entities have done so by demoting minority rights in the pursuit of nationalistic agendas. It bears reminding that all persons in Bosnia-Herzegovina are minorities, but that minority is a feature of geographical location. While the status of individual-as-minority is relative in Bosnia, legal affiliation should strive to be normative and not dependent here. Such a leap is still missing, absent on grounds of political expediency.

International Standards and the Constitution

A notable feature of the Constitution is its "internationalist" character. It is "international friendly," a clear consequence of the environment of its birth. Thus, it is a constitution which attaches great importance to international rules and principles, with a notable emphasis on human rights.[39] Particular attention can be given to Article II, paragraph 2, whereby "the rights and freedoms set forth in the European Convention for the Protection of Human Rights and Fundamental Freedoms and its Protocols shall apply directly in Bosnia Herzegovina. These shall have priority over all other law."[40]

There can be no doubt that the status given to the European Convention on Human Rights (ECHR) is of great symbolic value in the new legal order. However, there are inherent shortcomings to be acknowledged, both of the Convention itself and of the deep-seated problems within the local legal order which need to be resolved within the European Convention framework. There is a grave danger that a failure of the Convention in Bosnia would undermine the credibility of the ECHR protection system itself. The ECHR has been the leading regional human rights system since its inception in 1953.[41] It has been stalwart in creating an accessible human rights structure with a marked emphasis on the protection of individual rights,[42] a hallmark of the system. The Convention has developed a sophisticated jurisprudence, marked by a commitment to due process and an expansion of the boundaries of entitlement for the singular person.[43] The ECHR is not a system or a jurisprudence marked by a pre-occupation with group or minority rights, nor is its jurisprudence noted for confronting situations of gross and systematic violations of rights.[44]

A number of commentators have remarked upon the limited capacity of the European system to confront mass violations of human rights.[45] If we acknowledge that the European human rights order is struggling to gain institutional capacity in confronting massive human rights violations, premised not only on individual denials of rights but instead upon destruction polices aimed at a group, Bosnia will be a testing ground. In order to confront adequately the kinds of violations that have taken place in Bosnia, the European Convention has to learn a language and develop mechanisms for systematic violations, either by adjusting individual rights or by the creative absorption of group issues into the individual rights prism. The European Convention has been "smuggled into the legal order of Bosnia and Herzegovina."[46] There should be no expectation that it contains tailor-made solutions to the scale and type of human rights violations that took place during the war in Bosnia and which accompany the post-war phase.

Positively, the use of the Convention in Bosnia may set a new and innovative course for the European system in its dealings with the hard issues of group identity in divided societies and the appropriate remedies necessary to confront gross violations of rights. These are the kinds of issues that lie ahead of the European Convention as it expands eastwards and absorbs the former Soviet states under its mantle.[47] For Bosnia, it should be evident that there is no panacea to confront its human rights violations, past and present. The Convention is a tool that gives a concrete language to human rights in the domestic sphere, but needs adjustment and creative expansion if it is to meet the expectations that have been set for it. Equally important to grasp is the reality that notwithstanding the impressive rights and freedoms imported from international human rights law, these alone cannot undo the deleterious effects of the establishment of entities with single or dominant ethnies, whose very existence continue to undermine the most basic of rights.

Finally, the importation of international standards that take precedence over local law is a reminder of the international community's anxiety over the parties' willingness to comply with the commitments they were undertaking. International standards and oversight mechanisms were an insurance policy for domestic failure.[48] Unfortunately, it remains the case that these impressive human rights protections are held hostage by political fortunes: they can be completely paralyzed by the strong political institutions in the entities which cement the country's ethnic divisions.[49]

Constitutional Evolutions?

Given the limitations described above, what hope is there for the Constitution to ameliorate the status of the rule of law and the protection of rights in post-Dayton Bosnia? First, despite its limitations and the uncomfortable compact it contains, a written constitution carries enormous symbolic importance in the post-war period. It stands as a commitment to legalism and structure, a stark contrast to the trenchant engagement in military politics that characterized political life in Bosnia since 1991. Installing a constitution is a signal to society that the rules on political and social behavior are being regulated and will bear scrutiny. The absorption of that basic creed by a state's citizenry may have a crucial sociological impact on their perception of the state and their status within it.

Second, constitutions can also be subject to change and evolution. The Bosnian Constitution specifically includes provisions for amendment.[50] The procedure requires a decision of the Parliamentary Assembly, with a two-thirds majority of those present in favor of any change. Article X(2) specifically limits constitutional amendments from extinguishing or limiting any rights set out in Article II of the Constitution. It is clear that in the current, polarized political climate, constitutional amendment is unlikely in the short term. Nonetheless, with greater public awareness of the extent to which the Constitution itself is responsible for the tripartite fragmentation of the state along ethnic lines, some movement may be possible. Equally, the international community must play its part. A greater acknowledgment that the Dayton Constitution does little to facilitate an integrative multiethnic state may encourage the international community, which is in a *de facto* position of trusteeship in Bosnia,[51] to foster domestic politics that seek to outgrow the nationalistic straitjacket that the Constitution produced. Like in my proposals for the Dayton Agreement overall, significant portions of the Constitution should be viewed as transitional. As Bosnia progresses away from violence, society and the Constitution ought to evolve towards a more homogenous framework premised on multiculturalism and multiethnicity. The goal should be to create conditions that will facilitate positive constitutional growth. This would require carving out a space for the non-ethnic "middle" political voice, which is entirely excluded from the current political spectrum.

It would also require another step, the more pervasive project of creating and building constitutional consciousness and consensus within the state.

This long-term educative process would seek to involve citizenry intimately in the legitimization and building of the bedrock for a constitution. It requires political elites and the international community to seek out and inform local communities and ordinary citizens about their constitution. This project, demonstrated concretely in the South African transition, gives citizenry a sense of ownership in their constitution.[52] It promotes knowledge, encourages input into the unfolding constitutional structure and encourages litigation. In the context of concrete physical needs in Bosnia such an enterprise bears an air of luxury. This is not the case. If Bosnia is to be transformed into a rule-of-law state, ordinary citizens must be co-opted into the process. Equally, if state building is viewed as a fluid, cooperative exercise, movement upon and participation in the constitutional process is an assertive addition to the endeavor.

The Common Institutions—A Closer Look at the Constitutional Court

Just as it has been ill-conceived to perceive of ethnic conflict in unidimensional terms, so too must the international community avoid the dangerous path of conceiving of reconstruction too simplistically. Clearly, the unification of Bosnia-Herzegovina has little prospect for success without more to hold it together than the "common institutions," which receive minimal funding and only grudging support from the Republika Srpska. No intensive thought has been given to the extent to which legal institutions constitute "common institutions."[53] Foremost among such legal structures is the Constitutional Court. At best, this body could operate as a standard bearer for rebuilding confidence in the rule of law, a meaningful symbol of a functional unitary Bosnia. At worst, it could degenerate into a squabbling forum for the hand-picked representatives of the entities, a means to subvert rather than support the interdependency of the state.

Article VI of Annex 4 of the DPA sets up the Constitutional Court. Its task is to uphold the Constitution. The Constitutional Court of the Federation was officially inaugurated on January 11, 1996 in Sarajevo.[54] Its mandate includes determining whether laws made within the legislative competence of the entities are consistent with the Constitution. It also has appellate jurisdiction over European Convention issues that arise out of any judgment from a court in Bosnia-Herzegovina. Three of its nine members are selected by the President of the European Court of Human Rights, and after consultation with the Bosnian Presidency, the other six are to be elected by the entities.[55] All of the members of the Court are to be appointed for an initial term of five years and are not eligible for reappointment. As nationalist political personages dominate the institutions and political hierarchies in both entities, there can be real concern that the judicial appointment process will reflect that politics. Other power-sharing institutions in Bosnia-Herzegovina, based on the principle of ethnic quotas, have resulted only in gridlock. The tempering feature of the Constitutional Court is the external appointment mechanism, which may have a neutralizing effect on politically motivated appointments designed to subvert cooperation.[56]

The role of an independent judiciary in a society which has experienced and continues to experience violence is paramount.[57] Discharging that obligation is most difficult for judges in states like Bosnia, which still manifest the ongoing effects of a prolonged conflict and a difficult peace. Under the Bosnian Constitution, the judiciary retains significant space for recognizing fundamental rights when interpreting statutory provisions, implementing provisions that conform to principles of fundamental justice and conducting judicial proceedings. Doing so impartially and professionally is pivotal to maintaining and securing confidence in the rule of law and justice itself. In particular, the judiciary itself must be aware of its obligations. In order to meet these requirements, officials appointed to the judiciary must at least hold the minimal degree of training and be appointed with a view to their independence. Appointed judges themselves have a special responsibility to act in a manner that furthers both the perception and the reality of their independence from the state. The legacy of violent internal conflict will burden judges in Bosnia-Herzegovina in the form of distrust and skepticism about law and legality. This is a burden that only their active participation and collective integrity may overcome. The Constitutional Court stands at the judicial apex. The example set by this body will have certain effect on others courts and the response of the watching public.

The Court is one of the common institutions envisaged by Dayton as a means to mesh the entities into a state-like existence and force reliance and interdependence. Nonetheless, political cooperation between the entities has been sparse and intermittent with respect to both common institutions and other matters.[58] While the Court has been less subject to interference than other bodies, it still remains in a precarious position, another hostage of the political fortunes of nationalistic agendas.

The Role of Internal International Actors

The role of the High Representative is crucial to any analysis of rebuilding in post-conflict Bosnia. The Office of the High Representative (OHR) has primary responsibility for promoting "full compliance with all civilian aspects of the peace settlement."[59] In addition, the High Representative is to oversee the efforts of the parties to rebuild the structures and institutions of government and their endeavors to promote human rights.[60] The High Representative may call on international donors, including the World Bank and the European Union, and may withhold aid from those who fail to live up to their Dayton commitments. The High Representative's function is a hybrid of executive and enforcement responsibilities. On the one hand he is a political troubleshooter, on the other he is a mere civil servant overseeing the formal agreements the parties themselves have consented to enter. In seeking to mend the broken structures of the Bosnian state, external actors like the OHR play the critical role in holding the pieces together. The potential for success is predominantly linked to the willingness of the fragmented entities to be thus bound.

Nevertheless, the High Representative has some independent capacity to enforce compliance by the parties to the Dayton Agreement. Security Council resolution 1022 gave the OHR the power to recommend the immediate reimposition of sanctions should the parties fail to fulfill their obligations. The High Representative has been subject to some criticism for his narrow interpretation of that power and for remaining silent "in the fact of mounting evidence of the parties' non-compliance with crucial parts of their civilian obligations under the peace agreement."[61] An early lack of confidence in the OHR is also blamed for the paucity of investment in materials and diplomatic resources in that agency, which contributed to robust criticisms of its effectiveness in the field.[62]

The OHR is also responsible for drafting a quick-start program of legislation aimed at piecing Bosnia-Herzegovina back together. This has been haltingly implemented. The quick-start program includes provisional laws on international economic relations, citizenship and passport provisions, a provisional central bank, the duration of the parliamentary mandate, immunity, presidential succession, air traffic regulations and the 1997 state budget.[63] In addition, other international non-governmental organizations have concerned themselves with drafting domestic legislation. The Central and East European Law Initiative (CEELI), for example, has been advising the Bosnian government with respect to its criminal procedural and penal codes.[64] While these international efforts are well-intentioned attempts to transform the framework of law inherited from the former Yugoslavia, a word of caution is warranted. Fundamental structural changes to the legal order need to maintain a delicate balance between intrusion and genuine assistance. For such changes to take root in the local legal and political culture there must be an attempt to build a "bottom up" consensus that such changes are warranted and will be supported by domestic legal actors and institutions. It is insufficient for outsiders to create perfect paper rules, if they are meaningless to and suffer a lack of support from the community that they intend to benefit.

The Human Rights Commission

The Human Rights Commission ("the Commission") was established under Annex 6 of the Dayton Agreement. It consists of an Ombudsperson and a Human Rights Chamber.[65] The task of both institutions is to investigate alleged violations of the Human Rights protections entrenched by Dayton. In essence, this means that both bodies have the duty of ensuring that the European Convention on Human Rights, its Protocols and all additional rights protected by the international agreements listed in the Appendix to Annex 6, are observed and enforced in the post-war Bosnia.

The creation of the Commission testifies to the reality that external standards and actors were essential to facilitating the protection of Human Rights in post-war Bosnia. The intimate responsibility of the international community for the day-to-day upkeep of legal protections is illustrated by the Human Rights Commission, one of its creations. The indefinitely-envisaged appointment of eight members of the Human Rights Chamber by the Council of Europe is indicative of the long-term tutelage the domestic legal system faces.[66] The Commission is an example of the lack of faith in the domestic state's ability to run certain affairs to international satisfaction, thereby creating a need for international personnel to do the job instead.[67] While this ambivalence about domestic capacity and good will may well have been warranted at the time of the Dayton Agreement's signing, there are some inherent dangers in choosing the path of internal trusteeship for the international and local community. External responsibility may create a monopoly that does not encourage internal capacity building. The international community cannot hope (nor wish) to act *in loco parentis* to the Bosnian state indefinitely. However, the path to genuine rather than superficial reconstruction will be even slower if local responsibility for the enforcement and oversight of legal protections is not encouraged.

The Office of Ombudsperson

The Human Rights Ombudsperson is authorized to investigate "alleged or apparent violations of human rights."[68] Her role is to take cases only where an individual complainant is prepared to come forward. She has no authority to investigate violations on behalf of a class of complainants. The findings of the Ombudsperson are to be made public, and where a party in violation fails to adhere to the conclusions and recommendations made, this is to be brought to the attention of the High Representative. Jessica Simor has argued that the decision by the Ombudsperson to adopt procedural rules of admissibility mirrored upon the European Convention (Articles 26 and 27) creates doubts as to the efficiency and accessibility of her office.[69] She suggests a number of internal reforms, including, first, that the Ombudsperson take a less onerous position on admissibility procedures, thus being able to exert jurisdiction over human rights violations clearly outside the less expansive mandate of the Human Rights Chamber. Secondly, she suggests that there be no expansive report for non-review in cases in which the Ombudsperson decides not to proceed with investigation: this would allow the office greater time and resources for cases that merit serious and committed investigation. In this context, the Ombudsperson would be well served by taking note of the imaginative approach taken by the ECHR in relation to admissibility criteria in the recent past, particularly in relation to cases which demonstrate elements of administrative practice. Finally, the Office of the Ombudsperson should proceed with investigation prior to deciding whether case information discloses a violation.[70]

The Office of the Ombudsperson has the potential, given some procedural reforms, to become a tool for responding directly to human rights violations in an immediate and efficient manner. However, the role of the Ombudsperson cannot be detached from the extensive international "takeover" of domestic legal functions. The Ombudsperson is appointed by the Organization for Security and Cooperation in Europe (OSCE).[71] There can be no doubt that the selection procedure is designed to remove bias and partisan appointments—a commendable intention. However, in this wider examination, it raises serious issues about the ability of the domestic legal system to become self-reliant in the short and long term.

The Human Rights Chamber

The Human Rights Chamber is composed of fourteen members, four from the Federation, two from the Republika Srpska and the remaining eight appointed by the Committee of Ministers of the Council of Europe.[72] The Chamber holds the power to decide upon complaints of human rights violations referred to it by the Ombudsperson or on the basis of complaints made directly by individuals.[73] The propagation of accountability mechanisms such as the Ombudsperson has created overlapping layers of legal structure that, to some extent, have similar aims. Significantly, the DPA does not spell out the relationship between the Ombudsperson and the domestic prosecutorial system. Proliferation does not necessarily mean efficiency or improved accountability. One strong image is that of a two-tiered system of legal accountability. This consists of an existing and insufficiently funded domestic system, the supranational system of the International Criminal Tribunal for the Former Yugoslavia and a domestic-international structure which overlays the indigenous legal system. The linkages between the three structures remain imprecisely defined and subject to much local ambivalence.

Policing—Internal and External Dimensions

In at least two ways, the rehabilitation of domestic police forces is a crucial aspect of transition in a society that has experienced conflict. First, civilianized police forces in post-war societies frequently absorb demilitarized soldiers as a means of containing the discontent that results from demobilization. This may create a surplus of unsuitable police officers and a public perception of their lack of professionalism. In addition, where police forces may have been partisan to a particular "side" of the conflict, their function mandates a restoration of neutrality and an appearance of evenhandedness. Second, police officers fill an important confidence-building role by demonstrating impartiality between communities and satisfying the requirements of representativeness in ethnically mixed and divided communities. The international community can be instrumental in advancing both goals.[74] In practice, the Implementation Force (IFOR, now SFOR) has had only a limited involvement in the civilian implementation, including the establishment of the police force, and the UN International Police Task Force (IPTF) has interpreted its mandate in a limited manner.

The role of the IPTF is outlined in Annex 11 of the Dayton Agreement, entitled the "Agreement on International Police Task Force."[75] Annex 11 states that the parties to the peace agreement were to request that the Security Council establish a UN civilian police operation to assist with law enforcement training, local law enforcement and the facilitation of a transition to civilian policing.[76] Once the Dayton Agreement was signed, the Secretary-General sent a police reconnaissance mission to Bosnia. He subsequently outlined that "... the Task Force will not exercise any executive law enforcement functions. Its effectiveness will depend, to an important extent, on the willingness of the parties to co-operate with it in accordance with article IV of annex 11 to the Peace Agreement."[77] Based on this cooperative principle, the mandate of the IPTF was confirmed by Security Council resolution 1035 of December 21, 1995.

The IPTF has deployed more than 1,600 policemen from thirty-four countries in forty stations around the country.[78] Their primary function is to advise and monitor the local police, based on the principle of consentual interface with local police forces. Owing to his influence with donors regarding aid to the Bosnian police forces, the IPTF Commissioner has much leeway with the Ministers of Interior of both entities. In many localities of Bosnia-Herzegovina the IPTF is the visible face of the Dayton Agreement, having daily and minute connections with local authorities and communities alike.

Operational problems for the IPTF The IPTF has encountered a number of problems since its conception and actualization on BiH territory. One outstanding and consistent problem for IPTF has been the lack of sufficient resources to fulfill their obligations under Dayton. This was initially experienced as the limited deployment of police officers by donor states in the jurisdiction.[79] While the numbers deployed are now consistent with the original mandate, problems persist in the technical and material assistance provided to the officers on the ground.[80] In order to carry out their commitments in a complete and efficient manner, obtaining resources is a priority.

However, as with many mixed post-conflict missions, it is clear that international financial assistance is targeted to the high-profile actors, currently the SFOR contingent. It is harder to convince donors that equal assistance should be prioritized for "bread and butter" rebuilding, which over the long term will create the means and the stability to ensure that the high-profile military actors can actually withdraw.

Differences in legal culture A particular problem in the early stages of IPTF deployment was a notable lack of sensitivity to and knowledge of domestic legal culture and rules.[81] Examples were rife of IPTF observers stopping or interfering with local court proceedings, alleging an unfair trial. In many cases the IPTF observers simply had no knowledge of how court procedure in a civil-law system operated. They assumed that because it looked "different" it had to be unfair. These kinds of enforcement problems can create enormous obstacles to genuine cooperation and assistance. External legal actors must avoid imbuing their contact community with a sense of their own cultural and legal superiority. Rebuilding must incorporate a genuine appreciation for the validity of the local legal culture—not an attempt to override it with a foreign import.

Rebuilding local police forces Building confidence in the local police is a crucial component of reconstruction. The role of the IPTF is cuspidate in monitoring the work of local police forces, including the major task of screening and training them. This task is a delicate one, given the link that has emerged between political affiliation and the ability to gain state employment in areas dominated by nationalist politics which actively disfavor minorities.[82] Generally, local police forces are composed of members of the dominant ethnicity of the region. From the outset, their lack of representativeness is a burden in ethnically mixed communities. This factor is exacerbated by persistent allegations of human rights abuses by local police forces.[83] Given this lack of confidence in law enforcers, the role of the international overseer is vital. The IPTF spokesperson has stated that:

> These reports [of human rights abuses] will be independently investigated and the IPTF will demand disciplinary action to be taken against those found guilty of human rights abuses. The IPTF will not hesitate to publish the names of the officers involved and will ensure that they no longer serve as policemen.[84]

Despite these verbal commitments, difficulties persist. The cumbersome and slow process of vetting police officers has inevitably meant that abuses continue, thus threatening the objective of police impartiality. The vetting process is further encumbered by the additional need to reduce the numbers of policemen serving in the jurisdiction. In practice, the IPTF has been slow to publish the names of officers proven to have engaged in abuses of power.[85] Further, despite IPTF promises to teach police officers about ethics and human rights, such training has been slow to materialize on the ground.

The IPTF must also be seen as accessible to the ordinary citizen. Creating easy procedures for ordinary persons to submit information about police chiefs or officers that might render them unfit for their positions, including information about involvement in war crimes, would greatly assist the IPTF's work as well as its currency with local populations. Another crucial goal for the IPTF mission is that of transparency. Transparency in its oversight functions would demonstrate to the local political and legal communities how it undertakes its work. This could be furthered, for example, if the IPTF were to publish information about its processes of supervising the vetting and restructuring of the Federation police.

As with many other international organizations operating in Bosnia, the IPTF faces a dual task. On the one hand, the IPTF's function is to help rebuild and restructure a particular component of Bosnian society. The importance of rehabilitating the police is underlined by the reminder that it is local police who will be the standard bearers for law and order after the departure of international forces. On the other hand, the IPTF must remain attuned to the dangers of facilitating indefinite dependency by taking over too many of the powers of the local police forces. The object of international oversight is not to cripple domestic civilian capacity, but to encourage it to flourish.

Rebuilding the Bosnian Legal System

One of the central locales for institution building lies in the restructuring of the domestic legal system. For this to occur in the Bosnian context, some very practical measures must be put into place; most urgently, an increase of practical resources available to the legal system. For example, the main courthouse in Sarajevo, where a significant portion of domestic trials should take place, was severely damaged during the war. Many other Bosnian legal buildings have suffered similar damage. A practical program of rebuilding damaged facilities will be vital to capacity building. Internal legal resources are also scarce. Facilities for recording oral evidence in Bosnian courtrooms are grossly inadequate.[86] While the domestic legal system has so far only dealt with a handful of cases related to war crimes and war-related claims, the potentially huge number of impending cases will face monumental practical obstacles.

Current writing on democracy building notes that judicial and legal reform play a crucial part in democracy assistance and the prioritization of aid.[87] This has not been the case in Bosnia. The technical assistance required by the courts and their staff is glaringly absent.[88] In part, this can be explained by the emphasis placed on making sufficient financial resources available to the International Tribunal, while the domestic legal system lags behind in priority and visibility. While this is a matter of prioritizing resource allocation, there is also a need to recognize that technical support for the legal system is not a luxury.[89]

Some practical measures which might assist in re-prioritizing the legal sphere include convening a steering committee of donors to promote better coordination among funding programs. Greater international transparency and accountability in setting priorities for technical assistance would help to establish an empirical basis for allocating resources. For example, the World Bank, IMF and the European Commission should regularly publish information on their economic assistance packages, including criteria for starting or ending projects. Moreover, the resource needs of the legal system in Bosnia need to be made visible to the international donor community. Adequate resources are vital to rebuilding faith in civilian structures and the rule of law, serving to ensure that the rule of law can be delivered to the citizens it is intended for.

Resource allocation is a crucial issue with respect to the legal materials and training available to judges and lawyers. Article 142 of the Criminal Code of the SFRY covered domestic war crimes, but as this provision had never been litigated domestically, there is little guidance on its scope and interpretation. The domestic interpretative process can only turn to international jurisprudence and writing for clarification. Access to international material was and remains limited for many local legal actors. Many domestic judges are cognizant of the fact that they are making "new" law.[90] There can be no doubt that training programs, technical assistance and greater liaison with the ICTY would make this task much easier for both judges and lawyers. If the domestic system fails to apply the international standards correctly it will, no doubt, be roundly criticized. But by failing to give the domestic legal system sufficient information to meet its expectations, the international community has fated the system to fail at its task, through no absolute fault of its own. The war crimes trials will be viewed as the testing ground for rebuilding the domestic legal system. But for the domestic system to traverse the chasm successfully, a knowledge gap needs to be filled.

At worst, a lack of resources might be prejudicial to open, fair and competent judicial procedures. The number of war crimes cases will increase domestically, thus increasing the resource strain. The Bosnian legal system will be closely watched (evident by the number of international observers present at any domestic war crimes trial) by the world. The Bosnian Federation has demonstrated genuine good will to conduct these trials openly, fairly and competently. However, it lacks the assistance sorely needed for doing so.

The Republika Srpska's attitude poses specific problems for the processing of domestic war crimes trials. In short, concerns pervade about the willingness of the Republika Srpska to undertake genuine and fair accountability boundaries. Specific problems encountered there include inadequate monitoring of due-process violations, including access to counsel during the investigation stage of criminal proceedings. In addition, following the Dayton signing, an early practice emerged of arresting ethnic minorities on what appeared to be weak grounds for political considerations.[91] Given the overall lack of cooperation by the Republika Srpska with the Dayton process, law has been one among many causalities of an unwillingness to support accountability and transparency in the entity. Effective legality in the Republika Srpska poses a threat to the hegemony of political forces who were the principal actors in the war project. Reestablishing the primacy of law is one of the most effective means to channel international resources to those constituencies within the entity committed to resuming safe and normal lives.

The Link Between Local and International Accountability

Ultimately, rebuilding legal capacity aims to make law enforcement meaningful to citizens. Building confidence in the rule of law in Bosnia has many components. Not least of these, establishing accountability for past crimes is an obvious starting point for any forward progress. The legal obligations of the state parties and the guarantor states in this respect remain unambiguous. The UN Security Council had stated that "...compliance with the requests and orders of the International Criminal Tribunal for the Former Yugoslavia [to arrest and surrender to the Tribunal people indicted for war crimes] constitutes an essential aspect of implementing the Peace Agreement."[92] This obligation also follows from the Genocide Convention, the Geneva Conventions of August 12, 1949, its Additional Protocol 1, and Security Council resolution 827 of May 25, 1993. This has clearly not been the case in Bosnia so far. The initial paucity in numbers of those indicted for war crimes at the Hague attested to the lack of international will to make these commitments fully meaningful.[93] While there has been a substantial improvement in the number of arrests made in recent years, nonetheless the task is ongoing and incomplete. What must be consistently reiterated is the extent to which international inaction in this sphere has profound, long-term impact within Bosnia on domestic confidence in legal processes. The appreciation for the rule of law in the local setting depends on meaningful accountability on the international plane, and vice-versa. The international component must remain consistently self-aware, attuned not only to its own demands but to the pulse of the system it supports.

Conclusions

Whatever our views on the preexisting legal and political order in the former Yugoslavia, some aspects of its legal structure should remain in the fore as Bosnia-Herzegovina is reconstructed. First, Yugoslav space (both literally and physically) comprised a multinational environment. Multiple and incompatible claims on the territory and identity of its many nations were accommodated, partly or significantly (depending on one's views), through a layered-rights discourse of complicated constitutional arrangements.[94] Bosnia must also accommodate multiple and incompatible claims of territory and identity. Its choice is threefold: first, separation of the internal political entities (unidimensional statelets within the state); second, long-term international cuckolding; or third, the precarious route of accommodation and intersection. In this context, to dismiss entirely the relevance of the forerunning state entity may be to discard potential solutions to a problem that is not new to the Balkans.

At this historical moment, the idea of a Bosnian state has little internal cohesion. Three statelets bundled into coexistence have mutually exclusionary ideas about what being a part of the state called Bosnia means. The territory of the Republika Srpska still clings to secessionist principles, aggravated by ideological nationalism that fluctuates between rejection and conciliation to the Dayton Agreement. The Croat-Bosnia Federation is a fragile détente with grave disjunctions between two political leaderships as to the conception of their mutual coexistence. As Hansen points out, "whereas Croats regard it as a federation of two political administrative units and emphasize the importance of links to Croatia, Bosnians see their partnership as a community of two constituent peoples, who underline the integrity of Bosnia, as essential."[95] Out of these mutually exclusionary visions of the state there seems little room for maneuver or compromise.

Yet, despite all the shortcomings illustrated throughout this article, Dayton itself is testament to the capacity for finding a middle ground, albeit a narrow one. The real challenge lies in widening that narrow ledge, and with it creating the means to ensure a functional, not a deformed state. For the short term, Dayton has provided a home to group identity, and created spaces in which some (though not all) people may feel secure enough to rebuild. Ultimately, as Miroslav Volf reminds us, "the homes which group identities provide can be stifling."[96] Rebuilding Bosnia in a meaningful way requires modalities of transition, starting from a settlement premised on the cohesion of the group, and reaching, eventually, a society that nurtures the individual and celebrates its multiethnicity, multiculturalism and diversity. Legal structures are one bridge for this passage. The rigidity of the Dayton agreements could leave one pessimistic towards its capacity to encourage this kind of societal transformation. Thus, much depends on encouragement by the international community to view Dayton as a means to a much more inclusive end, rather than as an end in itself.

Notes

*   Some of the ideas for this article were developed while the author was the Special Representative of the Prosecutor of the International Criminal Tribunal For the Former Yugoslavia (ICTY), observing domestic war crimes trials in November 1996. This article does not reflect the views of the ICTY, all opinions expressed are the author's own. However, I would like to note my acknowledgments to all those I met during my visit to Bosnia in the fall of 1996 including Prof. Zavko Grebo, Zdravka Grebo-Jevtić, Amra Kapetanovic-Steers, Prof. Cazim Sadiković, Michael

O' Flaherty and Amira Sadiković. My appreciation to Professor Colm Campbell and Dr. Moshe Hirsch for their helpful comments. The final product remains entirely the responsibility of the author.

1 The Dayton Peace Agreement (DPA), The General Framework Agreement for Peace in Bosnia and Herzegovina was initialled in Dayton on November 21, 1995 and signed in Paris on December 14, 1995. Available at: http://www.oscebih.org/documents/dayton.htm.

2 See generally, Dick A. Leurdijk, "The Dayton Agreement: A Tremendous Gamble," *International Peacekeeping* 3 (Dec 1995-Jan 1996), p. 2.

3 See UN Security Council Resolution 1021 (November 22, 1995); UN Security Council Resolution 1022 (November 22, 1995); UN Security Council Resolution 1026 (November 30, 1995).

4 See *generally*, Cherif Bassiouni, et al.: *Guiding Principles for Combating Impunity for International Crimes* (Draft), (On file with author).

5 Remarks attributed to the Director of the Program on African Governance at the Carter Center, Working Papers, 2nd annual seminar of the African Governance Program (Atlanta, Carter Centre, 1990), p. 202.

6 David Williams & Tom Young, "Governance, the World Bank and Liberal Theory" *Political Studies* 42, no. 1 (March1994), p. 85.

7 See Thomas Carothers, "Democracy Assistance: The Question of Strategy," *Democratization* 4, no.3 (1997), p. 116.

8 See Boutros Boutros-Ghali, *An Agenda for Peace – Preventative Diplomacy, Peacemaking and Peace-Keeping Report of the Secretary-General*, UN GAOR/SCOR,47th Sess., Preliminary List Item 10, at 55, UN Docs. A/47/277 & S/24111 (1992).

9 See Zoran Pajic, "A Critical Appraisal of Human Rights Provisions of the Dayton Constitution of Bosnia and Herzegovina," *Human Rights Quarterly* 20, no. 1 (1998), pp. 125-138.

10 Francis Boyle who argues that "Bosnia was sacrificed on the alter of Great Power politics to the Machiavellian god of expedience." See Francis A. Boyle, "Negating Human Rights in Peace Negotiations," *Human Rights Quarterly* 18, no. 3 (1996), pp. 515-516.

11 See Michael N. Barnett, "The Politics of Indifference at the United Nations and Genocide in Rwanda and Bosnia," in *This Time We Knew: Western Responses to Genocide in Bosnia*, Thomas Cushman & Stjepan Mestrovic (eds.). (New York: New York University Press, 1996), pp. 128-162.

12 See International Crisis Group, "Beyond the Ballot Boxes: Municipal Elections in Bosnia and Herzegovina" (September 10, 1997). Available at: http://www.crisisweb.org/projects/bosnia/reports/bh26rep.htm. See also Daniel J. Blessington: "From Dayton to Sarajevo: Enforcing Election Laws in Post War Bosnia and Herzegovina," *American University International Law Review* 13, no.3 (1998), p. 553.

13 As Bosnia has not been able to draft new legislation since independence in 1992, the applicable law is still largely the legal codes of the Socialist Federal Republic of Yugoslavia.

14 As Hansen points out: "Neither of the successor states has traditions of multiparty democracy, free elections and independent media as laid out in the new Bosnian Constitution. In addition, there is a deep mistrust towards security forces, the police and the judicial system." Annika S. Hansen, "Political Legitimacy, Confidence-building and the Dayton Peace Agreement," *International Peacekeeping* 4, no.2 (1997), p. 75.

15   The situation of Kosovo highlights all the deficiencies of the pre-existing constitutional structure of the former Yugoslavia. See *generally*, David L. Phillips, "Comprehensive Peace in the Balkans: The Kosovo Question," *Human Rights Quarterly* 18, no. 4 (1996), pp. 821-832.

16   See Susan L. Woodward, *Balkan Tragedy: Chaos and Dissolution After the Cold War* (Washington DC: Brookings, 1995), p. 31.

17   See Sophie Albert, "The Return of Refugees to Bosnia and Herzegovina: Peacebuilding with People," *International Peacekeeping* 4, no. 3 (1997), p. 1.

18   In some ways this problem is already being encountered in the attempts to reintegrate refugees into their former communities. See Chris Hedges, "Fearful Serbs Fleeing Last Enclave in Croatia," *International Herald Tribune*, December 18 1997. See also R. Jeffrey Smith, "Legal Ethnic Cleansing Keeps Sarajevo Muslim," *International Herald Tribune*, February 3 1998.

19   Arend Lijphart, "Consociational Democracy," *World Politics* 21, no. 2 (1969), pp. 207-225; Arend Lijphart, *Democracy in Plural Societies: A Comparative Exploration*. New Haven: Yale University Press, 1977; "Democratic Political Systems Types, Cases, Causes, and Consequences," *Journal of Theoretical Politics* 1 (1989), p. 33.

20   For Lijphart, the behavior of elites is crucial to creating a stable democracy in a highly plural society. Citing Claude Ake he argues that as a result of overarching cooperation between elites, a divided society can 'achieve a degree of political stability quite out of proportion to its social homogeneity." See Lijphart, "Consociational Democracy", p. 212.

21   See e.g. "Legal Ethnic Cleansing Keeps Sarajevo Muslim," *International Herald Tribune*, February 3 1998.

22   Liberalization in the guise of democracy is not a phenomena unique to the Dayton Peace Agreement. See *e.g.* Hanna Y. Freji, and Leonard C. Robinson "Liberalization, the Islamists, and the Stability of the Arab State: Jordan as a Case Study," *The Muslim World* 86, no. 1 (1996), p. 2.

23   See Liah Greenfeld, "War and Ethnic Identity in Eastern Europe: Does the Post-Yugoslav Crisis Portend Wider Chaos?" in *This Time We Knew: Western Responses to Genocide in Bosnia*, Thomas Cushman & Stjepan Mestrovic (eds.). (New York: New York University Press, 1996), p. 309.

24   The EC countries had moved to recognize Bosnia on 7 April 1992. See generally, Roland Rich, "Recognition of States: The Collapse of Yugoslavia and the Soviet Union," *European Journal of International Law* 4, no. 1 (1993), p. 50. Prior to this, the Arbitration Commission of the Conference on Yugoslavia (the 'Badinter Arbitration Commission') had concluded in its Opinion No. 1 of 29 November 1991, that Yugoslavia was in the process of dissolution. See Alan Pellet, "The Opinions of the Badinter Arbitration Committee: A Second Breath for Self-Determination of Peoples," *European Journal of International Law* 3, no.1 (1992), p. 182.

25   See DPA, Annex 4, Article I, para. 2.

26   Paolo Gaeta, "The Dayton Agreements and International Law," *European Journal of International Law* 7, no. 2 (1996), p. 161.

27   See DPA, Annex 4, Article I, para. 7. By this, citizenship is granted at two levels, the national and the entity level, and the entity has the first right to issue a passport. Only those not covered by their entities will receive their passport from the national government of Bosnia-Herzegovina.

28   See *Ibid.*

29   As pointed out to me by Dr. Zoran Pajić, the word citizen does not appear in the normative portion of the Constitution.

30 Wolin notes that a constitution in setting limits to politics also sets limits to democracy, frequently constituting it in ways compatible with and legitimating of the dominant power groups in the society. See Sheldon S. Wolin: "Fugitive Democracy," in *Democracy and Difference. Contesting the Boundaries of the Political*, Seyla Benhabib (ed.). (Princeton, Princeton University Press 1996), p. 35.
31 See generally Wolin, *ibid*.
32 Defence issues are of course also subject to the Dayton Agreement, in particular Annex 1-B of the same. See *generally*, Bonnie Jenkins: "The Enhancement of Political and Military Stability in the Former Yugoslavia through the use of International Law: Annex 1-B of the General Framework Agreement," *Fordham International Law Journal* 19 (1996), p. 1920. See also Chester A. Crocker, and Fen Osler Hampson, "Making Peace Settlements Work," *Foreign Policy* 104 (Fall 1996), pp. 68-69.
33 See Hansen, "Political Legitimacy," p. 80.
34 In addition, each entity was given the autonomy to enter into special parallel relationships with neighboring states. See DPA, Annex 4, Article III, para. 3b.
35 Domination by national parties has been particularly apparent as exemplified by struggles between hard-line and marginally more moderate nationalist politicians for political control of the Republika Srpska. See "Hard-Liners Tie Up Bosnian Serb Entity," *International Herald Tribune*, December 29 1997.
36 As Hansen points out ,"The only characteristic of a state denied to the entities is the right to patrol or in any way enforce the inter-entity border." Annika S. Hansen, "Political Legitimacy," p. 80.
37 See Pajic, "A Critical Appraisal," p. 134.
38 Woodward, *Balkan Tragedy*, p. 108.
39 These include the International Covenant on Civil and Political Rights, International Covenant on Economic and Social Rights, and, the Universal Declaration.
40 See generally, Eric Stein, "International Law in Internal Law: Towards Internationalization of Central-European Constitutions?" *American Journal of International Law* 88, no. 3 (July 1994), p. 429.
41 *Convention for the Protection of Human Rights and Fundamental Freedoms*, Nov. 4, 1950, 213 U.N.T.S. 221, Europ. T.S. No.5.
42 See Christian Tomuschat, "Quo Vadis, Argentoratum? The Success Story of the European Convention on Human Rights and a Few Dark Stains," *Human Rights Law Journal* 13, p. 406 (describing the European system as focused on individual applications).
43 On due process rights as the hallmark of the Convention, see generally Conor Gearty, "The European Court of Human Rights and the Protection of Civil Liberties," *Cambridge Law Journal* 52 (1993), pp. 89-127.
44 See Oren Gross, "'Once More unto the Breach': The Systemic Failure of Applying the European Convention on Human Rights to Entrenched Emergencies," *Yale Journal of International Law* 23, no. 2 (1998), pp. 500-508. By contrast, the American Convention on Human Rights, adopted in 1969, was born out of the experience of the hemisphere. See Dinah L. Shelton,: "The Inter-American System for the Protection of Human Rights: Emergent Norms," in *International Human Rights Law Theory and Practice*, Irwin Cotler and F. Pearl Eliadis (ed.), Montreal, The Canadian Human Rights Foundation, 1992. The Inter-American Court was formally instituted in 1979, and consists of 7 judges elected by State Parties to the Convention. Arts 52, 53, O.A.S.T.S. No. 36, at 16, 9 *International Legal Materials* at 673. As I have previously pointed out: '... it should be pointed out that the Inter-American Commission, as a body of the O.A.S. Charter, has functioned reasonably

well in its dealings with situations of gross and systematic violations of human rights occurring in the territory of Member States'. See Fionnuala Ni Aolain, "The Emergence of Diversity: Differences in Human Rights Jurisprudence," *Fordham International Law Journal* 19 (1995), p. 131.

45 See Aisling Reidy et al., "Gross Violations of Human Rights: Invoking the European Convention on Human Rights in the Case of Turkey," *Netherlands Quarterly of Human Rights* 15, no. 2 (1997), pp. 161-173. See also Meno T. Kamminga, "Is the European Convention on Human Rights Sufficiently Equipped to Cope with Gross and Systematic Violations?" *Netherlands Quarterly of Human Rights* 12, no. 2 (1994), p. 153-164.

46 Pajic, "A Critical Appraisal," p. 131.

47 On the issues related to Russia's accession to the Council of Europe see generally, Bill Bowering, "Russia's Accession to the Council of Europe and Human Rights: Compliance or Cross-Purposes," *European Human Rights Law Review* 6 (1997), p. 628.

48 See generally Ustinia Dolgopol, "A Feminist Appraisal of the Dayton Peace Accords," *Adelaide Law Review* 19 (1997), pp. 59-71.

49 A Bosnian journalist highlights the point admirably: "Everyone swears on the Dayton peace agreement, on an integral Bosnia, on human rights and respect and pluralism, on the importance of free and fair elections and a dozen nice similar phrases, which are tomorrow supposed to turn Bosnia into a Balkan Switzerland. However, the contrast between reality and words is increasing. Today's Bosnia is nothing but a castle in the air, whose parts are still being held together by some curious miracle." *Dani* (Sarajevo), April 26 1996.

50 See DPA, Annex 4, Article X, para. 1.

51 International law recognizes many kinds of dependant states, the status of the state being largely governed by the facts of each state's own situations. Various terms can be employed to describe dependant states. They include vassal states, protected states, protectorates, colonial protectorates or trusteeships. On these entities see *generally*, G.H. Hackworth, *Digest of International Law*, vol. 1. (Washington: Gov't Printing Office, 1940), pp. 74-97; Oppenheim, L.[assa] *International Law*, H. Lauterpacht (ed.), 8th ed. (London, New York: Longmans, 1995), pp. 90-94. Trusteeship may be one appropriate analogy for the situation of the Bosnian state. See, J.L. Brierly, *The Law of Nations. An Introduction to the International Law of Peace*, Sir Humphrey Waldock (ed.), 6th ed. (Oxford: Oxford University Press, 1963), p. 181.

52 See generally Alexander Johnston, "Introduction: South Africa Since February 1990," in *Constitution Making in the New South Africa*, Alexander Johnston, Sipho Shezi, and Gavin Bradshaw (eds.), (London and New York : Leicester University Press, 1993), p. 1; *Constitutional Guidelines for a Democratic South Africa* (1989) reprinted in *Columbia Human Rights Law Review* 21, no. 1 (Fall 1989), pp. 235-246.

53 International Crisis Group, "Aid and Accountability: Dayton Implementation" (November 24 1996), available at: www.crisisweb.org. Carl Bildt, the first High Representative for the implementation of the Dayton Agreement outlined the difficulties of the common structures in September 1996. See *UN Chronicle* 33, no. 3 (1996), p. 59.

54 See American Bar Association, Central and East European Law Initiative Annual Report (1995).

55 This description draws heavily on that provided by James Slone, "The Dayton Peace Agreement: Human Rights Guarantees and Their Implementation," *European Journal of International Law* 7, no.2 (1996), p. 215.

56 The three members selected by the President of the ECHR are not to be citizens of Bosnia-Herzegovina nor of a neighboring state. The Constitutional Court asked for CEELI's assistance in organizing its first session to hear cases in July 1997. See *CEELI Update* 4 (1997), p. 8.
57 See, *Basic Principles on the Independence of the Judiciary*, G.A. Res. 146, UN GAOR, 40th Sess., Supp. No 53, at 254, UN Doc A/40/53 (1985).
58 Inter-ethnic cooperation is still sparse and subject to political dictates. Many of the common institutions outlined in the DPA have not seen the light of day, and institutions of the wartime Bosnia-Herzegovina are still in place. The international conference on Bosnia held in Paris on November 14, 1996 saw this as one of its major points of concern. For example the Human Rights Chamber has been faced with almost a complete lack of cooperation from the Entities governments. See Decisions on Admissibility, Human Rights Chamber for Bosnia and Herzegovina, May 1997. Recommendations by the Ombudsperson for Human Rights have equally remained impotent. Some progress has been made. For example, following extensive negotiations the central government (the Council of Ministers) with the two co-prime ministers was formed on January 3, 1997 by the Parliamentary Assembly. This was the first time that the representatives of the three communities sat down together in the Assembly. It remains the case that neither the Presidency nor the Assembly fulfill their constitutional roles.
59 The DPA, Annex 10, Article II para. 1.
60 See *Ibid.*
61 Human Rights Watch, *Human Rights in Bosnia and Hercegovina Post Dayton: Challenges for the Field* (1996), p. 2.
62 See Elizabeth M. Cousens, "Making Peace in Bosnia Work," *Cornell International Law Journal* 30, no. 3 (1997), p. 815.
63 See United Nations, *Report of the High Commissioner to the Secretary-General*, UN Documents S/1996/814 (1996), para 86.
64 See *CEELI Update* 4, 5 (1997), p. 8.
65 For a thorough discussion of these bodies, see Jessica Simor, "Tackling Human Rights Abuses in Bosnia," *European Human Rights Law Review* 6 (1997), p. 644. The Ombudsperson is Dr. Gret Haller. *Ibid*, pp. 649-650.
66 The eight members were appointed by the Committee of Ministers of the Council of Europe, pursuant to resolution (93)6, as foreign members who were not citizens of neighboring states.
67 DPA, Annex 6, Chapter 2 sets out the framework of the Commission on Human Rights. It is to consist of an Ombudsperson and a Human Rights Chamber. The first appointee, who is to hold office for five years (non-renewable term), is not to be a citizen of Bosnia-Herzegovina or any neighboring state. The Ombudsperson is to appoint his own staff. The appointment is to be made by the 'Chairman-in-Office of the OSCE' after Consultation with the parties. See *ibid*, Art. IV, para 2.
68 *Ibid*, Annex 6, article V, para 2.
69 Simor, "Tackling Human Rights Abuses in Bosnia," pp. 651-2.
70 See *ibid*, at 649-50.
71 See DPA, Art. VI.
72 Again, these members cannot be citizens of Bosnia or Herzegovina nor of neighboring states.
73 See DPA, Art. VIII, para 2.
74 See Stephen P. Marks, "Preventing Humanitarian Crises Through Peace-Building and Democratic Empowerment: Lessons From Cambodia," *Medicine and Global Survival* 1 no. 4 (1994), available at: http://www2.healthnet.org/MGS/MarksMGS1-4.html.

75 DPA, Annex 11.
76 Article III of Annex 11 sets out the role of the IPTF *Ibid.*
77 U.N. Documents S/1995/1031, para. 27.
78 As Human Rights Watch point out, deployment of manpower was extremely slow. See Human Rights Watch, *No Justice No Peace, The United Nations International Police Task Force's Role in Screening Local Law Enforcement* (1996), p. 8.
79 See Human Rights Watch, *Human Rights in Bosnia and Hercegovina Post Dayton: Challenges for the Field* (1996), p. 2.
80 The station commander reported to Human Rights Watch/Helsinki that IPTF in Sanski Most was unable to perform at even the most rudimentary level due to these resource problems." See Human Rights Watch, *No Justice No Peace*, p. 15D.
81 Interview on file with author. (The author conducted a number of interviews while serving as the Special Representative of the Prosecutor of the ICTY. These interviews were granted on the condition of complete anonymity.)
82 Human Rights Watch have documented patters of employment discrimination against individuals based on their political affiliation or ethnic identity. See Human Rights Watch, *Politics of Revenge, The Misuse of Authority in Bihac, Cazin, and Velika Kladusa* (1997), pp. 16-22.
83 *Ibid*, p. 31-37. See also human rights abuses by police forces documented by Simor, "Tackling Human Rights Abuses in Bosnia," p. 660, with specific reference to Mostar.
84 Human Rights Watch, *Politics of Revenge*, p. 40.
85 There are currently approximately 20,000 policemen serving in the Bosnian-Croat Federation, and about 12,000 in Republika Srpska. See Human Rights, Watch, *No Justice No Peace*, p. 9.
86 Interviews on file with author. Autumn 1996.
87 See Thomas Carothers, "Democracy Assistance: The Question of Strategy," *Democratization* 4, no. 3 (1997), p. 113.
88 Not all prosecutors have a telephone, many do not have computers, and most of the computers in the Prosecutors offices do not have data-base facilities. The lack of data-base capacity means that it would be impossible (without long hours of manual labor) to cross-reference and compile information. Such process is crucial to the prosecution of war crimes cases, concerning command and control responsibility.
89 In theory, the amount of inward investment to Bosnia Herzegovina will be massive. In 1996, under the auspices of the World Bank, a framework for investment was put in place to jump start the economy of the Federation and that of Republic Srpska. A total of $1.8 billion was pledged for Bosnia Herzegovina at two donor conferences in 1996, of which $1.5 was fully committed. Reconstruction contracts worth $1.02 billion had been signed by the end of 1996, of which $950 million had been spent by the end of that year. See International Crisis Group, "Aid and Accountability: Dayton Implementation," p. 10.
90 Interviews on file with author. November- December 1996.
91 Interview on file with author.
92 U.N. Security Council Resolution 1022.
93 As of June 15, 2000, 67 suspects have been indicted by the UN International Criminal Tribunal, 40 have been apprehended and 27 suspects remain at large. See www.un.org/icty.
94 See Woodward, *Balkan Tragedy*, p. 210.
95 Hansen, "Political Legitimacy," p .82.
96 See generally Miroslav Wolf, *Exclusion and Embrace: A Theological Exploration of Identity, Otherness, and Reconciliation* (Nashville: Abington Press, 1996).

4 Social Reconstruction and Moral Restoration

DŽEMAL SOKOLOVIĆ

That social reconstruction is feasible solely under the rule of law can be taken for granted. Law has, however, two sources: morality and force, and it is dependent on both. Which of these sources is preferable depends on what type of society one idealizes. The social reconstruction of Bosnia requires moral restoration of a society that has undergone horrible moral damage. I take as axiomatic the fact that those who do not differentiate between right and wrong, good and evil, are not able to make good laws. Many present-day lawmakers in Bosnia are the same ones who bear some responsibility for the tragedy. The Bosnian Parliament itself has recently designated for the position of Head of its Human Rights and Refugee Affairs Board a man who was denounced in 1992 for having organized rape camps and other atrocities. Social reconstruction cannot ensue from a law-making body that lacks the ability to make basic moral assumptions and distinctions. The question is, where are we to search for the source of morality which is to be the foundation for the rule of law in Bosnia? An external model of the rule of law might be the most effective base for the reconstruction of Bosnia. In order for law to spring from morality it may have to do so with the protection of force. If this is the case, Bosnia needs both military protection and an educational protectorate in order for an authentic social reconstruction to commence.

The Rule of Just Laws

Disappointed by the state of the *ancien régime*, which was also under the rule of Law, Voltaire exclaimed: "Burn up your laws and make new ones! Where will the new ones come from? From the mind!"[1]

Law is an elemental part of human culture. There is no inborn human propensity to be just. Just as the stone axe was one of the greatest achievements in man's technological history, so too is law one of the greatest achievements in his social history. And yet, whether man is going to use an axe in order to facilitate his survival or to smash the head of his fellows does not depend on the axe but on the hand that holds it. There is nothing in an axe that disposes it to be used in this or that way. How the law is used does not depend only on the law but on the hands that hold it.

The establishment of the rule of law depends solely on two suppositions: 1) that Law is made by moral people and 2) that it is in the hands of moral people. Otherwise, what happens to law, as is so often the case in human history, is what has happened with axes: the worst people, armed with axes, cut off the best heads. Even the best laws in the hands of unjust people might become transformed into the instruments of evil. We have convened under the title "Justice and Social Reconstruction" to discuss the possibility of establishing the rule of law in Bosnia. That social reconstruction of Bosnia is not feasible without the rule of law is taken for granted. But the setting up of a rule of laws does not guarantee that they rest on morality; laws will not necessarily contribute to social renewal and might even elicit new clashes. Inasmuch as these facts are not entirely apparent, they should be considered.

Plato once observed that there are no laws without mores. I would extend that insight and note that there are no laws without moral people. Laws ought to be made primarily by moral people and then given to moral people. But then, why did Voltaire insist that laws be taken from the mind? Why did not he simply say that laws ought to be made by moral people?

Like law, morality and justice are not given by nature, but are both achievements which man attains only by dint of his mind and agency. When Plato claimed that "power belongs to reason, as it is wise,"[2] he had in mind that only wise men or philosophers could be just. However, as I, while writing, remember the idea about philosopher-rulers or ruler-philosophers, I am reminded of the words of the great Bosnian political philosopher Hasan Kjafija from Prusac. In contrast to Plato, he noted 450 years ago, "The best ruler is the one sitting with scholars, and the worst scholar is the one sitting with rulers".[3] The question of whether power should be given to wise humans or not is one of mankind's biggest temptations and dilemmas. If society is to be just, should science and wisdom rule? And if this is the case, will not wise scientists who are in power be spoiled by it?

Mind and science ought to be the source of laws, for, as Voltaire thinks, only wise humans might make society and the state (or power) just. But Plato is not right when he says, even while speaking simply of an ideal state, that wise men should rule. Power and, therefore, laws as well, are to issue from the mind, but there are dangers when wise men embrace power. It spoils people and, hence, should never be given to the best among us. For that reason Hasan Kjafija is right: it is in the scholars' interest—but more importantly in the interest of the state and the interest of us all—not to give power to scholars, but to obtain power and laws from their minds. Wise men are to be members of our parliaments if we wish our laws to be just. But scholars should never be in power and take the laws into their own hands. This is actually in accordance with Plato's idea of justice (the fundamental idea of his just state), that everybody works at what he is naturally capable of. Yet it opposes his derived idea that power should be in the hands of philosophers.

Dayton, or The Rule of Unjust Laws

Can the people sitting in the Bosnian Parliament carry out the restoration of society, set up the rule of law, or create a just state? Let us ponder this question in light of some recent events in the Bosnian Parliament.

In September 1997 the Parliament of Bosnia-Herzegovina (thus not only the supreme lawmaking body, but a contemporary symbol of democratic order) voted to designate "ultranationalist Velibor Ostojić" as Head of its Human Rights and Refugee Affairs Board. Ostojić had been actively involved in the Serbian insurrection and the ensuing violence. In defense of these actions, he declared that the worst atrocities in the war had been committed against Serbs and that "...We are defending Christian Europe against Islamic fundamentalism".[4] In the very beginning of the war he had been heavily involved with Radovan Karadžić's inner circle of ministers in arming Serbian Democratic Party extremists and planning and executing the invasion and brutal ethnic cleansing of Foča, Kalinovik, Čajniće, Goražde and Višegrad.[5] Bosnian television claimed that he had played football with human heads, while the refugees from Eastern Bosnia consider him to be the organizer of rape camps and of the expulsion of tens of thousands of non-Serbs. Ostojić still opposes the return of refugees to their homes.

All the representatives of the three ruling national parties voted for Ostojić's election, including those from the HDZ and the SDA. That the

SDS representatives voted for him is not surprising, since he was an inner-circle activist and among the leaders of that party. It appears that only a few representatives from small opposition parties from both entities voted against Ostojić's appointment. Sejfudin Tokić, the representative of the United List and one of leaders of UBSD (one of the 38 social democratic parties in Bosnia and one of the two social democratic parties represented in Parliament), was first to react. Another social democrat, Zlatko Lagumdžija, the leader of Social Democratic Party (SDP) of BiH and a parliamentary representative, did not vote for Ostojić's designation. According to him he left the session immediately before the vote took place.

After the Parliamentary session, the shameful news spread to the public. Among a few citizens' organizations, the Society for Threatened Peoples and the Association of Bosnian Podrinje Citizens reacted most firmly. They demanded the immediate and irrevocable resignation of all who voted for Ostojić (which would mean the resignation of the Parliament!).[6] The Board of Mothers of Killed and Lost Children addressed a message to Parliament noting that the "perpetrators of crime in BiH feel more and more safe and powerful".

Among the firmer (though unexpected) accusations of the public, Avdo Campara, the Chairman of the Bosnian Parliament's House of Peoples and a former apparatchik in the communist regime, retaliated publicly. Indeed, he answered in the manner of the "old regime," stating, "The Party of Democratic Action (SDA) and the Party for BiH (the party of Haris Silajdžić) should self-critically acknowledge their mistake". However, Campara claims that none of the representatives—from either the ruling or the opposition parties—reacted to Ostojić's election. Haris Silajdžić, a long-time favorite of the West, acknowledged, "Nobody reacted. If someone else had, I would also have reacted". No Parliamentarian resigned after this event.

(The situation in the Parliament of BiH reminds one irresistibly of the German Reichstag of January 1933. Then, despite a majority held by communists and social democrats, the representative of the national socialists was able to form a government while the communists and social democrats were disagreeing over programmatic issues. As you might recall, the name of the chancellor was Adolf Hitler.)

From the standpoint of this conference, however, the most interesting reaction to the BiH Parliament's decision was that of the international community. It simply ignored the event. Neither its official representatives in Bosnia nor outside of it commented on it at all. The West treated

Ostojić's appointment as an internal affair of a sovereign state—as if anything relevant in that state is still an internal affair.

Since the Dayton agreement, nothing in Bosnia is its own internal affair. The meaning of all political events has become relative to the specific parameters of Dayton, but especially so a decision of Parliament that a man who kicks human heads and banishes people from their homes should be responsible for human rights and refugees. This horrible episode, indeed, is just a consequence of the sophisticated and far-reaching democratic procedure that allowed Velibor Ostojić to become a *member* of the Parliament of BiH in the first place. This procedure of reconstructing democratic life in BiH commenced in November 1995 in Dayton.

For that reason, the international community should have reacted; and for that very reason, the international community, whether one calls it the OSCE, the UN or the USA, did not react.

I would not wish to engender misunderstandings about my attitude toward the Dayton agreement. From the very moment it was signed I considered that the agreement achieved two extremely positive things. First, it ended the war. Second, it divided Bosnia in an untenable and unfeasible way. The division of Bosnia (an actual consequence of the Dayton agreement which is a negation of Bosnia and therefore a negative matter) in an unsustainable and unrealizable way (thus the negation of a negation—let us play at dialectics a little bit) is also an achievement of Dayton, thus the affirmation of Bosnia. This is to say that the Dayton agreement is indeed the product of powerful and ethical people, but taking its civic aspects into consideration, is it the fruit of wise enough people?

If the intention of Dayton, besides the cessation of the war, was to preserve Bosnia through a division that is not yet viable but which will inevitably lead towards its resurrection, then wisdom means that those who originally imposed the war and committed the genocidal division of the country (as well as their political arrangements) should be eliminated from the process of its reconstruction. If those who had been dividing Bosnia remain in power, they will continue to divide it in spite of the Dayton agreement's intention and tactics. This is not only true because one has reasons enough to doubt their sincerity, but also because we are quite sure that they haven't the necessary prudence for the task of reconstruction. Even if they now sincerely wish to preserve Bosnia—and it is quite possible for justice or goodness to be learned—it is certain that they lack the wisdom to do something like that. If they had it, they would not have begun the war and divided the country in a criminal way. With Ostojić and those who voted for him in the Bosnian Parliament, and with people like

Momčilo Krajišnik (of whom Miodrag Živanović, the leader of the opposition among Bosnian Serbs in the Republika Srpska, says is more extreme than Radovan Karadžić) as a member of the Presidency of BiH, Bosnia has no prospects. But neither has the Dayton agreement. And then it is no longer only the internal affair of Bosnia. The character of Parliament itself, as well as the fact that these men appear in the presidency and in the Parliament, indicate that the Dayton agreement, in spite of some incontestable achievements, has not been a wise solution.

The reason for the lack of effective international response, as I have noted, is that it is simply regarded as a matter internal to Bosnia. Nonetheless, the consequences of Dayton are already being felt in the West. For the position of Bosnia's ambassador in Washington, Momčilo Krajišnik proposed Jovan (formerly John and Omer) Zametica, the one-time spokesman for indicted war criminal Ratko Mladić. SFOR and OSCE will probably be able to implement the results of local elections in Bosnia, for it is in tune with the Dayton agreement; American and EU perceptions of democracy perhaps must lead them to accept Ostojić as a member of the Bosnian Parliament. But can the United States accept this man recommended by a member of the tri-partite Presidency (another provision of the Dayton agreement) as the Bosnian ambassador?

Zametica's tutor and Ph.D. advisor at the London School of Economics published the following in *The Observer* in July 1995:

> Whatever the outcome of the present fighting in Bosnia—even if your murderous bands of desperate 'ethnic cleaners' win and set up your Bosnian Serbian state—you can never come back here. We thought we had taught you something about the international community, about war and war crimes, about the consequences to a state if its rulers deliberately choose to put themselves outside the bounds of civilised behaviour. We did not teach you to preach hatred for your neighbours as a basis for unity among Serbs; to enlist their guilt and horror at the crimes they have committed to be a bond between them; to tell blatant lies openly and in the knowledge that your every audience will know them to be lies.
>
> We thought we had taught you that those who support murder and rape and the harrying of unarmed men, women and children neighbours to exile and despair, even if they do not commit the acts themselves, make themselves by that support accessories after the fact. You have joined the murderers; and I will not say you welcome at LSE...

We cannot, nor would we wish to, take away your degree. It was given you for work fairly done and fairly examined.

But you cannot use it any more as a badge of achievement. What you are now doing has removed its credibility.

As these things go, you are still a youngish man. You can look forward to years of contempt and loathing. Stay where you are and rot in the realisation of what you have become. But do not, repeat not, expect us to forget or welcome you. Do not come back.[7]

This is how a wise man speaks. I am 100 percent sure that the American government will also refuse to offer hospitality to such a man, even though his appointment would be in tune with the Dayton agreement. But this is still not evidence that wisdom stands behind Dayton. The American government must also apply the same principle of the implementation of Dayton agreement to events internal to Bosnia: solely insofar as it is just!

If one wants a just implementation of the Dayton agreement, the agreement itself, as I have said, has to be more wise than it is. It should be applied in a way that will provide solutions in harmony with the fundamental moral norms that form the basis of human rights and democracy. Zametica should not be allowed to come to Washington, as he was not allowed to appear at a conference at Yale last year.

But what about the other unjust consequences of Dayton? Ostojić as the Parliament-appointed combatant for human rights, and an indicted war criminal's spokesman as Bosnian Ambassador to the United States, are not the only evidence that Dayton is not a wise solution. Searching for the cause of these things leads us to some inevitable questions: who has elected a Parliament that would designate Ostojić? Who elected Krajišnik, who appointed Zametica to be ambassador? And eventually, who elected those who consented to sit in Bosnia's Presidency together with Krajišnik?

As one should be cautious to whom to give an axe, one should ponder to whom to give power, even in a democracy. The cardinal consequence of the Dayton agreement is not the election of Ostojić, it is the election of the Parliament and Presidency of BiH. It is the "people" of BiH who are accountable for the decision to elect such representatives in the Parliament, who are then responsible for electing Ostojić, and who do not then resign from pricks of conscience or principles. Here I would like to make a bold assertion: perhaps the Bosnian people are not ready for the power that has been given to them. In fact, it may not even be possible to speak of a "Bosnian people" in a country in which the people act as a tri-national electorate. Power also implies the likelihood of making laws and the rule of such laws. If a country's people are not wise enough, then neither will the laws its Parliament makes be wise. I fear that the pragmatic outcomes of democracy in Bosnia mean that we have perhaps hastened too much with octroyed democracy: one can only expect that events such as Ostojić's election will be followed by similar events and the inertia of events will yield anti-democratic consequences. Herein lies the basic fault, accountability and lack of wisdom of the Dayton agreement: it was too ambitious and unrealistic. I have never quite agreed with Thomas Jefferson's words that every people has the government it deserves. I actually believe that every people deserves a better government than it has. Yet recent developments in Bosnia also corroborate that Jefferson's words are at least partly accurate. To the question of whether Bosnia is ready for a true democracy, my answer is still negative.

Ostojić, the Parliament of BiH, Krajišnik in the Presidency of BiH, Zametica in Washington, and so forth, are fruits of last year's elections in Bosnia. What the consequences of this year's September elections will be, one can only forebode.

Educational Protectorate

Who might accomplish the moral restoration of Bosnia, establish there the rule of moral laws and undertake the reconstruction of its society? The Bosnian authorities? The "people" of BiH? The intellectual elite of Bosnia? The international community?

In their report "Beyond Ballot Boxes: municipal elections in Bosnia-Herzegovina," issued immediately before the September 13–14 1997 elections, the International Crisis Group (ICG) claimed that these elections had little to do with democracy.[8] For our discussion, these words are also considerable: "The International Crisis Group (ICG) is concerned with the agreement signed on 2 September between US Major-General Grange—Commander of SFOR troops in the northern sector (MND North)—and hardline Pale leaders loyal to Radovan Karadžić. The agreement undermines the international community's credibility, throws into question the international community's commitment to the rule of law in the Republika Srpska (RS), and seriously jeopardizes the ability of candidates and citizens opposed to the Pale hardliners to participate safely in the municipal elections".[9]

After the elections, Stephen Bowen and Sandra Mitchell resigned from their positions in the OSCE and warned the public of election manipulations: "Having resigned as senior legal counsel to the Election Appeals Sub-Commission (EASC) to express our deep concern over the Organization for Security and Cooperation in Europe's (OSCE) decision to accommodate Bosnian Serb hardliners led by Radovan Karadžić, we are more concerned than ever that the international community and the OSCE's policy of appeasement and disregard for the rule of law has undermined the peace process in Bosnia-Herzegovina".[10]

If nothing can be done in order to protect law and justice, perhaps resignation is the wisest decision. And evidence of moral persuasion. All this time there were just a few resignations in Bosnia.

That Bosnia needs the rule of law in order to begin social reconstruction, nobody disputes. But where are the laws to come from if Bosnia is morally damaged? As a sociologist I cannot resist pointing to a stable society as the most fruitful ground for morality to spring from. Conversely, a turbulent social situation demolishes all moral norms, and makes even the most just laws inapplicable. I myself come from a town in Bosnia where people almost never used keys for yards, houses, rooms, wardrobes. And then suddenly they began to lock up all the doors. In the interim, something occurred that totally shifted their moral persuasions. Down the river a hydroelectric plant and a lake were built. It caused the migration of inhabitants of a neighboring town, some of whom came to our town. This brought tremendous turbulence to the life of the city. Many of the newcomers could not withstand the temptations of change and led their hosts to a situation of mistrust that caused them to begin locking their yards and homes. Bosnia, however, has experienced a tremendous macro-social turbulence.

When I visited a relative of mine this year, an 80-year-old former World War II partisan, he told me a truth which all those wishing to help restore Bosnian society should be aware of: "When the Germans bombarded us we hid in the forest and returned after three days. Nobody was missing a single egg from his henhouse. In this war, many lost their lives because they did not dare to leave their houses and flats to be seized by others". He meant by *their own others*. All scruples had vanished, no moral norms were sacred anymore. In such a morally destroyed society, the border between good and evil, between right and wrong, is not just blurred, it is lost. To give to such a society the opportunity to make laws must inevitably lead to the designation of Ostojić as a fighter for human rights and Zametica as ambassador in Washington.

Can Bosnia establish a rule of law if the laws are to be made by its own wise men? In a situation where not a few Bosnian intellectuals sit with the rulers, are rulers themselves, or cling to the national-collectivistic ideas, it is hard to expect that they can make just laws.[11]

Bosnia has to learn democracy, the rule of law, what is just. Besides military protection, which could last for a long time, and political supervision, which might be futile, Bosnia needs what I would call an *educational protectorate* designed by the international community.

Humans cannot become wise unless they already are. But goodness can be learned. An educational protectorate would ensure that the reconstruction of society can begin from moral foundations. Bosnia desperately needs help from outside world. I have in mind not only help of the *institutional* global community, but help from the *international civil society* and the wisdom it brings with it. This conference, as a non-governmental action, is an act of the international civil society and aims to compensate for what official actions often miss.

Actually, Bosnia is *de facto* already under the protectorate of the international community. Otherwise, how do we explain the fact that the High Representative of this community decided after the Bonn conference to put into function the law on BiH citizenship from January 1, 1998 "until both houses of the Parliament of BiH pass into the law in its full form, without amendments and without conditions".[12] Bosnia is thus not a sovereign state, either. In every sovereign state the chief of the state is the carrier of its sovereignty. The collective Presidency of BiH, as the chief of the state, and therefore every member of the Presidency as well, although the carrier of only 1/3 of sovereignty each, should be the sovereign of the State of BiH. But how can one speak of the Presidency of BiH as a carrier of sovereignty if the High Representative can threaten to remove one of its members if he does not cooperate in the implementation of the Dayton agreement? The *de facto* sovereign of Bosnia is, accordingly, the international community, and the representative or carrier of its sovereignty is the High Representative.

Bosnia, however, is not *de jure* under the protectorate of international community; Bosnia is *de jure* a sovereign country. Moreover, the High Representative, i.e. the international community, does everything to make it look *as if* there is no *de facto* protectorate, and *as if* Bosnia is *de facto* a sovereign state. It is clear to the author, as a man of theory, why the international community is anxious about the protectorate and sovereignty over Bosnia. But as a man who probably lacks a sense of political pragmatism, it is not clear to me at all why the world is so anxious about the simulation of Bosnian sovereignty and a naive pretense that there is no protectorate.

If this is a version of educational protectorate over Bosnia, for which I have just pleaded, then it is very ineffective. The cause of the ineffectiveness of the Dayton agreement, that is, its civic part (and especially concerning the right to return and the obligation to provide the basic conditions for return) lies perhaps just in the lack of a *de jure* protectorate. This lack enables the authorities in Bosnia, in spite of real supervision by the international community, to govern in a manner in collision with the Dayton agreement. The *illusion* held by the Bosnian authority—from the level of the "unique state" of BiH, over two "multiethnic entities,"[13] down to cantons and municipalities—that it is sovereign in relation to the external world, transmutes into a real sovereignty of this authority over its own people. The reality of Bosnian sovereignty vividly recalls the medieval feudal state in which, after all, the idea of sovereignty as a specific system of relationships among states originally emerged. All that is certain, when who is sovereign and who has a protectorate over whom is in question, is that the people are not sovereign—and this is the basis of the *"nouveau régime,"* that is, democracy, which the international community reportedly favors. In Bosnia in particular, everyone else has power over the people. However, the "unique state" of BiH is *de jure* sovereign in relation to "two multiethnic entities," while the entities have avoided *de facto* the vassal relation towards the central authority and become sovereign, even in their relations to the international community. Clinton did not, during his recent visit to Bosnia, teach his Christmas lesson to the chiefs of "two multiethnic entities," as the vassals of his own vassals, but to the chiefs of the central authority, that is, to his vassals. So it happens that, just as in the Middle Ages, a feudal principle is in place in Bosnia whereby "the vassal of my vassal is not my vassal". The same principle also applies to the relationship between the central authority and lower political units, cantons and municipalities. Municipalities are vassals of cantons, but the governments of entities have no real direct power over municipalities.

Therefore, it is good that the High Representative proclaimed the law on citizenship of BiH. This act is proof of the protectorate of the world over Bosnia, and thus of the security of its citizens. Is it good to further foster the illusion of sovereignty of the central authority of BiH as a "unique state"? I am not sure, for it really fosters the sovereignty of its entities and so furthers the division of Bosnia and its disappearance as a sovereign state. For this reason I maintain that it would be in the best interests of the international community, of Bosnia itself, and of realizing the positive sides of the Dayton agreement, to desist from the illusory sovereignty of

BiH as a "unique state" and set up a *de jure* protectorate, and in doing so, prevent and halt the process of shaping three sovereign entities as ethnically-genocidally "pure" states. Otherwise, it will be the international community who will share responsibility for that.

A protectorate over Bosnia, which the international community primarily fears (because it recalls the old, colonial days), in Bosnia frightens only the current authority. This is not because it would lose sovereignty with respect to the external world (it already lacks this now) but because it would lose a dictatorial sovereignty over its own people(s).

A protectorate in Bosnia's case has nothing in common with the protectorates of the colonial period. A protectorate of the international community over a country (state) is something entirely different from the protectorate of a state over another country. As such, an *educational protectorate over Bosnia* would be something totally new in the political history of humankind and, accordingly, a political achievement. The one condition is that its aim would really be not to position Bosnia as a persistent vassal of the world (that is, a permanent loss of sovereignty), but instead to educate Bosnia, that is, to create assumptions that will enable Bosnia to carry on living as a country in which its own people, and not national groups or their parties, will be the carriers of sovereignty.

The octroyed law on citizenship (the act undertaken by the High Representative) has been a great step towards this. But it is not enough. An educational protectorate over Bosnia would have to commence from the moral renewal of Bosnian society. It is difficult to teach the generation which is currently in power what is good and what is evil, what is right and what is wrong. It is possible to do it with forthcoming generations. An educational protectorate, with moral renewal as its dominant dimension, must begin the process of social restoration by using the force of law towards the following directions:

1. Education laws (which are, nowadays, more a source of hatred and preparation for new future strife, than they had been before this tragedy) must make criminal any incitement of interethnic and inter-religious hatred in textbooks and in teaching.[14]
2. Media laws must make criminal any incitement of inter-ethnic and inter-religious hatred.
3. Laws on property must pledge the right to property not only without regard to ethnic or religious background, but also regardless of membership in different political-administrative units or formations.

4. Not only laws, but also the judiciary must play an educational role in Bosnia. In order to attain this, the judiciary must be in the hands, and not only under the supervision, of foreigners for the time being.

Law, therefore, which in many societies is the goal and the consequence of a long moral development, in Bosnia has to become a device and the cause of society's moral renewal. Regardless of whether the law rests on morality, it has, at times, to be applied by force. This is a risk for the rule of law. It was the risk for stone axe too. But law has to undertake this risk. If the international community does not undertake this risk, the risk of lawlessness in Bosnia will enlarge even more.

Notes

1. From Bergbohm, *Jurisprudenz und Rechtsphilosophie*, quoted from Georg Lukács, *Povijest i klasna svijest* (Zagreb: Naprijed, 1970), p. 179.
2. Plato, *State*, book IV, 441, XVI.
3. Hasan Kjafija, "Temelji mudrosti o uredjenju svijeta," *Behar* Vol. III, no. 13 (1994), p. 20.
4. *The Independent* (London: August 11, 1992), p. 6.
5. "Newsday Report," *St. Louis Post-Dispatch* (April 19, 1993), p. 9A.
6. *BBC Summary of World Broadcasts* (September 20, 1997), EE/D3 029/A.
7. Donald Cameron Watt, "You are a liar and an outcast," in: *The Observer* (London: July 30, 1995).
8. International Crisis Group, "Beyond the Ballot Boxes: Municipal Elections in Bosnia-Herzegovina" (September 10, 1997), available at: http://www.crisisweb.org.
9. *Ibid.*
10. See http://www.balkaninstitute.org.
11. It is not difficult to imagine how intellectuals and politicians would regard such an approach in a country where a 19th Century author wrote an ironic fable entitled "The Wisest Men in the World". See Dr. Muhsin Rizvić, *Panorama bošnjačke književnosti* (Sarajevo: Ljiljan, 1994), p. 271.
12. See ONASA, December 18, 1997.
13. The expression "unique state with two multiethnic entities" was invented at the Sintra conference.
14. The Bologna-based *Centro per l'Europa Centro-Orientale e Balcanica*, with the cooperation of DIECEC (Development of Intercultural Education by Co-operation between European Cities), plans to submit a project to the ERASMUS program whose goal is to take nationalism out of all history textbooks. What they will find in the textbooks currently used by the pupils of the "two multiethnic entities" of BiH remains to be seen.

5 The Challenge of Democracy in Divided Societies:
Lessons from Bosnia—Challenges for Kosovo
FLORIAN BIEBER

The past decade has been marked by two seemingly contradictory trends on the global scale. With the fall of the Berlin Wall and the regimes associated with it, Europe and many other regions of the world experienced an unprecedented wave of democratization. The world had to tackle a sharp increase of ethnic conflict at the same time, sometimes in the very societies that had set forth upon the path of democratization only shortly before. The relationships between plural societies and ethnic conflict, on one side, and democracy on the other, have often been misunderstood and misjudged, frequently to the detriment of those plural societies engaged in a process of democratization.

This paper will argue that the understanding of democracy and ethnic diversity, as two contradictory premises on which to build a society, is a misleading one. The building of a multi-national democracy requires that its institutional engineers discard the hope of "solving" nationalism. At the same time, such a political system requires careful attention in order not to exacerbate ethnic tensions. International attempts to develop multi-ethnic institutional frameworks for Bosnia and Kosovo shall serve as a test-case for the Western understanding of multiethnic societies, especially in former Yugoslavia, and its inadequacies in trying to develop a mechanism for (re)building plural society. As early as 1993, Donald Horowitz announced the failure of Western governments to address the special democratic needs of plural societies: "As the recent wave of democratization now runs its course, it is not too soon to say that a major opportunity for constitutional planning for interethnic accommodation has been largely lost, and the emerging results are there for all to see. This is a serious foreign-policy failure for the United States and for the Western World more generally."[1] This paper will argue that this pattern has been repeated in Bosnia and Kosovo and begs the question of Western and liberal policy towards plural and divided societies in general.

Theoretical Constraints to Democracy in Multiethnic Societies

The very conception of group rights—specific privileges given to a group on the basis of common descent—contradicts the essence of democracy and its principle of equality. It may even seem reactionary, since "liberal democracy emerged in part as a reaction against the way that feudalism defined individuals' political rights and economic opportunities by their group membership."[2] The transition from feudalism to democracy has, however, never been as clear-cut as this conceptual contradiction might imply. The second half of the 19th century was marked in most West and Central European countries by a constant enlargement of the segment of the population eligible to vote. Nevertheless, it was only the experience of the first World War, which was global not only in its territorial component, but also in its effects on social classes, that gave rise to universal suffrage in most European countries.[3] Even in the Europe of the interwar period and since the end of World War II specific groups were excluded from democratic rights. In the years following 1918, after the dissolution of the old empires, millions of Europeans lost their citizenship and were unable to receive new "entrance tickets" to the young democracies (most of them soon to become authoritarian). After the Second World War a similar phenomenon again occurred in Europe, with the addition in several countries of a ban on voting for former members of the German National Socialist Party (i.e. in Austria in 1946). Thus, cases of "pure" democracies are difficult to find and the phenomenon of discrimination against groups has accompanied the development of democratic societies since their beginnings. The conceptual difference between feudalism and democracy lies in the fact that in feudal societies the different groups lived on the same territory and in a hierarchical relationship to one another.[4]

Democracy, on the other hand, seeks to eliminate the rigid divide of these groups. In its very conception, however, it creates new ones. While the medieval state attributed very little significance to the border and the idea of the state as a firmly defined unit with citizenship for its inhabitants and distinctly reduced rights for non-citizens, the democracy required a state as a unit in which the old divisions could be eliminated. The unifying criteria for these states became the nation. I do not seek to retell the history of the development of nations. But the overlap of nation, state and democratic development have created a tight interlinkage between all three components of modern states. Thus, when authors point to causes of ethnic conflict such as the transformation of *"Ethnos* becomes *Demos"*[5] or a switch in voting from a "political to a national choice,"[6] it involuntarily disguises the fact that that in most countries the *"Demos* and *Ethnos"* coincide and a political choice will inevitably be a national choice. In countries populated by a strong majority and only few and small minorities, the politics of the state are the politics of the nation. An election in Germany is not only an election for or against the 'rulers' of the country of Germany, but also of the German nation. Thus, the development of democracy in most countries carries a national bias. In many Western European countries, this bias has become less visible as the multinational elements have disappeared through assimilation, expulsions and other malign as well as benign factors. Nevertheless, in recent decades, immigration to Western European countries forces them to readdress the previous overlap of nation and *demos*. Jürgen Habermas has addressed this challenge in his recent writings:

> The nation-state must rid itself of the ambivalent potential which once provided its propulsion... In the past, the nation-state created a blend of political discourse which made it possible to absorb the thrusts of abstraction and, through national consciousness, to embed the population, torn from its traditional life-connections, in a context of widened and rationalized *Lebenswelt*. The more the legal status of the citizen coincided with his cultural identification with the nation, the more easily this integrative function could be fulfilled. Today, with the nation-state internally challenged by the explosive power of multiculturalism..., the question must be posed whether there exists a functional equivalent for the combination of *Staatsnation* and *Volksnation*.[7]

The conflict between group rights and democratic rights becomes an even greater issue in countries that encompass several national groups and can take the form of minority rights, or in multinational societies that lack the outright predominance of one particular nation.

In Yugoslavia, diversity of ethnicities and divisions in society were never forgotten during the Communist period, but were carefully taken into account by the federal and republican administrations. Tibor Várady effectively points to the alternation in the pages of Sarajevo newspapers between the Cyrillic and Latin alphabets, and the informal requirement of university rectors to be members of different groups in turn. These are acknowledgments of the "existence of ethnic rivalry. The preestablished sequence of rectors would not have made sense without the supposition that there was an undercurrent of ethnic bias..."[8] These mechanisms, however, did not just indicate the presence of ethnic politics in a country without ethnic parties; they also served to "both resolve and perpetuate the problem."[9] This recognition, that any mechanism which formally or informally grants collective rights to a group on the basis of its national or ethnic origin might not only solve the tension (or rather subdue it) but might also ensure the continuing presence of collective rights on the political agenda, raises the question of the continuity of ethnic and national affiliation in general.

Nationalism has largely been seen by its academic analyst with suspicion, and usually with dislike and even disgust. As an ideology with strong emotional appeals, scholarly investigations of nationalism are rarely performed out of sympathy for the phenomenon, but rather out the urge to understand and eventually "solve" nationalism. Nationalism thus was generally conceived as a tool for certain political elites to ensure their hold to power. This approach, in the words of Ivelin Saradamov, is based on most scholars' temptation "to 'package' nationalism and ethnic conflict in a way that would make them look 'curable'".[10] If one accepts the premise of a possibility to eliminate nationalism and ethnic politics,[11] and the desirability of such a development, any system which instead perpetuates it hardly seems viable or positive.

Some scholars, such as Danilo Zolo, would thus advocate the withdrawal of plural politics and plead for assimilation, the only alternative to ethnic politics.[12] Zolo argues that "there can be little doubt that the regulation of social risks is better guaranteed the more efficaciously the political system exercises its systemic function of exclusion/inclusion, i.e. the more it succeeds in making the internal bond of political fidelity both *organic and exclusive* and in introducing it into the consciousness of its subjects."[13] Zolo's conception of a democratic political system based on an organic— i.e. "natural"—bond of the population highlights the danger of ignoring national politics in any intellectual endeavor on the subject. The nation offers itself as the most "organic" and natural state of society, thus running the danger that the space opened by a negation of plural ethnic or national politics will actually be filled by the national conception of the predominant group, and not by anational politics. As a consequence, scholars, even when attempting to overcome nationalism, must work within a conceptual framework which accepts and elaborates political systems that perpetuate the society's national and ethnic component(s).

As I pointed out earlier, democratic politics are inherently "national" in their historical development, including in cases where nation and state do not perfectly overlap, and in particular in the countries of Southeastern Europe. While national rights as collective rights challenge the democratic rights of the individual, both are closely intertwined and inseparable. The horrendous experience of national politics in the former Yugoslavia, propagated by ethnically homogeneous parties, has rendered the concept of "nation-based" politics suspect and undesirable. This conclusion, however, is misleading. The key lies in determining a set of institutional and political tools which are inherently "ethnic," but which at the same time preclude exclusive and divisive politics. In order to prevent divisions, we have to seek strategies to build united societies *with* ethnic politics.

When discussing the tools needed to preserve the interests and identities of individuals in plural societies through collective rights, we should bear in mind the inherent difficulties and challenges of institution building. In order to evaluate the effectiveness of the international community's attempts at institution building on the territory of the former Yugoslavia, we have to pose the following questions:

1. To what extent do collective rights infringe on individual rights?
2. Do the group rights undermine basic prerequisites for democracy?
3. Are the group rights flexible enough to wither away when the groups no longer deem them necessary, and are they rigid enough to endure when one group wants to do away with them to the disadvantage of others?

Does the Dayton Model Offer an Adequate Balance Between Democracy and National Rights?

When peace was established in Bosnia through the negotiations at Dayton and the institutional framework developed there, it was clear to all parties concerned, from Bosnia, Croatia, and Yugoslavia, as well from the Contact Group (United Kingdom, Germany, France, Italy, Russia and the United States), that the biggest challenge for peace in Bosnia was to find a mechanism that would enable the nations of the country to agree on living in Bosnia. While this observation seems self-evident, it should be emphasized as it demonstrates the elements that *did not* hold great importance during the attempts to end the war: minority rights and democracy.[14] The negotiations at Dayton involved the political representatives of the weakened central government of Bosnia and the presidents of Croatia and Serbia, all three of whom together hardly possessed the necessary legitimacy to represent the people of Bosnia.[15] The subsequent vote for ratification in the three respective parliaments was a forgone conclusion and scarcely added democratic legitimacy to the agreement. Nevertheless, the constitution (annexed to the agreement) claims to have been determined by the "Bosniacs, Croats, and Serbs, as constituent peoples (along with Others), and citizens of Bosnia and Herzegovina."[16] The preamble can claim most of its legitimacy not from its origins or authorship, but rather from the fact that it was later implemented by the institutions which form the state of Bosnia and Herzegovina.

The process of institutionalizing a multi-ethnic society (as was done in Bosnia) uses essentially three tools for ensuring adequate group rights: individual rights, ethnic federalism and consociationalism. Individual rights do not only encompass human rights, which are to be implemented in any working democracy. It also includes individual rights that relate to membership in a national group, such as the use of language in schools, media and all spheres of life, private and public. Often, these rights amount to cultural rights, or even cultural autonomy, which go beyond the individual, but avoid the territorial dimension of group rights. While some of these rights can be granted easily without conflicting with democracy and institutional functioning, some are more problematic. The possibility of using all languages in dealings with state institutions might burden the institutions and render them inefficient. The right to schooling in the language or culture of every group might not only be too costly, but also divisive. A common language is required in order to render a state functional, unless complete bilingualism is achieved.[17] While individual human and political rights might not be adequate to ensure a sufficient safeguard for the diversity of a state, "if minority members do not enjoy civil and political rights as individuals, their subjugation and assimilation is imminent."[18]

The constitution of Bosnia and Herzegovina does not only enumerate basic human rights—it also contains what is probably the most complete catalogue of human rights conventions the country promises to adhere to of any constitution in the world. The 15 agreements range from the Geneva conventions on the status of refugees, to numerous instruments of minority protection such as the "Framework Convention for the Protection of National Minorities."[19] This seemingly elaborate protective mechanism is, however, deeply flawed, as no group rights are listed in the constitution and the individual rights make no reference to individuals' rights as members of a group (use of own language, education in the culture of the group, etc.). The international agreements, despite their enumeration, lack direct applicability, as their implementation is not regulated.

Instead, group rights are taken into consideration at the second level mentioned above: ethnic federalism. The powers of the central state of Bosnia are extremely curtailed, to the advantage of the entities. These essentially ethnically-defined entities provide adequate protection for group members *within* their territory, but are incapable of providing an institutional safeguard for the rights of their group members in another entity. Moreover, the "emphasis on corporate entities reduces the significance of citizens; the principle of equality between groups promotes inequality between individuals; and group veto power confers a strength which is not necessarily in proportion either to the size or the wealth or the group."[20]

The final mechanism for accommodating different groups in a plural society is consociationalism, which signifies the cooperation of different groups in a non-territorial institutional structure, governed jointly by the elites of each group.[21] In Bosnia, the consociational model can be detected in the institutional framework of the state, in the chambers of parliament, and even more so in the presidency. While this system of government counters territorial aspirations and thus could limit sources of tension in a multiethnic society, it requires "mutual trust and the rule of applicable laws equally applicable to all groups"[22]—conditions hardly fulfilled in Bosnia.

The framework for national diversity offered by the Bosnian constitution thus can be seen as taking into account all available means of group accommodation, but only inadequately, while at the same time all-too-easily jeopardizing democratic principles. The rigid determination of the ethnic origins of the members of different central institutions, combined with their entity origins, closes the possibility for members of other ethnic groups, or for members of an ethnic group outside its "own" entity, to be representatives or to be represented in the central institutions of Bosnia.

Within this kind of institutional framework, the return of refugees to an entity in which they do not constitute the predominant ethnic group, and the development of parties that seek to represent several ethnic groups or to place other forms of ethnic cooperation in their programs, are difficult to achieve. Due to the excessive rigidity imposed by the constitution, the institutions must constantly confront the ethnic divide of the country, without recourse to any possible remedy that could foster cooperation. At the same time, some important elements of group rights are neglected, rendering the state's democratic development difficult.

Were the Lessons of Dayton Learned at Rambouillet?

While it is still to be determined which of the institutional arrangements discussed during negotiations at Rambouillet and Paris in February and March 1999 will be implemented in Kosovo under NATO control, Rambouillet provides another example of the international community's having charted an agreement to end a conflict between two nations in former Yugoslavia and having provided a territory with a new institutional framework. Here, an attempt was made to have the representatives of the state in which Kosovo lies—that is, Yugoslavia and Serbia—negotiate the agreements with the representatives of the minority dominating the province—the Albanians. While the representatives of the state easily achieved legitimacy because they were sent to the negotiations by the elected government of that country,[23] the representatives of the minority proved to be more problematic, due to the absence of internationally and state-recognized elections within the Albanian community of Kosovo and taking into account the political developments since the last unofficial elections held in Kosovo. Thus, the Albanian delegation included, besides the elected "president" Ibrahim Rugova and members of the party carrying the most votes in the election, the LDK, members of the Kosovo Liberation Army, and intellectuals, such as Veton Surroi, who had no formal political or military following.

Within the framework of the agreement for Kosovo, the projected constitution took a more prominent place (Chapter 1) than the constitution had in the case of Bosnia (Annex 4 of the Dayton agreement). In general, the constitution suggested for Kosovo is more detailed and elaborate than the six-page constitution for Bosnia. The document does not define the people enacting the legal text and in no other way does it determine the composition of Kosovo. Generally, it refrains from clearly dividing institutions between Albanians and Serbs. The term used in this constitution is "national communities," which avoids ascribing the status of 'minority' or 'majority' to either of the national groups in Kosovo. While the text refrains from a separate definition of the communities, the "national communities" are defined in connection with the composition of the assembly. Here the constitution differentiates between "[c]ommunities whose members constitute more than 0.5 percent of the Kosovo population" (and less than 5 percent) and those which "constitute more than 5 percent."[24] Hereby, both Serbs and Albanians would belong to the second group of communities, while all other minorities belong to the first group. As opposed to the main challenge at Dayton, to map out the relationship between the groups within their respective entity of predominance, the challenge of the negotiations at Rambouillet lay in codifying the relations between the province and the state, Serbia or Yugoslavia.[25]

Thus, as previously, the emphasis of the agreement did not lie with democracy.[26] Minority rights, however, did play a more significant role in the case of Kosovo than in the case of Bosnia. As in the Dayton constitution, human rights are safeguarded according to high standards. In Rambouillet, however, this chapter is supplemented by Article VII on National Communities, which lays out the non-territorial rights of Kosovo's national groups. This chapter foresees a degree (as yet undetermined) of self-government by the national communities, and democratic elections within each group. In addition, it established the right to bilingual official signs (street names, city names, etc.), the establishment of educational institutions, the use of national symbols, the preservation of religious and cultural sights, and a separate family law.[27]

Thus, the Rambouillet proposals pay greater respect to non-territorial national group rights. It remains vague, however, in contentious issues such as the degree of bilingualism of Kosovo, especially in education and other spheres of interaction with authorities. Most of the progress made at Rambouillet should be seen more as confirmation of the basic approach of the international community to the resolution of the conflicts in both cases. The state of the area under negotiations was taken as a basis for finding a solution which would be acceptable to all sides, without fundamentally departing from the *status quo*. The absence of a territorial division in Kosovo forced the authors of the agreement (which includes the constitution) to elaborate on the rights of national communities to a larger degree than their counterparts had in Bosnia, where a multinational society was replaced during the war by a three-way division of the state. Robert Hayden argues, accordingly, that the Western approach to Kosovo and Bosnia were similar also insofar as they were to a great extent concerned with preserving the "legal fiction" of an independent Bosnia and a Kosovo as part of Yugoslavia. "Legal fictions are often useful devices, and the pretenses that Bosnia has been preserved as a state and that Kosovo cannot be independent are useful to hide the discomforting truth that, if borders of the state really cannot be changed, then a population that rejects inclusion within them either must be expelled ... or ruled by brute force."[28]

Conclusions

The wars in Bosnia and in Kosovo should not be seen as the remnants of a delayed 19th century war, but as the embodiment of the challenges democracy and ethnic diversity pose to European and global societies for the years to come. Ethnic diversity has been on the rise in most of the countries of Western Europe in the past few decades, due to migratory movements which have transformed Western Europe into *de facto* immigrant societies. In addition, long-marginalized national and linguistic groups in Europe are making themselves heard. This new Western European diversity demonstrates the absurdity of attempts to create and uphold a "pure" nation-state.

The close interlinkage between national and democratic politics has brought a severe conceptual crisis to the institutionalization of democracy in multinational societies. Such institution building requires the recognition of ethnic diversity without viewing it as the "root of evil" in ethnic conflict. The abuse and instrumentalization of ethnic politics of personal power, absolute political predominance and hatred—not ethnic politics *per se*—are the causes of national conflicts.

Success in developing multinational societies, whether within the European Union, Bosnia or Kosovo, will require a different set of institutional tools than those chosen by the Western countries in the cases of Dayton and Rambouillet. Instead of a patchwork that essentially perpetuates existing cleavages, a dynamic system is needed that will enable development without endangering the essential balance of national and individual rights and the interests of different national groups. Without developing a blue print for such a system, it should include:

1. a clear and unambiguous set of group and individual rights;
2. instruments for inter-group cooperation on multiple levels of society;
3. tools to allow the plural society to adjust and readdress its development as inter-group relations change; and

4. a clear system of incentives for groups to cooperate in a plural society and to vest their interests in the multinational project.

The West's failure to address the challenges of plural societies through "creative application of Western precepts of ethnocultural justice"[29] have set a somewhat discouraging precedent for the success of multiethnic societies in Central and Eastern Europe, as well as for developing the multinational structure of the European Union.

Notes

1   Donald L. Horowitz, "Democracy in Divided Societies," in *Journal of Democracy* 4, no. 4 (October 1993): 35.
2   Will Kymlicka, *Multicultural Citizenship* (Oxford: Oxford University Press, 1995), 34.
3   Suffrage for women, however, was still frequently excluded from "universal" suffrage.
4   Julien Benda, in his study of intellectuals, describes this development in terms of a shift in "hatreds:" "The condensation of political passions into a smaller number of very simple hatreds, springing from the deepest roots of the human heart, is a conquest of modern times." Julien Benda, *Le Trahison des Clercs* (The Treason of the Intellectuals) (New York: W.W. Norton & Company, 1969), p. 8.
5   Bogdan Denitch, *Ethnic Nationalism* (Minneapolis-London: University of Minnesota Press, 1994), p. 51.
6   Vojin Dimitrijević, "The Post-Communist Apotheosis of the Nation-State," in *Religion & War*, ed. Dušan Janjić (Belgrade: European Movement in Serbia, 1994), p. 20.
7   "*Der Nationalstaat muß das ambivalente Potential, das einst als Schubkraft gewirkt abschütteln....Seinerzeit hat der Nationalstaat einen Zusammenhang politischer Kommunikation gestiftet, der es möglich machte, die Abstraktionsschübe der gesellschaftlichen Modernisierung aufzufangen und eine aus überlieferten Lebenszusammenhängen herausgerissenen Bevölkerung über das Nationalbewußtsein in die Kontexte einer erweiterten und rationalisierten Lebenswelt wieder einzubetten. Diese Integrationsfunktion konnte er um so eher erfüllen, als sich der Rechtsstatus des Bürgers mit der kulturellen Zugehörigkeit zur Nation verband. Heute, da sich der Nationalstaat im Inneren durch die Sprengkraft des Multikulturalismus...herausgefordert sieht, stellt sich die Frage, ob es für das Junktim von Staats- und Volksnation ein ebenso funktionales Äquivalent gibt.*" In his latest collection of studies, Habermas makes a strong appeal to include the "other" into societies, instead of basing the self-definition of communities on exclusion. His chapter "Der europäische Nationalstaat – Zu Vergangenheit und Zukunft von Souveränität und Staatbürgerschaft" (pp. 128–153) applies this approach to the concept of nation-state. Jürgen Habermas, *Die Einbeziehungen des Anderen: Studien zur politischen Theorie* (Frankfurt: Fischer, 1996), p. 141.

8   Tibor Várady, "Minorities, Majorities, Law and Ethnicity: Reflections of the Yugoslav Case," *Human Rights Quarterly* 19 (1997), pp. 42–43.
9   *Ibid*, p. 43.
10 Ivelin Saradamov, "Ethnic Warriors: Ethnicity and Genocide in the Balkan," paper presented at the *4th Annual Convention of the Association for the Study of Nationalities* (New York, April 15–17, 1999), p. 1.
11 Ethnic conflict cannot "disappear" without the simulatious end of ethnic politics.
12 See also Robert L. Simon, "Pluralism and Equality: The Status of Minority Values in a Democracy," in *Majorities and Minorities*, eds. John W. Chapman and Alan Wertheimer (New York and London: New York University Press, 1990), pp. 208–209.
13 Danilo Zolo, *Democracy and Complexity: A Realist Approach* (Cambridge: Polity Press, 1992), p. 57. (emphasis by FB)
14 See for example Richard Holbrooke's memoirs on the conspicuous absence of any discussion of democracy and minority rights. Richard Holbrooke, *To End a War* (New York: Random House, 1998).
15 The serious inadequacies of democracy in Croatia and Serbia raise the question of whether Tudjman and Milošević could democratically represent their citizens.
16 *Constitution of Bosnia and Herzegovina* (1995), preamble.
17 In the case of Belgium, one can observe the difficulty that only few Flamands speak French and even fewer Walloons speak Flemish, making English, not an official language, the most common language of communication between groups.
18 Vojislav Stanovčić, "Problems and Options in Institutionalizing Ethnic Relations," *International Political Science Review* 13, no. 4 (1992), p. 364.
19 *Constitution of Bosnia and Herzegovina* (1995), Article II and Annex I.
20 Stanovčić, "Problems and Options," pp. 366–367.
21 See Florian Bieber, "Consociationalism - Prerequisite or Hurdle for Democratization in Bosnia?" *South-East Europe Review* 2, no. 3 (1999): 79-94.
22 Stanovčić, "Problems and Options," p. 369.
23 The delegation, however, also included members of each of the national groups in Kosovo (Roma, Egyptians, Gorani, "loyal" Albanians and Turks), whose legitimacy and degree of representation were doubtful. See also the "Serbian Counterproposal," which was signed by all these groups and representatives of Serbs from Kosovo with similarly dubious legality. *Agreement for Self-Government in Kosmet* (Paris, March 18, 1999).
24 *Constitution, Interim Agreement for Peace and Self-Government in Kosovo* (February 23, 1999), Article II, 1.
25 The status of Kosovo is left ambiguous to the extent that it is not possible to determine clearly whether the province is autonomous within Serbia or Yugoslavia.
26 The American statements relating to Rambouillet emphasize "Democratic Self-Government" without elaborating on the problems of institutionalizing a multiethnic democratic society. The only detail is the implementation of elections by the OSCE. See U.S. Department of State Bureau of European Affairs fact sheet, "Understanding the Rambouillet Accords" (Washington, D. C., March 1, 1999).
27 *Constitution, Interim Agreement for Peace and Self-Government in Kosovo* (February 23, 1999), Article VII.
28 Robert M. Hayden, "The State as Legal Fiction: American Proposals for the Constitutional and Political Status of Kosovo," *East European Constitutional Review* 7, no. 4 (Fall 1998), p. 49.

29   Tibor Várady, "On the Chances of Ethnocultural Justice in Central-Eastern Europe."

6 Lessons from the Belgian Constitution for Multiethnic Societies*

RICHARD LEWIS

In the last few years, Bosnia-Herzegovina has undergone a traumatic experience on many counts. Not only has the country undergone the scourge of war and the consequences that it brings, but the nation state to which it belonged disintegrated into violence and enmity. This left a constitutional and social vacuum that has not yet been entirely filled. It is true that the Dayton Accords set out a constitutional model. Many, however, consider this model to be flawed. Subsequent events have born this out.

This paper discusses but one form of constitutional arrangement: that of Belgium. This country's checkered history, invaded and fought over for five hundred years, echoes in many ways that of Bosnia. And Belgium is also a divided society, in the same way as Bosnia. The constitutional settlement that the Belgians have worked out over the last century may not be the ideal model for Bosnia, but it certainly contains some lessons, which will be discussed in this paper.

It goes without saying, especially with regard to Bosnia, that there can be no more important and no more pertinent subject than how to govern divided societies. This subject has so many facets and the problems have so many possible solutions that it is hard to summarize in one sentence or title. Basically and in plain language, we can describe what we are going to discuss as follows: "Bearing in mind that practically no nation-state on earth is homogeneous and that people are all different, how do we organize societies that are as fair as possible to all?" Or, to put it in Benthamite language, "The greatest good for the greatest number."

I am confining this text to a discussion of the Belgian model, which has been described as one of the best examples of consociational democracy—though for the academically-minded I do not have the time to be drawn into the Lijphart versus Horowitz debate on whether consociation actually encourages élite-initiated conflict. However, I would like to quote Donald

Horowitz who, I think, poses a crucial question:

> The central question of political engineering is this. In deeply divided societies, which kinds of institutes and practices create an incentive structure for ethnic groups to mediate their differences through the legitimate institutions of a common democratic state? Alternatively, how can the incentive system be structured to reward and reinforce political leaders who moderate on divisive ethnic themes and persuade citizens to support moderation, bargaining and reciprocity among ethnic groups?[1]

And I would put the issue in yet another way. Minorities tend to distrust democracy as a legitimized means of oppression. How can this distrust be overcome? And, if it cannot, what can be done to keep the greatest degree of peace and harmony and, if necessary and in the best possible conditions, create new nation-states? Let me remind you that over 50 percent of wars since 1945 have been caused by the creation of new states. Of course, these are enormous issues and my example of Belgium is not going to answer one tenth of them. What it can do, perhaps, is to give food for thought, which will carry some of these themes into the rest of the conference.

Why Belgium As a Case Study?

The question "why Belgium?" can be divided into two aspects. First, why is the example of this particular country so interesting to the scholar and practitioner as far as conflict resolution is concerned? And second, how does the country exist as a nation-state at all? The two questions are inextricably linked to history.

In June 1794, the French Revolution spilled over into the Austrian Netherlands and the territory was annexed by France with instructions from Paris "to strip Belgium of its substance."[2] The period of Napoleonic rule in the country was characterized by a harsh regime. The Flemish language was forbidden not only as an official tongue but in all forms of public and cultural life. The seeds were sown to institutionalize French as the "national language" of Belgium, and a suspicion of French motives and methods hardened. This period also established French administrative traditions in the country.

After the Congress of Vienna and the restoration of the Belgian territories to the United Netherlands, William I set about the absorption of Belgium into the Netherlands, language and religion included. But the two countries had evolved differently, especially from a religious point of view. In fact, in spite of linguistic ties, the Flemish were more hostile to union with the

Netherlands than were the Francophones.

It can readily be seen from this all-too-brief analysis that there was little love between Belgium and its neighbors. On July 21, 1830 the Belgian Revolution was declared and some weeks of conflict ensued. When the British "midwife," Lord Palmerston, advocated a buffer state between France and the Netherlands, it took a short time to establish Belgian independence on October 4, 1830. It is noteworthy that the term "buffer state" is applicable in more than one sense, since it proved to be political, cultural and linguistic.

It is unnecessary at this juncture to consider in any detail the history of nineteenth century Belgium, since this is largely concerned with the Flemish movement. It is sufficient to emphasize that the early period of Belgian independence was not only concerned with the linguistic split and the domination of French culture, but also the emerging differences between Catholics and Liberals, the latter being resolutely anti-clerical. This split determined the course of political life in Belgium in the last century and is reflected even today in the Social Christian political movement and the "free" (as opposed to Catholic) universities. Kesteloot writes that in spite of both communities being Catholic, the Walloon movement seized on what was perceived as the clericalism of Flanders as a point of difference.[3] Thus, the cleavages in Belgian society that emerged in the twentieth century were not only linguistic. There was a Catholic/anti-clerical cleavage in addition to the classical political divide between right and left. For economic reasons, socialism gained more of a foothold in Wallonia, which is still present to this day, thus reinforcing the divide between French and Dutch speaking parts of the country.

Xavier Mabille, Director-General of the *Centre de Recherche et d'Information Socio-Politique* (CRISP), says that Belgium is a classic example of the construction of the nation-state. "There is a functional axis and there is a cultural and territorial axis in Belgium. The functional axis was determined by political evolution and the constitution of the nation-state. The cleavage between the Catholic Church and the state was an important factor as well." The result is a segmented society, which has actually built on the segments to reinforce different identities—religious, political and cultural/linguistic. This process is reflected in the Dutch word *verzuiling*, or segmentation. The country's institutions mirror politico-religious-cultural movements. For example, the *mutualités* health insurance schemes reflect the linguistic, political or religious affiliation of their members. However, "in some cases, important associations do not coincide with the *zuil* boundaries and here it is often the linguistic or regional factor that explains the discrepancy."

The Flemish Movement

There is no time to discuss in detail the Flemish movement, but there are some telling incidents, which should be mentioned. It was Hendrick Conscience and F.S. Snellaert who were among the first to give vent to feelings about the need for greater linguistic and cultural balance in Belgian national life. In 1847, they wrote their Declaration of Fundamental Principles Presented by the Defenders of the Netherlandish People's Rights to their Fellow-Country-Men:

> Belgium is an unnatural situation, which indisputably puts the very existence of the country constantly at risk. The large half of the nation is ruled by the other half. *Although this domination by the authorities and by our Walloon compatriots can probably not be regarded as a calculated aim, it nevertheless exists....While awaiting the dawn of unity and equality for all Belgians, we shall, gradually and with time, without wanting to harm the rights anyone has acquired, attempt to gain* instruction in the Dutch language... use of the Dutch language in national institutions... encouragement of Flemish writers... use of the Dutch language for and in the courts of law... use of the Dutch language in the administrations and councils of the Flemish provinces and towns... the obligation that army officers give evidence of their knowledge of Dutch.... (author's italics)

These rather moderate demands have taken 150 years to achieve. As time progressed, the fight to achieve equality and the bitterness that emerged to maintain that equality increased in fervor.

The years 1929 to 1932 saw a major turning point. Fourteen parliamentary deputies from Wallonia and eleven from Flanders published the so-called *"Compromis des Belges"* (The Compromise of the Belgians), declaring that Belgium was a national and international necessity, that the central government was incapable of effecting an understanding between the communities and that to safeguard the State there was a need for the basis of an amicable agreement. The *"Compromis"* went on to propose monolingualism for Flanders. The Walloons rejected bilingualism for the whole country as unacceptable and Flanders was understandably unwilling to accept an asymmetrical situation.

Thus, since 1932 and continuing to the present, the linguistic boundaries have been fixed "for ever," with no attempt at changes since 1962.

The Psychological Element

Thus far we have sketched the classic cleavages in Belgian society, without venturing into the minefield of the psychological fissures. These are important to understand in order to achieve a balanced view of how the country was turned, in the space of 30 years, from a highly-centralized state on the Jacobin model to what some commentators call the most decentralized State in Europe. The extent to which Flemish resentment is still felt is indicated by Ruys:

> For a correct understanding of the Flemish problem it is necessary to remember that the freedom to express oneself in one's own language and the ability to do so with confidence are essential to full individual development. For generations, Flemings lacked both. Living in a bilingual state, they found themselves confronted with another language and another culture... and since that other language was spoken by those who commanded the laws of the state, politically and economically, the language barrier became a social barrier... There is much in Belgium's present-day legislation... that may impress the outsider as narrow-minded or coercive... but if two unequal partners inhabit the same house, freedom becomes illusory for the weaker partner.[4]

It is impossible in a few words to convey what this has meant to Belgian society since independence. Its impact has ranged over the education debate (church education against "liberal" education, the violent split of the ancient university of Leuven into two linguistic parts in 1968 and the financing of schools), the split of the political parties into "families" of Flemish and Francophone wings and, above all, the controversial issue of economic transfers from Flanders (wealthier than Wallonia since the early 1960s).

It will suffice to take two poignant examples, simplified for the sake of clear understanding, as to how some of the issues were solved.

The first is the issue of the communes on the periphery of Brussels. When the language frontier was fixed once and for all in 1962, controversy raged over whether six Flemish communes with a substantial Francophone minority outside the nineteen bilingual communes which make up the Brussels-Capital region should have a special status (so-called *"communes à facilités"*) whereby Francophones could deal with the administration in French and have Francophone schools. This was eventually conceded, the Flemings having considered it a "temporary" measure to allow integration in succeeding generations. Indeed, the media in Belgium are currently writing of the debate to "reinforce the Flemish character of the periphery." Francophones feel themselves to be a beleaguered minority in these areas. Nevertheless, this was an important concession, illustrating the notion of compromise which is characteristic of the linguistic debate in Belgium.

Most recently, the so-called "Peeters memorandum" was published, indicating that the facilities are for one generation only. In other words, Francophones should stir themselves from their lethargy and learn Flemish despite their temporary linguistic rights.

The whole issue of Brussels is a key factor in the Belgian equation. The Flemish bargained for strong minority rights in the capital against institutional parity for the minority Francophones at the federal level. Some commentators would even go so far as to say that without "the Brussels factor," Belgium as a nation-state would have already fallen apart. Willy DeClercq, former Prime Minister, believes that in the unlikely event of a Belgian split, Flanders would "lose" Brussels, which would be too heavy a price to pay.

A second area of controversy has been the region of the Fourons (Voeren in Dutch), which became a *cause célèbre* nationally and even internationally. This is a case worth examining in some detail, since it illustrates the difficulties of government in a multi-cultural environment and the political compromises—some might say convolutions—for which Belgium is famous.

Briefly, according to José Happart, the former and highly controversial *bourgmestre* or mayor of the Fourons and now a minister, the problem affected government in Belgium for 30 years. "It is not simply a linguistic problem," he explained, in an interview with me, "it is a meeting place of three cultures, languages and beliefs. It is here that you see democracy played out, by which I mean the power relationship between the majority (Francophones) and the minority (Flemish)." Happart went on to describe how the six Fourons villages were transferred from Liège Province (Wallonia) to Limbourg in 1963, thus at the stroke of a pen creating an ostensibly Francophone minority in Flanders. The six villages became a symbol for both sides and Happart, because of his refusal to speak Dutch at the town council, became a figure of hatred in Flanders and a hero in Wallonia. It is difficult in a few words to convey the emotion behind the Fourons affairs, but some vignettes should impart the essential mood. The villages became a target for sometimes violent demonstrations by the Flemish *Taal Aktie Komitee* (Language Action Committee) and Happart and his family were physically and verbally abused. Shots were fired on at least two occasions and injuries caused on July 31, 1983. A Flemish pastor refused to conduct the burial service for José Happart's father in French. In short, the Fourons became a prime target area for Flemish nationalism.

The result of both the legal and political machinations surrounding the Fourons affair was that Happart stepped down as *bourgmestre* and became deputy *bourgmestre*. A legal function was created stipulating that the Francophones "belonged" to Liège Province and could vote there if they so chose. A comparable arrangement as a *quid pro quo* was agreed for the Comines region in Hainaut for the Flemish living there. Again, this typical Belgian compromise solution, with its trade-offs for both the major communities, is characteristic of consociational societies which live by consensus government.

The Constitutional Debate 1970–1993

The enterprise of turning Belgium from a unitary state into a highly decentralized federation—some would say confederation—began in 1970 and was accomplished in four stages. Brassine says that "Belgian federalism resulted from successive compromises over a period of time, a great deal of time, to conclude the negotiations which included reciprocal concessions."[5] As Uyttendale and Sohier write, the Belgian Federation was not imposed once and for all in a logical manner as, for example, in Germany or the United States, "but constitutes the finality, without any doubt provisional, of a narrative of various reforms provoked by political crises as yet incomplete."[6] In other words, the Belgian constitution will probably evolve further. Frank Swaelen, former President of the Belgian Senate, believes that in any case an entirely logical, Cartesian constitutional settlement does not suit the Belgian situation.

The first phase, in 1970, included dividing the two houses of the national parliament into linguistic groups in order to institute a so-called "alarm-bell system," whereby three-quarters of one linguistic group could suspend the process of legislation. This was also the beginning of regional and cultural autonomy. The second phase, in 1980, formulated the rules for regionalization under the "double-mandate system," whereby national parliamentarians sat in regional bodies holding limited "competence." An arbitration court was set up to determine disputes in case of conflicts of competence.

1988–89 saw the creation of a system that is probably unique, which is the division of competence between the national government, the Regions (Flanders, Wallonia and Brussels-Capital with special provisions for the 60,000 German speakers in the east of the country) and the so-called "Communities." The Communities govern the linguistic, cultural, educational and other powers relating to the Flemish, Francophone and German-speaking populations. Thus, three major centers of power were created, two of which were territorial (the whole nation and the regions) and one of which was derived from cultural identity. The 1988–89 changes reformed state finance to allow revenues to flow to the Regions and the Communities. Finally, the 1992 "*Accords de St Michel*" paved the way for the 1993 Constitution, which states in Title I:

1. Belgium is a Federal state which consists of communities and regions;
2. Belgium consists of three communities: the French community, the Flemish community and the German community;
3. Belgium has three regions: the Walloon region, the Flemish region and the Brussels region.

The constitution then proceeds to define the powers of each federal unit, retaining defense, external relations, social security, finance and justice for the national government.[7] The Regions are responsible for housing, the environment, the economy, public works, external trade and international cooperation. It is these last two which are considered controversial, since they allow a great measure of autonomy for negotiating international agreements and give Flanders free rein for the first time to use its considerable economic muscle. Finally, the Communities are responsible for so-called "*matières culturelles et personnalisables*:" education, health, cultural and media matters and tourism.

Professor Delpérée of the *Université Catholique de Louvain* says that this constitutional arrangement adds up to a uniquely Belgian compromise. "The originality of Belgium," he says, "is to organize everything on a 50/50 basis. We refuse the word 'minority'... We took our time, but we have a system which works for us. It may not work for others, but there may be lessons."

In the original conception of the Belgian State, there were two approaches. The Flemish took the view that territory determined the linguistic rights of the people. The Francophones held that linguistic rights were attached to the person concerned and that that person belonged to a "community." That is the origin of the concept of the division between "region" and "community" in Belgium, the latter being a cultural concept.

Why Does Belgium Work?

All the markers that are present in other conflictual community situations can be seen in Belgium. Most authors and politicians came up with similar key words. Frank Swaelen, former Senate President, used the expressions "compromise and coalition" and "will to live together." "We are a tolerant people. You can laugh at our compromises, but they work." He and others explained that the British political system of "winner takes all" could never operate in Belgium because the country runs by consensus government. "All shades of opinion, even extremes, are represented," he said.

Leo Tindemans and Manu Ruys, former editor of *Standaard*, talked at great length of the historical influences on Belgium. Ruys says that the country "is *not* a melting pot. There is a clear frontier between the two main communities... We are like a big house, one apartment for the Flemish and one for the Walloons. We respect each other... We are partners, not adversaries." He emphasized that the conflict was between the Flemish *speakers* and the Walloons and in that respect against the French-speaking Flemish bourgeoisie, the unpopular *fransquillons*. "We were never enemies, and Walloon intellectuals understood our (Flemish) demands."

Ruys says that "Flemings are Latins who happen to speak a Germanic language." This is echoed by Wily de Clercq, former Deputy Prime Minister, who dismissed the Dutch as "Calvinists" whereas "we Belgians are Burgundians and like to enjoy life." Many speak of the Flemings and Walloons as "sharing values" and point out that they continually rely on improvisation.

McRae discusses the Belgian case in detail.[8] He asks two pertinent questions. Why has the language issue been so intractable and why has this prolonged and severe conflict not propelled the Belgian political system into mass violence, civil war or political separation? He indicates that there is evidence of collusion between the two sides, that they are pragmatic and willing to compromise and that there is consensus on the rules of the political game. McRae indicates that:

> The institutional devices that work towards moderation are many, but virtually all may be classified under four headings:
> 1. Those promoting fair representation of the language communities
> 2. Those promoting cultural autonomy for those communities
> 3. Those designed to secure compliance from unwilling individuals or groups
> 4. Those designed to improve intergroup linkages across language lines.[9]

But is it only the character of the people that has saved Belgium from the worst type of communal conflict? A senior United States diplomat whom I interviewed on the subject reiterated that it comes down to Western values. "I think that inter-ethnic conflicts within Western countries tend to get resolved in relatively peaceful ways because of a respect for humanity, a sense of common citizenship, a sort of civic idea which doesn't exist in other countries." If this is true, one other factor has to be added, namely relative affluence. Former President of the Belgian Senate Frank Swaelen believes that the Belgian conflict would have been much worse had the country been at a lower economic level. The heated discussions over social security and other economic issues would tend to bear out the exacerbating factor of a sheer lack of resources.

John Fitzmaurice, a noted author on the subject, says that the Belgian method is tortuous and full of complex interlocking compromises, which bind and commit the parties and deflect violence. They are, however, costly in resources and duplication of effort, and only a wealthy society can afford this luxury. There is a further downside. The process of consensus building may eliminate conflict, but it makes political change difficult and the total system unwieldy, which in itself can create disaffection.

What makes Belgium work can be summed up in three expressions: common history and culture, consensus building, and constitutional compromise. If you could approximate these conditions in other countries, then it would be possible for different ethnic groups to live together.

The Policy Implications

Belgium is a prime example of the way a broad normative consensus is built. What is involved is identifying divergent interests before conflict emerges between communities and, sooner rather than later, recognizing aspirations. Given that, according to U.S. Institute of Peace figures, about 900 million people in 233 increasingly assertive regions around the world are seeking the separation and sharing of power, the matter is more than urgent.

So let us look at some of the policy implications:

1. Early identification of the potential problem is important (The Belgians, for example, revised their constitutional framework over 25 years, if not longer). The "hot" issues must be isolated and action taken. It may seem obvious but often there are words without action until it is too late.
2. The issue of the kin-state must be tackled from the outset. If the Netherlands had interfered in Belgian politics, the story of Flemish nationalism would have had to be rewritten. The wisdom of this implication can be seen, for example, in the Baltic States, where the

issue of the Russian minorities was addressed before it became inflamed.
3. Identity issues, such as religion and language, are crucial. Combining these issues with battles over resources increases the likelihood of open conflict. This is especially true if you deprive a group of people of a perceived identity marker, such as language rights or educational facilities.
4. The only remedy is small changes constantly repeated until the overall result is obtained. But the cost of doing this is often seen as too high for politicians who care little for the morrow.

Conflict between communities in most instances comes from a failure not of foreign policy (as in the case of large-scale war) but of domestic policy. It is, therefore, domestic policy in potentially conflictual situations that need to be examined early. Domestic policy is often a sensitive area in the state concerned and is frequently shielded under the maxim "this is an internal affair." Thus, often, non-governmental mediators or policy formulators are better situated to assist than are other governments. Again, more than a century of politics in Belgium demonstrates the failures of domestic policy on community issues, which were corrected only very recently.

Another observation, amply illustrated by the Belgian model, is that successful multiethnic societies can be democracies with a considerable measure of regional autonomy.

I am not advocating nor do I find feasible the wholesale transfer of the Belgian constitutional framework and style of political compromise to other states. What I am saying is that there are clear lessons to be learned from it. Among them is one unique feature, which should be emphasized. This is "the functional axis and the cultural/linguistic axis," that is, the split between the functions of the Regions and the functions of the Communities. This split might well be a transferable commodity. There are other cases—for example Lebanon—but Belgium is the outstanding model.

I would like to add two general summary thoughts before I close. The Belgian example shows just how important it is to ensure that constitutional agreements are clear, unambiguous and negotiated down to the last detail. Of course, this is tortuous and difficult. Of course, there is a temptation to "fudge" issues to get the signatures on paper. But in the end, as has been shown here in Bosnia and now in Northern Ireland, creating false dawns leads only to more misery.

The Belgian example is also—it may seem obvious but it is worth restating—but one method. No one method fits all. Everything in this field has to be tailor-made. Nevertheless, examples as to what has worked in one place can always be usefully examined in another context.

If we can increase international understanding of the issues, we will go a long way down the road of preventing dissension in nation-states, which embrace more than one community. Nothing could be more important at the dawn of the new millennium.

Notes

* Parts of this text were published as an occasional paper by the Center for International Studies, Duke University, in 1996. It has been revised and updated. Quotations by individuals are based on interviews with the author.
1 Donald L. Horowitz, *Ethnic Groups in Conflict* (Berkeley: University of California Press, 1985).
2 Georges Henri Dumont, *Histoire de la Belgique* (Paris: Hachette, 1977), p. 324.
3 Chantal Kesteloot, "Mouvement Wallon et Identité nationale," *Courrier Hebdomadaire* n° 1392 (Brussels: CRISP, 1993).
4 Manu Ruys, *De Vlamingen, Een Volk in Beweging, Een Natie in Wording* (English Edition) (Tielt: Lannoo, 1981).
5 Jacques Brassinne, *Belgique Fédérale* (Bruxelles : CRISP, 1994), p. 98.
6 Marc Uyttendaele and Jérôme Sohier, *La Belgique Fédérale—Fondements Constitutionnels et Légaux* (Brussels: Quorum, 1994), p. 11.
7 J. de la Guérivière, *Belgique: La Revanche des Langues* (Paris: Editions du Seuil, 1994).
8 Kenneth D. McRae, *Conflict and Compromise in Multilingual Societies: Belgium* (Waterloo, Ontario: Wilfrid Laurier University Press, 1986).
9 *Ibid*, p. 331.

7 The Building of Civil Society by "Core" Europe?

ARIYOSHI OGAWA

The collapse of the communist bloc in Europe revolutionized the notion of regions in Europe. What was once a dualistic, divided Europe was replaced by a single geopolitical order that created a new "core-periphery" Europe. Similar to what Stein Rokkan called "territorial structuring of Western Europe," with its "polycepharic" central trade-belt surrounded by strong territorial states and weaker peripheries,[1] current Europe is characterized by varying degrees of transnationality and of the presence of individual nation-states. Today, even a grand-scale state formation—i.e. territorial consolidation with a certain centralization—at the EU-level is being discussed, though its prototype seems rather different from the conventional structure of nation-states.[2]

What geographical areas, then, are the peripheries of this emerging EUrope? Although it is difficult to predict its future boundaries, there is little doubt that the EU and its members are actively concerned about the Central and Eastern European countries (CEEC), the Newly Independent States of the former Soviet Union (NIS) and the Mediterranean countries.[3]

The European core's concern over its peripheries is not only directed to their progress in market integration, but also to the condition of their democracy and rule of law. Nor is the concern limited to the scope of the formal enlargement of the European Union, as is indicated by the broad coverage of the PHARE program for CEEC and the TACIS program for NIS. This study examines the political cooperation between the core and peripheries of Europe toward the aim of bolstering civil society, a process that tends to depend on a common repertoire similar to that used for conventional development assistance in developing countries. Consequently, the former is experiencing contradictions and difficulties similar to those that the latter has faced.

At the beginning of the transition in Eastern and Central Europe, the European Community had no concrete pan-European policy other than trade agreements of an anti-dumping character.[4] Nevertheless, the

European Commission readily accepted the role of coordinator of Western assistance, as endowed by G24. The PHARE program of the EC—later the European Union—became the largest instrument of grant assistance from the West to CEEC. Although the greater part of this program was allocated to such areas as infrastructure and enterprise support, the program eventually attached increased emphasis to the building of "substantial" democracies and civil societies.[5]

Under the auspices of PHARE, the PHARE Partnership Programme was launched in 1993, focusing upon relatively large organizations such as trade unions, professional and trade associations, chambers of commerce as well as education/training and environmental NGOs. The Democracy Programme was launched in 1992 with the aim of promoting parliamentary practice, non-governmental activities and the rule of law. The NGO and LIEN programs, initiated in 1993 and 1994 respectively, dealt mainly with social aspects and smaller, grassroots-level NGOs. The PHARE Democracy Programme emphasized what are regarded as the distinctive features of a 'civil society,' highlighted in the following segments of its program description: "The programme will focus on issues where governments are not or should not be active.... Projects of a partisan nature or involving single political parties will be ineligible."

There was good reason to emphasize the building of civil societies in post-Communist countries. First, it was the intellectual and social movements that originally challenged the police-state regimes characterized by passive subordination, and that became hallmarks of newly-achieved democracy. Second, the transition from socialist welfare institutions to market economies left behind a vacuum of social services. Third, in some of the post-transition societies that suffered from ethnic division and xenophobia, the building of social trust (or "social capital") was considered crucial.

In this way, the emergence of civil societies has become an intellectual rediscovery in Eastern Europe. But similar arguments are being brought forward by major international developmental donors. Recent discussions of "good governance" stress "demand-side," "bottom-up" or "participatory" approaches, where non-governmental and non-profit actors would play key roles.[6] One World Bank expert stated, "NGOs may keep their distance from the state and run their projects parallel to those of the state; in some countries NGOs effectively play an oppositional role, while elsewhere NGOs seek to represent the voice of the weak and help them organize in their communities to achieve a more powerful voice in the making of decisions and the allocating of resources. The latter NGOs are emerging as critical ingredients of a civil society."[7]

The Conundrum of Building Civil Society From the Outside

Building civil society by way of NGO assistance, however, puts the legitimacy of both NGOs and the fledgling democratic system at risk. First, NGOs dependent on outside funding become more responsive to external concerns while losing independent values and broader partnerships. Second, NGOs may convert from voluntary social actors to mere contractors for donors. Third, to the extent that NGOs substitute the roles of the state, especially in the social sector, the legitimacy of an already weak government is diminished.[8]

Not surprisingly, this diagnosis resonates the criticism of internationally-supported democracy in post-Communist Europe. In the following sections, unexpected caveats of civil society development aid will be examined. First, the gap in external-local responsiveness of non-governmental organizations will be examined, using the case of the environmental organizations in CEEC, and second, the substitution of state by international NGOs, through the case of the social sector in Bosnia-Herzegovina.

Environmental NGOs in Central and Eastern Europe

Environmental activities in CEEC have been subject to the skepticism of officials and a lack of coordination among movements, two obstacles which partially stem from their "anti-political" ideologies. Yet they gained leverage from international agreements and support from international bodies such as UNEP, IUCN, WWFN, major American foundations, and international NGOs such as Greenpeace, Friends of the Earth and Nordic organizations. Moreover, the Regional Environmental Center for Central and Eastern Europe (REC) was set up in Hungary to facilitate the coordination of programs and projects in the region.

However, the development of local environmental NGOs is constrained by the complexities of their adaptation to foreign support and their "Western" modes of lobbying, a process that inevitably encourages standardization and competition among NGOs. For instance, applications for the REC's earmarked grants include such requirements as an account of the action plan, a financial estimation and the relevance in light of the REC's own priorities, all of which must be written in English. Janckar-

Webster asks, "how many people in ECE know sufficient English or [have sufficient] knowledge of administration or science to write a grant of this complexity, even with REC help?"[9]

The PHARE Partnership Programme's evaluation process, based on face-to-face interviews with local partners and consultation with NGOs, has revealed opinions stating dissatisfaction at the project level with the "heavy burden" of procedures and the stagnant bureaucracy of the program. While scientific groups enjoy increasing influence by being consulted on a regular basis, groups with political profiles find difficulty in participating in policy-making, and are even being shunned by the authorities.[10] Michael Waller laments that external assistance has thus obviated the role of NGOs as voices of the opposition, a role that had been thought to be appropriate for NGOs within the new democratic systems.[11]

The State-NGO Relationship in Bosnia-Herzegovina

The international community has made resolute efforts towards nurturing inter-entity trust and building a substantial democracy in Bosnia. Those in charge of democratic assistance have tried their best to cultivate a civil sector which will eventually foster vigorous opposition forces. But the outcome has turned out to be rather modest. One OSCE Democratization Branch Reporting Officer deplored in an interview, "The Citizens' Alternative Parliament, the Shadow Government and the Coalition for Return are basically the same 20 people when you scratch the surface a little. There is really no depth to this."[12] A more recent evaluation report of the OSCE Mission to Bosnia-Herzegovina indicated the successful involvement of local NGOs in the monitoring of elections. Yet it also adds that this is "the exception than the rule."[13]

Civil society has not been rebuilt in Bosnia-Herzegovina, but 'newly-feudalized,' argue Bob Deacon and Paul Stubbs.[14] The term "new feudalism" is defined by the emergence of a strong state that carries with it ethnic discrimination, patron-client relationships, and Mafia-like power. The circumstances are further aggravated by globalism, which lends a disjointed structure to the NGO sector. According to these critical authors,

> the role of large multi-mandated INGOs such as the International Rescue Committee (IRC), which implement their 'own brand' of programmes in the social welfare and health sectors, makes the development of sustainable social provision in the post-emergency phase much more difficult. Their acts such as ignoring governmental services, or recruiting the best public-sector

workers to work for higher salaries, can distort and hinder subsequent recovery as well as alienate public policy makers....[15]

The growing mid-level NGOs seem to contribute to the new-feudalization of society while touting the universal values of their foreign donors. Micro-level local NGOs, most sensitive to local social needs, are often alienated from funding processes.[16]

These examples do not describe the whole situation in Bosnia-Herzegovina, but instead illustrate its worst parts. Undoubtedly, however, one can see the danger of the NGO sector becoming a substitute, rather than a catalyst, for an ideal state–civil society relationship.

An Evaluation Model for Building Civil Society

Is the building of civil societies on the path to failure? The more one envisions an ideal civil society, the more disillusioned one will become in light of reality.[17] However, is it not even more absurd to expect that an organization, or even the whole non-governmental sector of a country, can provide its primary services, monitor government policies, represent its citizens at the grass-roots level, and foster trust between society's various groups, all at the same time?

Figure 7.1 Non-Governmental Organizations Values and Strategy

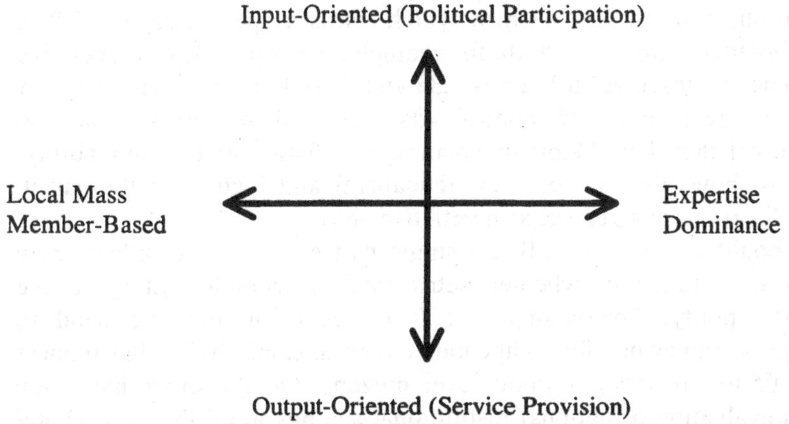

```
              Input-Oriented (Political Participation)
                            ↑
                            |
Local Mass       ←──────────┼──────────→     Expertise
Member-Based                |                 Dominance
                            |
                            ↓
              Output-Oriented (Service Provision)
```

Hence, the necessity to re-classify various NGOs is increasingly acknowledged by scholars and international donors, even beyond the current need to sift out QUANGOs (quasi–non-governmental organizations), MANGOs (Mafia-led NGOs) or FANGOs (fake NGOs).[18] Figure 7.1 is a simple plotting of NGOs with different orientations and organizational bases.

Non-governmental and voluntary sectors do not create civil society by themselves. They can only exist and work in international, institutional and societal contexts.

Figure 7.2 Linkages between International Supporters and NGOs[19]

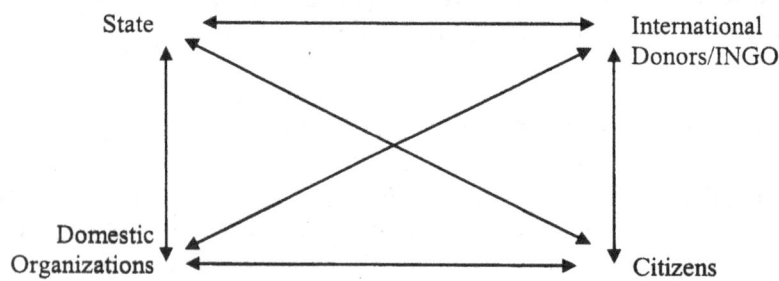

Phillippe Schmitter suggests that "consolidating democracies be conceptualized not as 'a regime' but as composites of 'partial regimes'..." For, Schmitter sees a democratic polity not as 'an' entity but rather as regimes with plural segments.[20] Figure 7.2 shows the linkages between the state, foreign supporters including international NGOs, domestic organizations and citizens, each of which forms a "partial regime." It is open to broader comparison with, for example, the corporate or associative democracies represented in Figures 7.3a and 7.3b. In some cases, the flow patterns of resources and control (as indicated by arrows) are so asymmetrical that they distort democratic articulation and accountability. Figure 7.4 shows the case of "new feudalism" and Figure 7.5 the gap in external-local responsiveness, as mentioned above.

What should be stressed is that a single part of the whole linkage may have its own function, whether detrimental or complementary to the democratic polity. The example of REC seems on the one hand to encourage a framework for indigenous environmental NGOs that renders them unfit to involve grassroots-level citizens. On the other hand, the Centre's evaluation of national institutional settings in all the Central and Eastern European Countries is likely to diffuse knowledge of international standards and practices among domestic NGOs, and thus enhance each group's capacity to participate in policy making and legislation.

Figure 7.3 Corporative and Associative Models of Democracy

a) Corporatism Model

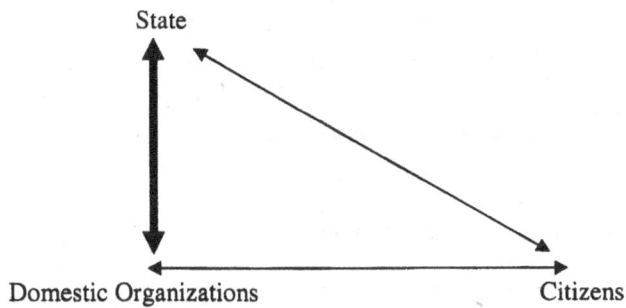

b) Associative Democracy Model

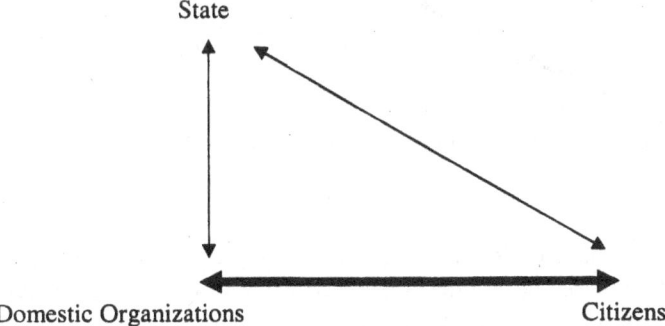

Here can be seen the potential to develop what Alsop and Farrington call a "nested" information system, where each stakeholder (including NGOs) has discrete information, but is open to inputting and accessing information to and from a common system.[21] In the context of today's information society, one may argue that non-governmental organizations which are no longer member-based and have lost their role as "schools for democracies," are still able to play an important democratic function.[22] On the other hand, the most efficient and effective international NGOs may hinder the reconstruction of democratic governance, as the case of "new feudalism" suggests. What is crucial is the aggregate function of all the "partial regimes," including formal and substantial institutions and organizations.

Figure 7.4 'New Feudalism'[23]

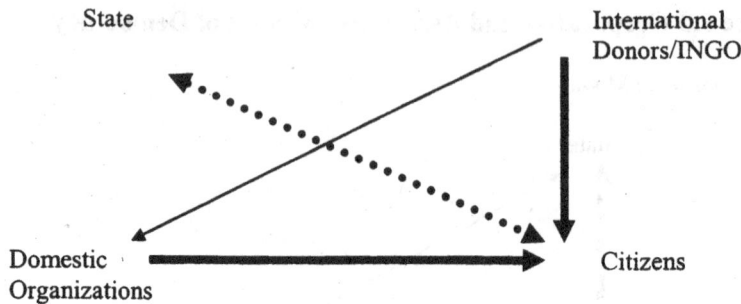

Figure 7.5 External-Local Responsiveness Gap

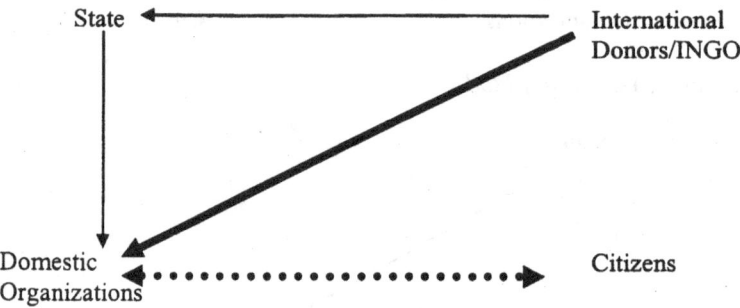

One must confront the paradox that the more disintegrated a society is, the greater its need for coherent coordination between the domestic democratic system and support from external sources.

Notes

1. Stein Rokkan and Derek W. Urwin, *Economy, Territory, Identity: Politics of West European Peripheries* (London: Sage, 1983).
2. Bartolini reflects on the EU as an emerging polity beyond the short-term discussion on "democratic deficit," asking: 1. Is the EU forming a state? 2. Will EU state-formation proceed without nation-building? 3. Will EU state-formation proceed without democratization? Stefano Bartolini, "Exit Options, Boundary Building, Political Structuring: Sketches of a Theory of Large-Scale Territorial and Membership 'Retrenchment/ Differentiation' versus 'Expansion/ Integration' (With Reference to the European Union)," *EUI Working Paper SPS* No.98/1 (1998).
3. Charlotte Bretherton and John Vogler, *The European Union as a Global Actor* (London and New York: Routledge, 1999), chapter 5.

4. Ulrich Sedelmeier and Helen Wallace, "Politics towards Central and Eastern Europe" in *Policy-Making in the European Union*, 3rd ed., edited by Helen Wallace and William Wallace (Oxford: Oxford University Press, 1996), pp. 354–355.
5. It should be noted that the US presence was much larger in the wake of the transition in terms of the amount of assistance for democratization, although USAID and American foundations have recently taken the "exit" strategy (*Evaluation of the PHARE Partnership Programme*, produced by Local and Regional Development Planning, commissioned by the European Commission, DGIA (November 1998), pp. 32, 41). Thus *EU-ropeanization* has two sides: Europeanization and Americanization of Post-Communist Europe. By national comparison, German foundations are second to US foundations in the volume of their support of democracy building in CEEC. See Ann L. Phillips, "Exporting Democracy: German Political Foundations in Central-East Europe," in *Democratization* Vol. 6, No. 2 (1999), pp. 70–98.
6. World Bank, *Governance: The World Bank's Experience* (Washington, D.C.: The World Bank, 1994).
7. John Clark, "The State, Popular Participation, and the Voluntary Sector," in *World Development* Vol. 23, No. 4 (1995), p. 593.
8. Michael Edwards and David Hulme, "Too Close for Comfort? The Impact of Official Aid on Nongovernmental Organizations," in *World Development* Vol. 24, No. 6 (1996), pp. 962–963.
9. Barbara Janckar-Webster, "Environmental Movement and Social Change in the Transition Countries," in *Environmental Politics* Vol. 7, No. 1 (1998), p. 81.
10. Adam Fagin, "Environment and Transition in the Czech Republic," in *Environmental Politics* Vol. 3, No. 3 (1994), p. 491.
11. Michael Waller, "Geopolitics and the Environment in Eastern Europe," in *Environmental Politics* Vol. 7, No. 1 (1998), p. 42.
12. David Chandler, "Democratization in Bosnia: The Limits of Civil Society Building Strategies," in *Democratization* Vol. 5, No. 4 (1998), p. 87.
13. OSCE Mission to Bosnia and Herzegovina Democratization Department, *Semi-Annual Report*, July–December 1998, p. 9.
14. Bob Deacon and Paul Stubbs, "International Actors and Social Policy Development in Bosnia-Herzegovina: Globalism and the 'New Feudalism'," in *Journal of European Social Policy* Vol. 8, No. 2 (1998), pp. 99–115.
15. Ibid., p. 110.
16. Ibid., p. 111.
17. Theoretically, an ideal state–civil society relation could be described, for example, as follows: 1. the state provides an encouraging institutional framework for civic organizations; 2. the organizations have internal accountability and democracy; 3. both vertical and horizontal linkages develop between different organizations. These conditions should be facilitated by constructive support, but without donor dependency (Axel Hadenius and Fredrik Uggla, "Making Civil Society Work, Promoting Democratic Development: What can States and Donors Do?" in *World Development* Vol. 24, No. 10 (1996), p. 1636). Such ideal levels of state–civil society relations are not very likely to be realized in the Eastern and Southern societies in the foreseeable future. Even the great majority of the West has not reached and probably will not reach such a ideal condition, with the exception of, for example, Scandinavia.
18. Anna C. Vakil, "Confronting the Classification Problem: Toward a Taxonomy of NGOs," In *World Development* Vol. 25, No. 12 (1997), pp. 2057–2070.
19. Arrows indicate the flow of resource and control.
20. Phillippe C. Schmitter, "The Consolidation of Democracy and Representation of Social

Groups," *American Behavioral Scientist* Vol. 35, No. 4/5 (1992), p. 427. See also: Andrew T. Green and Carol Skalnik Leff, "The Quality of Democracy: Mass-Elite Linkages in the Czech Republic," in *Democratization* Vol. 4, No. 4 (1997), pp. 63–87.

21 Ruth Alsop and John Farrington, "Nests, Nodes and Niches: A System, for Process Monitoring, Information Exchange and Decision Making for Multiple Stakeholders," in *World Development* Vol. 26, No. 2 (1998), p. 253.

22 Per Selle and Kristin Strømsnes, *"Medlemskap og demokrati: Må vi ta passivt medlemskap på alvor?"* in *Politica* Vol. 29, No. 1 (1997), pp. 31–48.

23 The dotted line indicates the most problematic juncture.

PART II

RECONSTRUCTING MULTIETHNIC BOSNIA

8 How a Quota Borda System of Elections may Facilitate Reconciliation

PETER EMERSON

> Driving across Bosnia in 1990 just prior to the elections afforded me a brief glimpse into the republic's miserable future. One village drowning in a sea of green crescents, which proclaimed the (Muslim) Party of Democratic Action..., would give way to another, where the šahovnica was sovereign (denoting the Croatian Democratic Union...), or where every wall was covered with the four Cs and the acronym SDS (Serbian Democratic Party).... Many doomed settlements were a jumble of all three.
>
> Misha Glenny[1]

> The elections in Yugoslavia in 1990, rather than being a regular instrument of popular choice and expression of political freedom...became the critical turning point in the process of politicaldisintegration.
>
> Susan Woodward[2]

Those elections, then, made everything worse. But, if a different electoral system had been in use, there could well have been a different result, different persons elected, and by now, a very different history. Ante Marković, for example, "remained phenomenally popular"[3] and "opinion polls indicated that voters would support parties espousing nonethnic or cross-ethnic progress."[4] But because the electoral system allowed the voters to express only one preference, that election became a cause of war. The electoral system used in Bosnia since Dayton has also, in effect, been little more than a sectarian head count.[5]

At the moment, the chosen electoral system often exacerbates the situation it is supposedly meant to heal. If democracy is to be an integral part of the peace process, the structures used in that democracy must themselves be peaceful. Hence, the purpose of this paper is to outline what I hope you agree is a peaceful electoral system: peaceful in that it encourages each individual voter to engage him or herself in a personal process of reconciliation, and peaceful in its outcome of an inclusive, proportional and balanced chamber of representatives.

Proportional Representation and Alternative Principles

Many people think proportional representation (PR) is a good thing. It is, granted, better than first-past-the-post, simple majority or plurality voting, but it is still adversarial. He or she who gets the support of a quota gets elected, and what other voters think about his candidature is irrelevant. Indeed, in torn societies, a candidate's success sometimes depends on the extent to which he has managed to antagonize those other voters not in his or her own ethnic group or quota.

In pure democratic theory, the candidate—that is, the person who, dressed in white, is literally 'candid'—should, if elected, represent everyone in his constituency. In first-past-the-post, a candidate may sometimes represent only 'his own,' leaving many, if not indeed a majority, with the feeling that they are underrepresented. In simple PR, he may represent only his quota, but because there are now several as opposed to just one winner, the number of persons feeling underrepresented will be fewer.

Ideally, however, an electoral system should be not divisive and exclusive, but cohesive and inclusive, leaving no one with a feeling of alienation. Accordingly, those elected should represent the entire constituency. The chosen electoral system should be one in which the success of any one candidate depends upon the opinions (preferences) of every voter in that constituency.

The principle of proportionality is important, of course. But so too is the principle of inclusivity. Indeed, any list of principles upon which an electoral system should be based is quite long. In the case of post-Dayton Bosnia, the list should include the following electoral principles:[6]

Every sane and law-abiding citizen should have the right to stand as a candidate, either independently or as a member of a particular party. We are all sophisticated creatures, so the electoral system should allow voters to express more than one preference, if they so wish. Ipso facto, of course, the procedure used in the count must take all of these preferences into consideration. The number of preferences to be cast will vary according to the number of persons to be elected although, for practical purposes, it need seldom exceed the figure of six.

While divisions in the count along ethnic lines may be necessary (because of the Dayton Agreement), they should not be allowed to interfere with the voters' rights to full expression of their preferences.

In expressing a second preference, a voter is in effect saying that, inter alia, he or she is prepared to compromise, and compromise should be an essential part of any peaceful democratic process. But more than that, a second preference allows the voter who so wishes to actively pursue a cross-party, cross-ethnic and/or cross-gender rapprochement.

The electoral system should be less antagonistic than a majoritarian contest; instead, it should actually encourage a certain amount of cooperation, both between parties and/or independent candidates within an ethnic community, and between communities. Any system which allows for the above principle will probably also comply with this principle. In a word, electoral contests should be based more on the win-win principle than on an adversarial win-or-lose basis.

In the Republika Srpska presidential and vice-presidential elections, for example, instead of one party winning both the presidency and the vice presidency, the winner should become the president and the runner-up the vice-president, regardless of their affiliation. If a party or candidate wishes to stand on a sectarian or ethnic platform, then of course it may. But this should not be an obligation. After all, other parties and candidates may wish to stand on a non-ethnic platform. As a matter of principle, therefore, no electoral system should put the non-ethnic at a disadvantage to the ethnic.

As has been the case in post-Dayton Bosnia, any count must be based on a principle of proportional representation, and this in turn should involve a reasonably low threshold. The measure of proportionality, however, should be based on more than just the voters' first preferences. Furthermore, in an ideal world, proportionality should be determined by the voters themselves. If a quota of voters wishes to vote for candidates of one particular gender, or for candidates standing on an anti-nuclear power ticket, for example, even though such a policy may not be regarded as topical, they should be able to do so. The constituency principle should help to ensure that any regional or national minority may still gain representation in all local, regional and national chambers, and overall proportionality can best be ensured by either a second-tier or a top-up electoral system. A top-up of an electoral system is the second part of the count; the first part takes place in local constituencies, and may be first-past-the-post or PR-list or PR-STV or anything else; the second part considers either those same votes or a second ballot paper on a regional or national level, and is normally conducted as a PR-list count. It is an attempt to ensure that, on a national scale, and despite any local quirks, the electoral system is proportional overall.[7] The effect of such a PR + PR system is to ensure that while any small constituency will inevitably have a high threshold - in a 4-seater constituency, its about 20%, and any party with less than 20% support may not get elected; in the regional/national top-up, however, the constituency is obviously large, and the threshold correspondingly small, which means even the small parties can gain representation.

A good electoral system will enable or indeed encourage the voter to vote 'sincerely'—that is, as he or she would really want to—rather than 'tactically,' as is the case when a bad system is deployed. Since in a good second-tier system, the voters would invariably vote in exactly the same way in both tiers, a better approach would be to use a top-up system based on a second, different count of the same poll information. While any electoral system to be used in Bosnia must cater to all three ethnic groups, those not wanting to be too closely associated with any of those groups, not to mention those outside those groups altogether, should not be excluded. Ballot papers should allow the voter not only a choice of party, but also a choice of candidates within the party. Moreover, there should only be one type of ballot paper in any one constituency. In Bosnia's presidential elections, for example, the ballot paper in both RS and the Federation should be one and the same. All apparentements should stand as one undivided contesting bloc, alliance or coalition. The ballot paper, therefore, should list independent candidates as well as candidates belonging to parties or coalitions.

Finally, in the current atmosphere, the chosen electoral system must be Dayton-compliant. Nevertheless, it should be designed in such a way as to provide for a natural evolution into a system ideally suited for the perfect 'multi-multi' society, or a society in which candidates are elected and policies are chosen regardless of the ethnicity, religion or gender of the persons involved.

The Quota Borda System

The Quota Borda System (QBS) complies with the above principles. In the years leading up to 1789, the year of revolution, it was obvious to certain members of the French Academy of Sciences that the simple two-option vote could not be used to identify the average opinion. Majority voting was used in what was, at the time, the only existing democracy, England, so no wonder that country was thus divided into two, whigs and tories. The democratic principle suggests only the wishes of the majority should be enacted; but the methodology, the so-called majority vote, is erroneous.

Accordingly, while Le Maquis de Condorcet suggested his criterion, Jean Charles de Borda suggested a points system in a paper entitled "Sur la Forme des Élections" in 1770. The Academy adopted it in 1784; it worked very well for a number of years; but then it was thrown out by a new member of that Society, although this particular individual was not best known for his democratic idealism; his name was Napoleon Bonaparte.

To put it all in context, however, we must now add that de Borda was not the first to suggest this methodology. That honour goes to Nicholas Cusanus, a humble monk by trade, who was disturbed by the majority voting used by his beloved cardinals when electing a pope. Accordingly, he suggested the same good points system, in the year 1435, but alas, the church still believed in the much more tedious series of weighted votes, before the eventual puff of white smoke.[8]

The question, now, is how to adapt QBS to all of Bosnia's election requirements: presidential, parliamentary, cantonal or local. We will first look at the system in outline, and then work on particular examples, finishing with the municipal elections in Travnik.

The 'Sistem Bodove,' or points system (or rather, QBS), works on the following basis:

1. the success of the candidate will depend on all the preferences exercised in his or her favor;
2. any party or any other group of people gaining a quota will thus gain fair representation;
3. this proportionality principle shall be combined with the constituency principle, giving, where appropriate, multi-member constituencies of from three to nine representatives; and
4. while this would suggest a threshold from 25 to 10 percent respectively, a lower and more equitable threshold can be achieved by operating a simultaneous top-up system in a larger regional constituency.

Accordingly, voters shall be asked to vote for a fixed number of candidates, a number we will call n (in most circumstances, $2 < n < 7$). If the voter fills in a complete ballot, he gives n points to the candidate he likes the most, $n-1$ points to his next favorite, $n-2$ points to his third preference, and so on, down to 1 point for the candidate he likes the least.

If the voter fills in only a partial ballot, or if, in other words, he votes for only m candidates (where m is a whole number defined by $0 < m < n$), he gives m points to the candidate he likes the most, $m-1$ points to his next favorite, m–2 points to his third preference, and so on, down to 1 point for the candidate he likes the least.

The purpose of this is to encourage the voter to vote for more than one candidate. As far as any count of first preference is concerned, that makes no difference: the first preference, after all, is the candidate who gets m or n points. At this stage of the QBS count, a candidate only gets the maximum number of points, that is, n points, from a voter who hands in a complete ballot.

In so doing, as was mentioned earlier, the voter is expressing a willingness to compromise. Furthermore, the voter may thus vote across the ethnic divide. That is, he may well be expressing a conscious act of reconciliation. Granted, in many instances the voter will probably give his first preference to a candidate of his own ethnic group. But at least, in this system, he has the opportunity to concede at least some points to those of a different ethnic group.

QBS in Presidential Elections

As noted earlier, there should be one ballot paper, and one ballot paper only, in any Bosnian presidential election.

To be Dayton-compliant, and for as long as those Dayton provisions stipulate that each national community—whether Bosniaks, Serb or Croat—shall elect one member of the three-person presidency, it will be necessary for all candidates to identify themselves as belonging to one or another national community.

The voters, however, must be free to choose. And just as some Bosniaks may well have chosen to vote on the Croat list, so too, in theory, should all of the residents of the Republika Srpska be free to vote for whomsoever they wish.

I would suggest that each voter be allowed to cast three preferences, giving three points to his most preferred candidate, two points to his next favorite, and one point to his third choice. A vote will be considered valid if a clear preference is given to one candidate of one nation. A complete ballot will be considered altogether valid if points are cast in sequence for different candidates of different national communities.

One could say that a danger in such a system is that many voters may seek to cross the ethnic divide and influence the outcome not only of someone from their own nation, but also of a second or third person from another national community. This could indeed happen, but it should be seen not as a danger, but rather as an encouragement for others to do the same.

If there were any fanciful result, it would be an 'unholy alliance' in which three extreme nationalist parties come together to support each other. But that could only work if plans for it became widely known, in which case the press would have a field day. Furthermore, if the three normally antagonistic parties were still determined to cooperate, the result might just resemble the desired inter-ethnic cooperation.

QBS in Parliamentary Elections

Unlike presidential elections, parliamentary elections could work on the basis of a top-up system. Any party that felt it had a good chance of winning x seats in a particular constituency would want to field either x or x + 1 candidates. At this stage of a QBS election these candidates would be, in effect, competing against one another. In the top-up election, however, all the members of any one party would be competing with each other.

The advantage of this particular QBS feature is that the ballot paper will never be too long. In the Republika Srpska parliamentary elections, for example, if the Republika Srpska was divided into two constituencies each electing 5 persons with a 4-person top-up (see Table 2, below), I estimate that only four parties or coalitions, including the Socialdemocrats, would want to put up two candidates, and only two groupings, the moderate SLOGA coalition and the joint Serbian Radical and Serbian Democratic Party list would want to stand three candidates.

Table 8.1 Proposed Constituencies for Parliamentary Elections in Bosnia-Herzegovina[9]

Constituency	Area	Number of voters	Number of Seats	Voters per Representative
Federation	Total	1,461,400	23	
	Cantons 1, 7, 8 & 10	449,369	7	64,196
	Cantons 5, 6 & 9	455,640	7	65,091
	Cantons 2, 3, & 4	556,391	9	61,821
Republika Srpska	Total	1,195,358	10	
	West of Brčko	597,679 est.	5	119,536
	East of Brčko	597,679 est.	5	119,536

In 1998, the ballot paper in Republika Srpska listed 28 different parties, coalitions, alliances or independent candidates. If QBS had been used, all the advantages of open-list proportional representation would have been added, not to mention those of PR-STV and others of the Borda preferendum, yet the final ballot paper would have consisted of only 34 different names, either independent or belonging to one of only 25 different parties or coalitions.

Table 8.2 Proposed Top-ups

Constituency	Number of Seats	Number of voters	Votes per top-up
Federation	5	1,461,400	292,280
Republika Srpska	4	1,195,358	298,840

Table 8.3 Proposed Total Number of Seats

Constituency	Number of Seats	Number of Votes	Voters per Representative
Federation	28	1,461,400	52,193
Republika Srpska	14	1,195,358	85,383

Considering these factors, the parliamentary elections could be conducted as demonstrated in Table 1, 2 and 3. Given the disparities in the total number of seats to be awarded in the two entities, it is the final top-up figures of voters per top-up which are perhaps most important: 292,280 and 298,840 for the Federation and the Republika Srpska respectively.

QBS in Local Elections

For local elections, I have chosen the example of Travnik municipality, which has 31 members on its council. The area is divided into four roughly equal constituencies based on purely geographical considerations. Each constituency elects five, six or seven members, such that the number of voters required to elect one representative is roughly the same in each constituency. The corresponding threshold is of the order of 16 percent. In addition, there is a top-up to elect six further members, so as to give an overall threshold of about four percent. The obvious advantages of this arrangement may be summarized as follows:

Dividing the municipality into constituencies will ensure fair representation to both rural and urban areas, as well as to any pockets of land populated by different ethnic groups.

The exact location of constituency boundaries will not be a major point of contention, since any particular disadvantage perceived by any one party in any particular local constituency boundary will be seen as an advantage in the overall top-up.

To ensure the full benefit of the top-up, each party will want to stand in all the municipal constituencies, which will help to promote a more cohesive atmosphere. In addition, of course, such a top-up will ensure that the electoral system is equally fair to both big and small parties.

In most municipal elections, voters would be asked to vote for just three candidates, again on the basis of the QBS. Accordingly, most municipal counts would not be too complicated.

Conclusion

International human rights charters and similar documents have rarely gone beyond saying that every citizen shall have the right to vote in free and fair elections. Unfortunately, however, the expression "free and fair" applies more to the conduct of the election rather than to the electoral system. In consequence, many countries retain electoral systems that are far from fair. Examples come readily to mind, and range from consolidated democracies like the United States and the United Kingdom, to Serbia and others.

In the absence of rulings on the international level that would impose fairer electoral systems, each country can choose whatever system it wishes. Needless to say, many party politicians choose systems which are favorable to their own particular party. Whether or not they are also fair to the electorate is not regarded by politicized lawmakers as quite as important.

Given Bosnia's history, however, and the unfavorable if not potentially disastrous consequences of unfair electoral systems, a fair electoral system is absolutely essential here. Indeed, I would suggest that the very future of this land depends on an improvement of the electoral system based on careful consideration of its fairness to the currently fragmented electorate, as well on the opportunities it might provide for citizens to practice reconciliation through the vote.

Notes

1. Misha Glenny, *The Fall of Yugoslavia: The Third Balkan War*, New Edition (London: Penguin, 1993), p. 147.
2. Susan Woodward, *Balkan Tragedy: Chaos and Dissolution after the Cold War* (Washington, D.C.: Brookings, 1995), p 118.
3. Laura Silber and Allan Little, *Yugoslavia: Death of a Nation* (New York: TV Books & Penguin, 1996), p. 210.
4. Lenard J. Cohen, *Broken Bonds: The Disintegration of Yugoslavia* (Boulder: Westview, 1993), p. 146.
5. See International Crisis Group, "Is Dayton Failing? Bosnia Four Years After the Peace Agreement" (October 28, 1999). Available at: http://www.crisisweb.org.
6. For the OSCE-proposed electoral law, see http://www.oscebih.org/documents/draftelectionlaw/eng/del-eng.htm.
7. Germany's top-up system is first-past-the-post + PR-list, and is called Multi-Member Proportional (and sometimes, mistakenly, Additional member System). Sweden uses PR-List + PR-List. Malta uses PR-STV + PR-List.
8. See Michael Dummett, *Principles of Electoral Reform* (Oxford, Oxford University Press, 1997) and P J Emerson, *Beyond the Tyranny of the Majority* (Belfast: The de Borda Institute, 1998).
9. Canton 1: Una-Sana, Canton 2: Posavina, Canton 3: Tuzla-Podrinje, Canton 4: Zenica-Doboj, Canton 5: Goražde, Canton 6: **Central Bosnia**, Canton 7: Herzegovina-Neretva – Mostar, Canton 8: West Herzegovina, **Canton 9: Sarajevo**, Canton 10: Livno. Information on Elections is available at: http://www.oscebih.org.

9 Journalism in Post-Dayton Bosnia: How to Make the Media More Responsible
DUŠAN BABIĆ

No one can deny that the conquest of the news media was a precondition for territorial conquest in Bosnia and Herzegovina. In fact, this country was first shattered by aggressive media, and then by guns. Words can easily turn into bullets, and the mighty visual language of television is particularly apt for this. In brief, hate speech can kill and maim just as bullets do. Just recall what happened at Zagreb's Maksimir Football Stadium on May 13, 1990, at the derby match between *Dinamo* from Zagreb and *Crvena Zvezda* (the Red Star) from Belgrade.

Football hooliganism had been spreading across the former Yugoslavia and gained momentum during the "great four" derby matches, which pitted *Zvezda*, *Partizan*, *Dinamo* and *Hajduk*–Split against one another. But in the late 1980s, due to the high degree of politicization of fan clubs, inter-fan conflicts escalated into inter-ethnic conflicts. Indeed, it can be said that the war started at Maksimir Stadium. This fact is illustrated by the inscription on the monument to the "Bad Blue Boys," that is, *Dinamo* fans killed in the "War for the Homeland."[1] The monument, erected in 1994, reads: "Dedicated to all the *Dinamo* fans for whom the war started on 13 May 1990 at the Maksimir Football Stadium and ended on the sacrificial altar of the CROATIAN homeland. BBB ZAGREB, 13 May 1994."[2] Another issue is that sports violence in general is usually an indication of a long drawn-out social crisis, as was the case in the former Yugoslavia.

According to the 1991 census, 4.3 million people were living in Bosnia and Herzegovina (BiH). By current estimates, about 3.5 million people live there now. There are no reliable data as to how the population is divided between the Federation of Bosnia-Herzegovina (FBiH) and the Republika Srpska (RS), but approximately one third of the country's total population probably resides in RS. These brief demographic details are important for presenting the legal development of the media sector in Bosnia.

Despite all its weaknesses and imperfections, the Dayton Peace

Agreement (DPA) was a successful tool for preserving peace. In 1995, hardly anyone could have foreseen that a peace process initiated in Dayton, Ohio, heartland of the United States, would survive the dark years of war in Bosnia, since borders here are drawn with blood. According to the DPA, Bosnia is formally composed of two entities: the Republika Srpska (RS) and the Federation of Bosnia-Herzegovina (FBiH). But in reality there are still three entities: RS, Bosniak-controlled Federation territory and Croat-controlled Federation territory, better known as Herzeg-Bosna. This is an outcome of the political composition of the former Yugoslavia.

After its collapse, three nationalist parties in Bosnia—the Croat Democratic Union (HDZ), the Serb Democratic Party (SDS) and the Bosniak Muslim Party of Democratic Action (SDA)—became the successors to the communist party (League of Communists of Yugoslavia), taking over its mechanisms of political and economic control. Nationalist leaders still have a strategic interest in maintaining the conditions on which their power depends: lack of democratic accountability, absence of the rule of law, and division of the country through a widespread fear that another ethnic group is the enemy.

Unlike the nationalist leaders, the so-called international community had no strategy. Its steps in Bosnia were mostly taken haphazardly, in response to events on the ground rather than according to some strategic vision. This attitude has to be changed radically, and the change must include new priorities for Bosnia.

This political environment negatively affected the media sector, especially considering that the Dayton peace process was strictly focused on how to stop the war. The consequence was that the DPA simply omitted to deal with the media and related issues. The omission was rectified during the meetings of the Peace Implementation Council (PIC), first in Sintra, Portugal in June 1997, and then in Bonn in December 1997. Unfortunately, by 1997 the issue was more one of media control than of media development, and this trend has continued to this day.

The Yugoslav Context

A picture of the pre-war media scene in Bosnia-Herzegovina cannot be extracted without first placing the case in a wider Yugoslav context. Bosnia-Herzegovina was one of six republics and two autonomous provinces that made up Yugoslavia. Until the mid-1960s, Yugoslavia was a highly centralized state, and the mass media, of course, were an integral part of the communist regime. The situation changed substantially after the famed communist party plenum at Brioni[3] in the fall of 1966, where Tito's top aid, Aleksandar Ranković (at that time vice-president and chief of the secret police), was expelled from the Party, removed from office and discharged from all his duties.

The post-Brioni democratization process did not happen overnight, but the adoption of a new Constitution in 1974 marked the completion of Yugoslavia's new political course and the reshaping of its political structure. For many historians, academicians, political analysts, politicians and others, this was the beginning of the end of Yugoslavia.

Prior to Brioni, *Borba* (Struggle) was the central daily, and in the early 1950s it had an astonishingly high circulation of 600,000. It was the spitting image of its Moscow counterpart and idol, *Pravda*, a large sheet of paper of only four pages. Another Belgrade daily was *Politika*, regarded by some apparatchiks as the paper of the petty bourgeoisie. This condemnation was certainly nonsense: prior to the Milosevic period, *Politika* was an outstanding paper in professional terms with an average circulation of nearly 300,000 and a low rate of unsold copies.

Before the Brioni plenum, dailies in the republics and autonomous provinces strictly followed the party line. The Zagreb-based *Vjesnik* (Herald/Courier) had the highest circulation, of around 100,000; followed by the Ljubljana-based *Delo* (Deed/Action) and the Sarajevo-based *Oslobodjenje* (Liberation), each with a circulation of around 90,000. The Skopje-based *Slobodna Makedonija* (Free Macedonia), with a circulation of 40,000, was followed by *Dnevnik* (Daily) in Novi Sad, the capital of Vojvodina province (30,000), and *Pobjeda* (Victory), in Titograd (now Podgorica), the capital of Montenegro (20,000). With the emergence of a specific kind of so-called "socialist self-management economy," which reached its peak in the late 1970s, a specific kind of media market emerged, too. This resulted in a mushrooming of other dailies, weeklies and periodicals, including local print media.

As far as editorial policies were concerned, the Belgrade press was the most open and liberal in the country, with the exception of the Ljubljana-based weekly *Mladina* (Youth). Formally the newspaper of Slovenian youth, the weekly dealt with very serious issues of national significance in the mid-1980s.

Before television was introduced as a medium in the early 1960s, Radio Belgrade played the role of a central radio station, controlled by the Politbiro (Political Bureau) and Agitprop (Agitation and Propaganda), the arm of the communist party. Republic and province radio stations played roles similar to that of Radio Belgrade, but also included detailed coverage of political events of local significance.

Then came the stormy events of the past decade...

What will remain a mystery is the *salto mortale* in editorial policy carried out without almost any change in the decision-making individuals. Within a short period, once-ardent agitators of the communist party line were dramatically transformed into violent nationalists and warmongers, and then later into vocal peacemakers, supporters of the DPA, and even genuine cosmopolitans and democrats. Apparently, the Yugoslav communist *nomenclatura* had been transformed into a nationalistic *nomenclatura*. But what is amazing is that the *nomenclatura*'s rhetoric remained almost unchanged: only the terminology underwent some logical changes having to do with Marxist phraseology, which was dropped or placed into pejorative contexts. Public debates suddenly adopted new vocabulary: pathos, statehood, nation, people, religion, new history, epics, blood and soil concepts, and so forth. True, "the happenings of the people" began in Serbia, but others eagerly accepted it as an alibi for secession from Yugoslavia. The mechanism of rule remained identical, since the mental structure of the new-old protagonists remained unchanged.

It should be noted, however, that media in Yugoslavia were more varied and pluralistic before 1989 than those of any other Eastern European country. And private media ownership *did not* exist in Yugoslavia until 1989.

The Pre-Dayton Media Scene in Bosnia

Following the free elections in Bosnia-Herzegovina in 1990, control of the media went from the communist government into the hands of political parties based strictly on ethnic criteria. New laws on information allowed for the establishment of private media companies. But the privatization of state-owned media, based on the Law on Social Capital, was halted during the war.

Many private radio and TV stations were established during the war. Some print media emerged too, but many of them have already ceased to operate or have simply disappeared.

As was mentioned already, the media played a key role in fomenting the ethnic hatred, hate speech, intolerance, xenophobia, racism and related feelings and manifestations that eventually led to war. Bosnian journalists were also caught in the crossfire of both war and war propaganda. Many faced bitter dilemmas as to whether to comply with professional standards or to embrace patriotism. Many of them still suffer from this kind of dilemma or disease, and in some cases it has even become a syndrome.

The Post-Dayton Media Environment in Bosnia

Even after the war, hate speech and inflammatory reporting was widespread, and effectively endangered the DPA. Bearing in mind the destructive role media played during the war and after it, the international community decided to introduce a unique body, the Independent Media Commission (IMC). Established in June 1998 by a decision of the High Representative, the IMC is a regulatory and disciplinary body primarily in charge of broadcast media. Its provisions take precedence over all other legal acts in Bosnia-Herzegovina. By establishing this institution, the international community expressed its firm commitment to securing free and pluralistic media throughout the country.

The IMC provides broadcast licenses, monitors media performance, receives complaints about the compliance of media with IMC rules and regulations and gives support to media organizations. Some media and political circles greeted IMC's creation with bitter refusal, or at least grumbling, some complaining that, "new censors are coming..." But the dissenters were overlooking the fact that broadcast media worldwide have been regulated for decades. The real uniqueness of the IMC is that the agency is run by foreigners. But it is projected that as soon as it is feasible, the IMC will transfer its responsibilities and authority to an indigenous domestic agency.

The overall standards of Bosnia-Herzegovina's media products—both in terms of contents and appearance—are hardly comparable to media in other European countries or elsewhere in the world. In general, the media sector in Bosnia-Herzegovina still faces substantial structural problems: it lacks a reliable legal framework and a coherent and accessible media market.

Legal Framework

The actual legislative framework for the media consists of laws from three different periods:

1. laws adopted in former Yugoslavia;
2. laws adopted during the early 1990s (that is, after the collapse of Yugoslavia); and
3. post-war laws adopted separately by the two entities of Bosnia.

This is the main reason why the legal environment for the media in Bosnia-Herzegovina lacks a cohesive regulatory framework within which to operate. The international community is currently assisting the local authorities to develop a homogeneous legal framework for regulating the country's media.[4]

The country badly needs a regulatory framework that affects the media sector for two reasons:

1. to separate state and political party influence from the media; and
2. to facilitate the privatization process of the media sector.

The ownership of the media is particularly important for ensuring a broad-based representation of views. Separately, the creation of a cohesive and reliable framework is a precondition for a sound media market.

According to the Constitution of Bosnia-Herzegovina (Annex 4 of the DPA), only the telecommunications sector is the responsibility of Bosnia-Herzegovina (under the Council of Ministers), while the entities are entirely responsible for the media. But it should be kept in mind that provisions defined by the Office of the High Representative (OHR) or IMC take precedence over all other legal acts in Bosnia-Herzegovina. It is also projected that IMC will widen the scope of its responsibilities to include the allocation of frequencies.

An additional problem that makes the media scene in Bosnia-Herzegovina even more complex is the fact that unlike FBiH, the RS is a highly centralized entity with its own media laws. In FBiH, the cantons are responsible for the media sector. But again, this is mostly on paper, due to the strong roles of the OHR and IMC.

Self-regulation vs. Statutory Regulation

Hate speech and inflammatory reporting is not a local invention. Europe experienced it before and during World War II as well. This alone was the main reason why West European countries produced an outstanding document in the early 1950s: the European Convention on Human Rights (ECHR) represented a cornerstone in the protection of fundamental human rights and freedoms. Unlike the UN Human Rights system, which is generally declarative, the European or Strasbourg system uses a more legal approach. It defines human rights as being in no way negotiable: if there is a violation of one of the human rights guaranteed by the Convention, neither the political nor economic interests of a government can influence the decision of any court. However, after several decades in practice, mechanisms for the protection of human rights proved too slow, which led to the recent establishment of a permanent European Court of Human Rights. Despite the fact that Bosnia-Herzegovina is not yet a member state of the Council of Europe, the ECHR has precedence over domestic legislation. This is yet another vivid illustration of the uniqueness of Bosnia-Herzegovina.

For the media sector, Article 10 of the Convention, which deals with freedom of expression, is of particular importance. Some legal experts claim that Article 10 is only a skillful condensation of Article 19 of the UN Universal Declaration of Human Rights. Nonetheless, Article 10 does not include guidelines on the freedom to receive and impart information in the way that the International Convention on Civil and Political Rights (ICCPR) regulates it in Article 19. The conspicuous difference between the ECHR and the ICCPR is that the ECHR does not address the prohibition of war propaganda, or the dissemination of national, racial and religious hatred, in the way prescribed by Article 20 of the ICCPR.

Convention designers overlooked an important issue: if authority can be misused, so can freedom—in our specific case, freedom of press. Whoever has the freedom to inform may also exercise that freedom to misinform. If so, there is need to promote a sense of responsibility among journalists. Democratic societies have responded to the possibility of misuse of the media by establishing professional press codes or journalistic codes of ethics. The question is how to make self-regulation more effective, and at the same time to require only a minimum intervention of law to strengthen the process of self-regulation. The experience of journalists and media organizations shows that where law is used to monitor journalistic ethics, it leads to political interference.

Self-regulation is Not a Magic Formula

Rule of law is a precondition for self-regulation of the media. It is obvious that there is not yet rule of law in Bosnia-Herzegovina. If there were, what would then need to be done?

Despite its limitations, the value and advantages of self-regulation are great and should be exploited. In our Bosnian case, a good indicator might be that all the journalist associations have adopted the Press Code,[5] drawn from existing European standards of journalistic practice, as the basis of a self-regulation system. It should be emphasized that the Press Code is only for print media, since the IMC imposed the Broadcasting Code of Practice, effective as of August 1, 1998. Unlike the Press Code, which is only *morally* binding on reporters, editors, owners and publishers of newspapers and periodicals, the Broadcasting Code of Practice sets out rules and standards for broadcasters and includes sanctions in case of violation. These might include the requirement to publish an apology, the issuance of warnings, the imposition of financial penalties, the suspension of licenses, entry onto premises or seizure of equipment, the closedown of operations or the termination of licenses.

What has to be clear is the fact that Bosnia-Herzegovina media, at least temporarily, cannot follow the Western formula of news media. The well-known motto used as a creed for Western journalism, that "there is no bad news," is not entirely applicable in Bosnia-Herzegovina. This does not mean a blackout on news, but just a softening of reports of bad news. The point is to prevent news coverage that pours fuel on the flames of hatred. Once used as a destructive force, media must now foster reconciliation and tolerance. Recall that television in particular, as the most powerful medium, acted as a virtual front line, or "killing screens."[6] Or, a sarcastic adaptation of Clausewitz's dictum could be applied to the early 1990s: "War is the continuation of television news by other means."[7]

Closing Remarks

Apart from having stopped the fighting, the few successes of the Dayton Peace Agreement—the Central Bank, a common currency, common license plates, state symbols and customs reforms—cannot overshadow its massive failures. The return process has turned into a mass relocation process, and it is almost obvious that ethnic cleansers are winning the battle to shape post-Dayton Bosnia-Herzegovina. The economy has not yet reached even 50 percent of its pre-war capacity. Unemployment ranges from 40 percent in the FBiH to 50 percent in RS. Salaries and pensions are in arrears. Social discontent has already burst into the open, with demonstrators usually blocking highways. Many local politicians are desperately trying to channel this social unrest into nationalism.

All of this must affect the media sector—and badly. For example, it is estimated that less than five percent of the total population reads newspapers.

The big problem facing this country is an absolute disproportion between the number of media and the size of the population. While current estimates claim that some 3.5 million people live in the country, there are a total of 426 media outlets! Regarding the number of broadcast media (the IMC has identified 281), the Bosnia has the densest concentration of broadcasters in the world next to Uruguay. The new long-term licensing regime of broadcast media—if it is implemented—may decimate the number of broadcasters. How it may affect the BiH media environment is difficult to predict.

There are no laws in force that protect intellectual property, and audio-visual piracy is widespread. But the IMC's long-term licensing regime will carry out comprehensive and targeted monitoring of broadcasters in Bosnia to ensure compliance with its Rule on Copyright Obligations, which should be adopted soon.

In general, the overall quality of programming is poor, particularly in those operations created during the war, because the personnel running them lack professional experience in both radio and TV companies. Many media companies have not yet reached critical mass with respect to their technical, financial and staffing resources. All companies will soon face strict rules, imposed by the IMC, for the issuing of licenses, program content requirements, financial transparency, advertising and the copyright regulations mentioned above. Without recognition, these companies will be unable to compete or even to survive in the rudimentary media market.

Privatization and the transformation of the media sector in Bosnia will have to achieve much more than mere economic efficiency. An open and transparent media sector must be created that will play an active role in the country's democratization.

Committed journalism does not exclude responsible journalism. In my view, "responsible journalist" is a synonym for professional journalist. The real professional will not spread ethnic hatred, racism, xenophobia and war propaganda. Besides, all of this is not protected in international law under freedom of expression. Journalists and others must remember that freedom of opinion is absolute, but freedom of expression is not. However, freedom of expression is the best way for the media to guarantee accountability and credibility to their readers, listeners and viewers. Without it, journalists cannot fulfill their basic task—to inform the people.

Notes

1. Srećko Mihailović, "The War started on May 13, 1990," in *The War started on Maksimir: Hate Speech in Yugoslav Media*, eds. Svetlana Slapašak et al. (Belgrade: Media Center, 1997), p. 97.
2. "BBB" is the commonly used English acronym for Bad Blue Boys.
3. Brioni: islands near the Istrian cost, a favorite resort of the late President Tito.
4. See Office of the High Representative (OHR) Documents: Media Restructuring in Bosnia-Herzegovina.
5. There are six journalists' associations in Bosnia-Herzegovina: the Association of Journalists of BiH, the Independent Union of Professional Journalists of BiH (both in the Bosniak part of the FBiH territory), the Association of Croat Journalists, the Association of Croat Publishers (both in the Croat part of the FBiH), the Association of Journalists of RS and the Independent Union of Journalists of RS. Additionally, there is another association called the Syndicate of Professional Journalists of FBiH, but in fact this organization only serves the Bosniak part of FBiH, and it is expected that two extra unions will be established for the Croat and Serb sides.
6. Dušan Reljić, *Killing Screens: Media in Times of Conflict* (Düsseldorf: Droste Verlag, 1999), p. 7.
7. Mark Thompson, *Forging War* (London: Article 19, 1994), p. 1.

10 Reclaiming Kozarac: Accompanying Returning Refugees*

MARGARET VANDIVER

> I am fed up with everything. More and more frequently I feel a call from deep within me, the call of my world, the call of silence. I want to return to my room. My whole being yearns to return to grandmother's orchard. I wish to sit once again on the softest grass in the world, to hear the chirping of the birds, to feel the breath of the freshest wind, to eat the sweetest pears, to play with grandfather's lambs. I wish to run through the spacious meadows, I wish to pick primroses and dandelions, drink water at the cold forest spring, I wish... I wish. But wishes do not come true. Around me... collapse. And my world is falling down.... My dreams about the future are slowly sliding into a black abyss.[1]

Between 1992 and 1995, tens of thousands of Bosnians were killed and over two million were forced from their homes.[2] No genocide in history has been better documented and more publicized while it occurred. The world stood by while:

> ... the Bosnian Serb army—with the active assistance of the Yugoslav Army and paramilitary groups from Serbia proper—began a drive to "ethnically cleanse" all non-Serbian inhabitants from much of Bosnia. As part of its "ethnic cleansing" campaign, Bosnian Serb forces used tactics such as siege warfare, systematic persecution involving widespread torture, murder, rape, beatings, harassment, de jure discrimination, intimidation, forced displacement of people, confiscation and destruction of property, and the destruction of cultural objects such as mosques and Catholic churches.... The abuses perpetrated during the "ethnic cleansing" of eastern Bosnia constitute war crimes and crimes against humanity as that term was defined at the

Nuremberg trials and within the meaning of customary international law. Moreover, the fact that the abuses associated with "ethnic cleansing" were "committed with intent to destroy, in whole or in part, a national, ethnical, racial or religious group," and that such acts were perpetrated systematically, that no one was held accountable for such crimes, and that they appear to have been premeditated in some cases, would indicated that the "cleansing" of eastern Bosnia and of the Srebrenica "safe area" in particular was part of a larger attempt by Bosnian Serb forces to commit genocide against the Bosnian Muslims and other non-Serbs.[3]

Many of the survivors of these brutal events remain displaced from their pre-war homes four years after the fighting ended. This paper gives an overview of the problems facing returning refugees, and then focuses on efforts to rebuild and return to the town of Kozarac.

The 1991 census of Bosnia counted a total population of just under 4.4 million. Approximately 2.3 million people, slightly over half the population, left their homes during the war and soon afterwards. About 1.3 million of these people became refugees in other parts of the former Yugoslavia or in other countries. Another million people remained in Bosnia as displaced persons.[4]

In the years since the Dayton Peace Agreement[5] and the presence of NATO ended the fighting and imposed a tense and fragile peace, many Bosnians still have not been able to return home. The return of these refugees and displaced persons to their homes is one of the essential requirements for a stable and lasting peace in Bosnia. Despite the guarantee of the right to return contained in the Dayton Agreement, returning home is fraught with dangers and difficulties. Nonetheless, many refugees and displaced persons do desire to return, even if their homes are ruins in towns now dominated by people hostile to their return.

The international community can play an important role in supporting returns by pressuring local officials, targeting aid, and giving direct assistance to returning persons. More important, however, are the determination, persistence, and courage of the displaced persons and refugees themselves. The creation of groups such as the Coalition for Return, "a multi-ethnic pressure group which lobbies for the creation of an appropriate climate and conditions for return, and accepts as a principle that returns to original homes must be made possible for all" is a heartening development.[6] Despite the best efforts of courageous individuals and local and international organizations, however, returns to the areas where people lived before the conflict have not occurred on a widespread basis.

The Legal Framework for Return

The Dayton Agreement contains explicit provisions for the return of refugees and displaced persons. These provisions, insisted upon by the United States during the peace negotiations, are "a means of disguising the otherwise quite strong resemblance between the Dayton Accords and a partition plan."[7] The enforcement of the right to return is essential if Bosnia is not to devolve into separate ethnically-based societies.

Annex 4 of the Dayton Agreement[8] states:

> All refugees and displaced persons have the right freely to return to their homes of origin. They have the right, in accordance with Annex 7 to the General Framework Agreement, to have restored to them property of which they were deprived in the course of hostilities since 1991 and to be compensated for any such property that cannot be restored to them.

Annex 7, Art. 1–2, declares that people may return to their homes "without risk of harassment, intimidation, persecution, or discrimination, particularly on account of their ethnic origin, religious belief, or political opinion." Annex 7, Art. 1–4, further states, "The Parties shall not interfere with the returnees' choice of destination, nor shall they compel them to remain in or move to situations of serious danger or insecurity, or to areas lacking in the basic infrastructure necessary to resume a normal life."

The Dayton Agreement established the Commission for Real Property Claims of Displaced Persons and Refugees. The Commission was to consider any claims for real property in Bosnia and Herzegovina, where the property had not voluntarily been sold or otherwise transferred since April 1, 1992, and where the claimant is not currently in possession of the property. Claims may be for return of the property or for just compensation in lieu of return. The Commission may determine who owns property, appraise its value, determine if transactions were made under duress and invalidate them, and dispose of abandoned property.[9]

Further protections for persons who wish to return are offered under provisions of international law which are applicable to Bosnia through its Constitution and through Annex 6 of the Dayton Agreement.[10] The European Convention for the Protection of Human Rights and Fundamental Freedoms applies to Bosnia, as do 15 other international human rights instruments, including the International Covenant on Civil and Political Rights and the Covenant on Economic, Social and Cultural Rights.[11]

Domestic law relating to the return of refugees and displaced persons is complex and changes frequently. Because of the many movements of various populations during the war, a large number of displaced people wound up occupying the houses of other displaced persons or refugees. In some cases, this was done illegally, but often local officials would declare property abandoned and authorize new people to take possession. It also happened that people seeking better or larger accommodations sometimes moved into vacant houses, thus resulting in "double occupancy" by one family.

During the war, local authorities in the Federation were able to declare privately-owned property "temporarily abandoned," and to allow the temporary occupancy of other persons.[12] This policy preserved the original owner's rights, while allowing someone else to live in the property. While this may have been a practical policy during the war, great difficulties arise when the original owners wish to return, and the current occupant cannot or does not wish to leave. "Very few original owners have succeeded in regaining possession from temporary occupants. Invariably, municipal authorities assign temporary occupancy rights only to members of their own ethnic group [and will not evict them] in favour of an original owner from another ethnic group."[13] There is no provision for appeal of the local authority's decision in these matters. In the Serb-held territories of Bosnia, domestic law holds that the original owner cannot retake possession of the property until the person living in the property returns home or receives compensation. Few Serbs are attempting to return to their previous homes in the Federation, and there is no provision for compensation, making this law practically unenforceable.[14]

The following summarizes a recent overview by Peter Lippman of the situation concerning socially owned property:[15] In the Federation, people who left socially-owned apartments were required to return within six days to reclaim them. This was impossible; people did not even receive notification of this requirement before the time allotted had expired. In the Serb-held territories, there was no time limit imposed, but returning persons could reclaim their apartments only if the current occupants were able and willing to go back to the homes they had fled. In practical terms, this meant that in both entities socially-owned property was not returned to pre-war owners. In April of 1998, the Office of the High Representative annulled these laws and set up a system to process property claims. Cases which had been settled are now open to reconsideration. On paper, this development may result in people being able to reclaim their pre-war property; however, it is unlikely that decisions in favor of returning people will actually be enforced by local authorities.

The Reality of Return

The international community had three primary and essential tasks to accomplish in Bosnia after the Dayton Peace Agreement was signed: maintaining the cease-fire, gaining custody of indicted war criminals, and enforcing the right of return. NATO has successfully overseen the cease-fire, but has done less well in the other areas. In the first year and a half after Dayton, NATO ignored the movements of war criminals and went to some lengths to avoid arresting them; since the summer of 1997, however, SFOR forces have been involved in a number of arrests. Enforcement of the right to return got off to a similarly poor start:

> For the first year of its existence, the NATO force firmly resisted calls for it to become directly involved in assisting the return of displaced persons to their homes. NATO officials and its political leadership argued that these activities were outside the force's mandate, and properly the role of civilian agencies. On several occasions, troops actually restrained Muslim displaced persons from returning home out of concern that their return would spark armed clashes....
> The relative passivity of SFOR as regards the reintegration effort has changed somewhat since early 1997. In several key areas, international troops have begun to assist the return of ethnic minorities to their homes.[16]

The International Crisis Group recently gave the following summary of the current numbers and situations of displaced persons and refugees from Bosnia: "836,500 people are still internally displaced within Bosnia-Herzegovina.... 223,000 Bosnian Serbs are still refugees in FRY.... 30,000 Croats, mainly from Bosnia, are still registered as refugees in Croatia.... 128,000 people from Bosnia-Herzegovina are still living as refugees in Western Europe."[17] Amnesty International reported that at the end of 1998, approximately 1.2 million refugees and displaced persons still had not returned to their homes.[18]

UNHCR and other international organizations declared 1998 to be the "year of return." Through the use of targeted aid,[19] the international community tried to encourage local authorities to enforce the right of return within their jurisdictions. An example of such a program is the Open Cities initiative, begun in the summer of 1997 in an attempt to channel aid at the local level to reward those officials who supported the return of minorities. At the end of 1997, Bihac, Busovaca, Gorazde, Kakanj, Konjic and Vogosca had been declared Open Cities.[20] Unfortunately, the number of returns actually achieved was far below that expected. The "Sarajevo Declaration," a plan to have 20,000 minority returns in Sarajevo in 1998, resulted in only about 2,500 persons coming back by the end of September of that year.[21] A 1999 action plan put forward by the Reconstruction and Return Task Force has also met with disappointing results; the plan called for 120,000 minority returns in 1999, but in the first eight months of the year, only 13,916 such returns had been documented.[22]

A striking pattern is observable among the returns that have occurred, and it is not encouraging for Bosnia's future as a multiethnic country, or even as a unitary state. Human Rights Watch reports that about 475,000 refugees and displaced persons had returned by the end of 1998, but that of these, only about 15,000 were "minority returns," that is, persons going to areas where the majority is now of a different ethnicity than their own. By July 1998, only 1,920 non-Serbs had returned to their homes in territory currently held by the Serbs.[23] Bosniak authorities have permitted far more minority returns than have Serb or Croat authorities; still, "the number of minority returns [in all parts of Bosnia] represents less than 5 percent of all the refugees and displaced persons created by the war."[24]

If people continue to settle in areas where their group is currently in the majority, rather than in the areas where they lived before the conflict, this pattern of resettlement will tend to cement the effects of "ethnic cleansing," and will greatly complicate the rebuilding of a mixed multiethnic society. As the United Nations High Commissioner for Refugees has warned, "Without a concerted push to make [the rights of refugees and displaced persons] a reality, confidence in the peace process will waiver, relocation to majority areas will intensify owing to a lack of other alternatives, and the vision of a multiethnic Bosnia and Herzegovina will give way to the brutal reality of division."[25]

The obstacles to return remain formidable, despite the law and the efforts of international organizations. Among the difficulties facing returning persons are lack of housing, housing occupied by other persons, lack of employment and means to support themselves, dangers from hostile neighbors, dangers from land mines, and, not least, bureaucratic obstacles. These problems are discussed briefly below.

In many areas of Bosnia, property was systematically destroyed. This destruction went far beyond the damage inflicted by shelling and fighting. Houses were burnt and dynamited to ensure that their owners, should they survive, would not try to reclaim them. People who return to their homes often find only a pile of rubble where their houses stood. All their possessions were destroyed or stolen long ago. Refugees who have no money and no access to construction equipment are confronted with a problem they cannot solve alone. They must be assisted in the process of cleaning up the remnants of their homes and in rebuilding new houses. Several international organizations are constructing houses for refugees, but it will require years for them to complete rebuilding even in selected locations.

Owning a destroyed house presents great practical problems. But owning a house that was not destroyed often presents even greater difficulties, because that house is nearly certain to be currently occupied by someone who moved in during the conflict. The house may have been taken by members of the group who drove the owners out, and who are very unlikely to be willing to yield it to the rightful owners. Or someone coming into the area in a later wave of refugees may have moved into the house in a desperate search for safety and shelter. Refugees living in other people's homes often cannot return to their own homes, and thus the return of the rightful owner would mean displacing the current occupant again. In such situations, it is difficult to find a solution that does not harm an innocent party.

Fear is another great difficulty obstructing returns of persons to areas where their groups are now in the minority. In parts of Bosnia, there has been substantial violence and intimidation against returning persons: "In Drvar, a Bosnian Croat area, a protracted series of violent incidents (including arson, assault, and murder) ultimately forced hundreds of Bosnian Serb returnees to flee again in April [1998].... In Travnik, at least five Bosnian Croats were slain since the beginning of 1998, but no perpetrators arrested. In Stolac and Capljina, approximately one hundred Bosniak houses were damaged in 1998..."[26] In addition to the events at Drvar, Amnesty International reported a number of instances of violence, including the beating of an elderly Bosnian Serb woman trying to visit her home in Kljuc, and an explosion in a house owned by two Bosnian Croats, which injured them as they entered the house.[27] Besides acts of intimidation and harassment, returning refugees must also be mindful of land mines and unexploded ordnance on and around their property. People who farmed before the conflict may find that their land is no longer usable due to the presence of mines.

A practical problem facing returning refugees is the lack of employment opportunities. Bosnia's unemployment rate is very high, and minority returns may face discrimination in competing for those jobs that are available. In general, the flat state of the Bosnian economy makes moving and resettlement problematic. Some Muslims returning to their property in Serb-held areas have faced discrimination in the provision of utilities, including electricity and water. Some returning refugees find themselves in dire poverty, completely dependent upon aid from international organizations.

The complexity of rules governing property and return and the bureaucratic obstacles to enforcing those rules are further impediments for refugees and displaced persons:

> ... imagine the confusion of an uninformed displaced person.... the laws are all but surrealistic in their detachment from the reality of the return process. In practice they have turned out to serve as so many opportunities for discouragement and obstruction to return.
> Displaced persons are often unaware of their rights, and unaware of available legal assistance. They don't know which government body to turn to, and spend their days, if they have the endurance, going from one office to another trying to learn their fate.

Occasionally they are illegally charged exorbitant fees for forms they must fill out; when there is a change of law they may have to start from the beginning again. The maximum period for a decision usually becomes the minimum and then, even if a returnee receives a favorable decision, evictions almost never happen.[28]

In addition to all these problems, returning home may place refugees and displaced persons in the traumatic situation of having to encounter and deal with the very people responsible for their plight. They may have to face neighbors who actively participated in their persecution, or who witnessed it and did nothing. Some returning people may meet the torturers and murderers of their family members in the streets and shops. Women may encounter their rapists. For all returning persons, there is sure to be a heavy weight of bitter memories of expulsion, fear, and flight. Rezak Hukanovic reflected upon such feelings in his memoir of survival in the death camp of Omarska:

> I am only one of many whose eyes beheld unrelenting misery every day, whose entrails faced their incandescent barrels, whose skin was flayed by their truncheons.
> I am only one of many who still carries this heaviest of burdens wedged into the furthest reaches of my heart, these horrid scars, hoping that, in time, they will be rooted out and fade.[29]

Given the array of problems facing returning people, one might wonder why anyone even makes the attempt to go back. One reason is the profound attachment many Bosnians feel for their own homes and their villages, towns, or cities. They miss the particular place lost, and do not want to live anywhere else. And for many people, return is a moral imperative as well as a legal right. As Amnesty International found:

> As long as territories within Bosnia-Herzegovina remain ethnically exclusive the region will remain unstable, since victims of the war who were forcibly expelled from their homes are likely to dwell upon that injustice. This sentiment was clearly expressed to Amnesty International delegates by numerous displaced people in Bosnia-Herzegovina who see return to their homes of origin as a moral right which extends beyond any formal guarantees given in the Peace Agreement. Some spokespersons within displaced

communities stated that if they are not able to return to their homes peacefully they will do so in the long-term by retaking the area by force. Experience from other regions has shown that the urge to return home will not dissipate over time, and that future generations are likely to inherit the desire to right perceived wrongs.[30]

Kozarac

To us, Kozarac is beautiful, even if it is ruined. Your fathers may be gone. But you still have Kozarac. Go home; your fathers have paid the price of that home with their blood.
There will be no peace in our hearts as long as one displaced person who wants to return is not allowed to go home. And we must know where the bones of our beloved are so that we can rebury them.
I have been living in Kozarac for six months and I feel born again. I have lost six kilograms because I am enjoying life so much. I hope you feel at home in my, and now your, Kozarac.[31]

The remainder of this paper describes the expulsion of the Muslim population of the town of Kozarac in 1992, and the efforts of survivors to return and rebuild their city. The events that occurred in and near Kozarac in the spring and summer of 1992 are incomprehensible in their calculated brutality. The attack on the people of Kozarac was "one of the most vicious campaigns of civilian slaughter in the entire war."[32] According to Michael Scharf, Kozarac was "among the most abhorrent cases of 'ethnic cleansing.' Muslim women were herded into schools and warehouses and raped repeatedly. Those Muslim men who were not executed on the spot were taken to Serb-run concentration camps, which served as central locations to terrorize individuals and intimidate the entire target population."[33] Scharf reports that of Kozarac's Muslim residents, 2,000 were killed in the shelling of the town and another 5,000 were executed after the town's surrender. "The others were taken to the local concentration camps: Trnopolje, where rape was an evening sport; Keraterm, where several hundred men were machine-gunned in a single night; and Omarska, which became known as a 'death camp'."[34]

Kozarac lies between Prijedor and Banja Luka, in northwest Bosnia. Politically, it is part of *općina*[35] Prijedor. The area known as Kozarac contains the town of Kozarac and the villages of Kozarusa, Kevljeni, Kamicani, and Jakupovic.[36] In 1992, it was a town of some 25,000 people; the great majority (approximately 90 percent) were Muslim.[37] It must have been a beautiful town before its destruction. Even in its ruins one can catch glimpses of fine architectural detail and the attractive layout of the town square and streets.

The following is a chronology of events relating to the attack on the citizens of Kozarac in 1992. The information is taken from a thorough report by *The Washington Post*.[38]

Expulsion from Kozarac:

April 30, 1992	Serbs in Prijedor took over city government. They removed the democratically-elected mayor and police chief and replaced them with extremist Serbs. Roadblocks were set up in Prijedor.
May 9, 1992	Serbs gave Muslim leaders in Kozarac seven days to a sign loyalty oath or be considered a "paramilitary terrorist organization."
May 14, 1992	Phone service in Kozarac was cut and roadblocks put up. The town was sealed off.
May 16, 1992	A tank arrived in Kozarac. There were convoys on the highway and Serb military mobilization.
May 24, 1992	1:00 p.m. Residents were told to get out by 6:00 p.m. 2:12 p.m. Shelling began from 12 directions. 3:45 p.m. Radio announced a half-hour pause in shelling, but shelling resumed in 15 minutes.
May 25, 1992	People fled from the town while shelling continued. Many civilians were killed while fleeing.
May 26, 1992	All attempts at resistance ended. Civilians were ordered to go to the football field, and about 4,000 gathered there. The shelling continued. Community leaders were identified and separated. Some were killed on the spot; others disappeared; others were taken to concentration camps.

June 9, 1992	Hundreds of Kozarac refugees arrived in Banja Luka in sealed cattle cars on their way to a Muslim area. Serb guards refused them water.
June–July, 1992	Looting and killings continued in a more chaotic manner. Many residents of Kozarac were detained in concentration camps at Omarska, Keraterm, and Trnopolje.
November 1992	A *Washington Post* reporter visited Kozarac and found, "the ruins of Kozarac are still sealed, guarded by heavily armed and hostile Serb soldiers."

It is difficult to overstate the extent of the destruction that occurred in Kozarac. Mary Battiata saw "mile after mile of scorched buildings, collapsed red-tile roofs, and houses reduced to shoulder-high piles of rubble" when she visited in late 1992.[39] Several years later, Michael Scharf described Kozarac as a "ghost town. One visiting reporter described the scene as 'a roadside attraction from hell.' ... it is now just a collection of burned-out and dynamited houses straddling a highway."[40] When I drove through the town in July of 1996, the only sign of life in the Muslim section was a stray cat hunting in the ruins. Every house had been systematically destroyed. The mosque was in ruins and its minaret lay broken in the weeds. In the Serb part of the town, on the other hand, a football game was under way, meat roasted on spits, and people met in coffee houses and bars, while a block away the ruined homes of their former neighbors stood as testimony to the terrible crimes committed in Kozarac.

The destruction of Kozarac was not due to some sudden popular upsurge of ethnic hatred.[41] It was "clinical, calculated and comprehensive,"[42] and was done for political gain. In 1990, Bosnia had held its first post-Communist elections. In the Prijedor area, Muslims were the most numerous group by a slight margin, and their party won the election. The new mayor of Prijedor was Muslim, as were the police chief and many other officials of the općina government. Serbian nationalists determined to change the demographics of the area by forcibly expelling non-Serbs, thus ensuring that they could win future elections.[43] The use of extreme cruelty and terror in the campaign of expulsion was clearly meant to ensure that survivors would be too afraid and sickened to return.

The extremists' goals were not entirely met, despite the decimation of Kozarac and other Muslim areas of općina Prijedor. The goal of ensuring elected Serb officials by having an all-Serb electorate was undercut by the Dayton Agreements, which specified that people would vote based on their location before the conflict. Currently, the deputy mayor of Prijedor is Muslim despite the fact that almost no Muslims live in Prijedor. And the attempt to keep people from returning has been undermined by the tremendous courage of the survivors and their great desire to come home.

Efforts to return to Kozarac:

May 1996	A group of Muslim women attempted to enter Kozarac to plant a tree of peace. They were met by a mob of stone-throwing Serbs and forced to turn back.[44]
1997	Refugees tried again to return, this time accompanied by a large SFOR contingent. They were met by a hostile crowd, and turned back.[45]
Summer 1998	Hundreds of refugees returned together to begin cleaning up the town and their houses. German reconstruction organization began rebuilding houses.
May 1999	A women's peace conference was organized in Kozarac by Screm do Mira. Rebuilding continued. Lippman reports, "obvious progress has been made since I was first in Kozarac a year ago. Then, all was wreckage .... Now, there is much reconstruction activity, and the Muslims who have returned to their town stroll the main street."[46]

In the summer of 1998, it finally became possible for Muslim refugees and displaced persons to return to Kozarac to begin the long process of repairing the houses and other buildings of the city. A group of Kozarac's expelled residents had worked with extraordinary bravery and determination to open the city to returns. As Emsuda Mujagic, one of their leaders, said, "A year and a half ago, the idea of returning to Kozarac wasn't even in people's dreams, and now it's a free town." I was part of an international group[47] that worked in the area for a period of several weeks in the summers of 1998 and 1999.[48]

Kozarac was still in ruins in July and August of 1998, but seemed a different place from the eerily silent and deserted city I had seen two years before. We joined hundreds of people in cleaning the public spaces of the town. Men and women with rakes, shovels, and brooms began the formidable task of reclaiming their shattered city. Children and teenagers carried water, soda, and juice to the workers. Backhoes moved large heaps of trash and broken masonry. We raked and cut back six years' growth of weeds and underbrush along the main street, and swept the sidewalks and steps of ruined buildings.

When the public areas had been cleared, we joined families working on their own houses. We raked through the ruins, finding haunting reminders of people's lives before the genocide—torn, scorched pages of books and newspapers, tarnished silverware, bits of half melted glass, twisted bedsprings, fragments of broken china. We Americans were able to grasp only dimly the magnitude of the loss and the horror of what had happened in Kozarac, but at the end of the day of work, we understood much more than we had before.

After hours of work, we all met in the town square, and ate a huge lunch. This was a happy time, and the square was full of laughter and music, much as it must have been before the war. There was a sense of victory in simply being there, where Muslims had not been able to go for the previous six years. But the joy of return was mixed with a sense of all that had been lost, and with new grief at the recent discovery of a mass grave holding some 60 bodies.

It is important that internationals be involved in the return process in Bosnia. One reason is as an acknowledgment of the dismal failure of internationals to protect the residents of Kozarac from aggression in 1992. International organizations had been in the area, but left shortly before the attack. The UNHCR left the area after Serbs hijacked its buses; the International Red Cross and European Community teams also pulled out because of fears for their safety.[49] As one woman who survived confinement in the Trnopolje camp, interviewed while her husband and two brothers were still in Omarska, said, "I must ask you where the world is."[50]

Another reason it is important for internationals to be involved is that we need to learn the scope of the destruction in a deeper way than is possible by reading books and looking at television pictures. An afternoon spent doing backbreaking labor in the blazing sun, and accomplishing only the partial clearing of one room of one house in one town gives an unmatchable sense of the extent of what was done and of the task of reconstruction.

Finally, the presence of internationals may to a small degree lend the returning persons some safety from harassment and violence, especially in the first tense attempts to come back and to rebuild. While we were in Kozarac in 1998, several truckloads of Serb soldiers drove through the town, giving the three fingered Serb salute, and observing us with considerable hostility. The presence of international witnesses may serve as a buffer to prevent such hostility from escalating to attack.

Conclusion

Returning to one's town, rebuilding one's home, and reclaiming one's community are some of the few ways in which people can start to undo the damage of the war. Although repaired buildings and cities never fully replace those that were destroyed, at least the visible evidence of renewal sends a message to everyone—other victims, bystanders, and perpetrators—that those who were expelled have not been defeated. For these reasons, as well as for the very practical reasons of providing shelter and stability, return and rebuilding programs are at the center of efforts to strengthen Bosnian society and democracy.

Notes

*   This work was supported in part by a grant from The University of Memphis Faculty Research Grant Fund. This support does not necessarily imply endorsement by the University of research conclusions.

1   This is a quotation from a young refugee interviewed by Ines Prica and Maja Povrzanović, in "Narratives of Refugee Children as the Ethnography of Maturing," in *War, Exile, Everyday Life*, Renata Jambresić Kirin and Maja Povrzanović (ed.), (Zagreb: Institute of Ethnology and Folklore Research, 1996), p. 106.

2   Several excellent books have detailed the background of the genocide, the means by which it was carried out, and how the U.N. and the great powers of the world failed to intervene effectively, e.g., Norman Cigar, *Genocide in Bosnia: The Policy of "Ethnic Cleansing"* (College Station, TX: Texas A&M University Press, 1995); Roy Guttman, *A Witness to Genocide* (New York: Macmillan Publishing Company, 1993); David Rieff, *Slaughterhouse: Bosnia and the Failure of the West* (New York: Simon & Schuster, 1995); Laura Silber and Allan Little, *The Death of*

Yugoslavia (London: Penguin, 1995).
3   Human Rights Watch/Helsinki, "Bosnia-Hercegovina: The Fall of Srebrenica and the Failure of U.N. Peacekeeping," (October 1995), p. 5.
4   Marcus Cox, "The Right to Return Home: International Intervention and Ethnic Cleansing in Bosnia and Herzegovina," *International and Comparative Law Quarterly* 47 (1998), pp. 620–21.
5   For a thorough review of problems with the implementation of the Dayton Accords, see International Crisis Group, "Is Dayton Failing? Bosnia Four Years After the Peace Agreement," (October 28, 1999), available at: http://www.crisisweb.org.
6   Amnesty International, "Bosnia-Herzegovina. All the Way Home: Safe 'Minority Returns' as a Just Remedy and for a Secure Future," (1998), available at: http://www.amnesty.org/ailib/aipub/1998/EUR/46300298.htm.
7   David L. Bosco, "Reintegrating Bosnia: A Progress Report," *The Washington Quarterly* 21 (1998), p. 65.
8   Annex 4 is the Constitution of Bosnia and Herzegovina.
9   Cox, "The Right to Return Home," p. 606.
10 *Ibid*, pp. 604–5.
11 *Ibid*, p. 605.
12 *Ibid*, p. 612.
13 *Ibid*, p. 613.
14 *Ibid*, p. 614.
15 Socially-owned property consisted of apartments given to workers by their employers. These apartments could be held for life, and inherited, but they could not be sold or sublet. Socially-owned apartments constitute about 20 percent of Bosnia's housing. Cox, "The Right to Return Home," p. 613.
16 Bosco, "Reintegrating Bosnia," p. 70.
17 International Crisis Group, "The Balkan Refugee Crisis: Regional and Long-term Perspectives," (June 1, 1999), available at: http://www.crisisweb.org.
18 Amnesty International, "Annual Report 1999," (1999), available at: http://www.amnesty.org/ailib/Aireport/ar99/eur63.htm.
19 Targeted aid has been criticized as little more than a form of bribery to try to induce officials to do what they are already obligated under law to do. See International Crisis Group, "Preventing Minority Return in Bosnia and Herzegovina: The Anatomy of Hate and Fear," (August 10, 1999), available at: http://www.crisisweb.org/projects/bosnia/reports/bh50main.htm,.
20 United Nations High Commissioner for Refugees, *Bosnia and Herzegovina: Repatriation and Return, Operation 1998* (Geneva: UNHCR, December 17, 1997), p. 18.
21 Human Rights Watch, "Human Rights Watch World Report 1999: Bosnia and Hercegovina," (1999), available at: http://www.hrw.org.
22 The Reconstruction and Return Task Force is mandated by the High Representative to coordinate international support for refugee return and to apply pressure to local authorities. International Crisis Group, "Preventing Minority Return in Bosnia and Herzegovina."
23 Human Rights Watch, "World Report 1999."
24 International Crisis Group, "Is Dayton Failing?"
25 United Nations High Commissioner for Refugees, *Bosnia and Herzegovina*, p. 1.

26	Human Rights Watch, "World Report 1999."
27	Amnesty International, "Annual Report 1999."
28	Peter Lippman, "On the Record: Your Independent Link to the Refugees of Bosnia," (1999), available at: *The Advocacy Project*, http://www.advocacynet.org. See also cases described in International Crisis Group, "Denied Justice: Individuals Lost in a Legal Maze," (February 23, 2000), available at: http://www.crisisweb.org.
29	Rezak Hukanovic, *The Tenth Circle of Hell: A Memoir of Life in the Death Camps of Bosnia* (New York: Basic Books, 1996), pp. 163–4. For other accounts of survivors' memories, see Stevan M. Weine, *When History is a Nightmare* (Rutgers: Rutgers University Press, 1999).
30	Amnesty International, "All the Way Home."
31	These quotations are from refugees attending a conference in Kozarac in May 1999, as reported by Peter Lippman, "On the Record."
32	Peter Maass, *Love Thy Neighbor: A Story of War* (New York: Alfred A. Knopf, 1996), p. 38.
33	Michael P. Scharf, *Balkan Justice: The Story Behind the First International War Crimes Tribunal since Nuremberg* (Durham, NC: Carolina Academic Press, 1997), p. 29.
34	*Ibid*, p. 95.
35	An općina is a political unit including a municipality and surrounding district.
36	Ian Traynor, "How They Wiped out Kozarac," *The Guardian*, October 17 1992.
37	*Ibid*.
38	Mary Battiata, "A Town's Bloody 'Cleansing,'" *The Washington Post*, November 2 1992.
39	*Ibid*.
40	Scharf, *Balkan Justice*, p. 95.
41	Several excellent recent histories of Bosnia lay to rest the "ancient ethnic hatred" explanation of the Bosnian conflict so popular among Western politicians and reporters for the mass media. See Robert J. Donia and John V.A. Fine, Jr., *Bosnia and Hercegovina: A Tradition Betrayed* (New York: Columbia University Press, 1994); Noel Malcolm, *Bosnia: A Short History* (New York: New York University Press, 1994); Mark Pinson (ed.), *The Muslims of Bosnia-Herzegovina: Their Historic Development from the Middle Ages to the Dissolution of Yugoslavia* (Cambridge, Mass.: Harvard University Press, 1993). One of the hardest things for outsiders to grasp about Bosnia is the intimacy of the people divided by the conflict. Even when we have managed to get beyond "ancient ethnic hatreds," it comes as a surprise to learn how well people knew each other, how thoroughly their lives were intertwined, and how many things drew them together. Scholars have tried to understand the extremes of violence by looking at variables such as depersonalization, bureaucratic efficiency, the emotional and even physical separation of the victim from the killer; e.g. Herbert C. Kelman, "Violence without Moral Restraint: Reflections on the Dehumanization of Victims and Victimizers," *Journal of Social Issues* 29 (1973), pp. 25–61. While these explanations are probably valid for some situations, they do not fit what happened in Bosnia. The genocide in Bosnia was perpetrated against colleagues, neighbors, friends, and even family members.
42	Traynor, "How They Wiped out Kozarac," p. 23.

43 *Ibid.*
44 "Serbian Mob Stones Muslim Women's Bus," *Los Angeles Times*, May 28 1996.
45 Lippman, "On the Record."
46 *Ibid.*
47 The Fellowship of Reconciliation is an international group founded before World War I. During the Bosnian conflict, the Fellowship began a program to bring high school and college students out of Bosnia and provide them with homes and educations in the U.S. The purpose was not only to provide safety for the students, but to allow them to continue their educations during the war so that they could come back to Bosnia and assist in rebuilding when the war ended. Over 150 students were brought to America by this program, and their success in American schools was outstanding. After the Dayton Peace Agreement, the Fellowship of Reconciliation continued its concern with Bosnia by sponsoring workcamps allowing Americans to come to Bosnia for short periods of time and work on reconstruction and English teaching projects. The 1998 and 1999 summer workcamps assisted in Kozarac.
48 Dolores Gunter, "Women Reconcilers in Bosnia," *Fellowship* (November/December 1998), pp. 27–28; Doug Hostetter, "Ethnic Cleansing Cleansed," *Fellowship* (September/October 1998), p. 27; E. Tabakovic, "Bosanci Su Odlicni Studenti," in *Unsko Novine Sanske*, August 7 1998.
49 Traynor, "How They Wiped out Kozarac," p. 23; Battiata, "A Town's Bloody 'Cleansing,'" p. A1.
50 Blaine Harden, "The Yugoslav Gulag: Days in the Life of Bosnian Inmates," *The Washington Post*, August 7 1992.

11 Women in Between: "Where do I belong?"*

ENIDA DELALIĆ

> And even if hope transcends horizons only after they have been substantially broadened by the knowledge of reality gained through practice, it is still through hope alone that one can attain an understanding of the world that is not only inspiring and consoling, but also more solid and potentially concrete than any other.
>
> Ernst Bloch[1]

For people who have become refugees, hope was and is often the only thing that inspires them to take steps that might lead to something better. Even those who have been able to relocate to other European countries have been and continue to be forced to return or move elsewhere, without any consideration of the political and economic situation in their countries of origin. This is particularly true in the Federal Republic of Germany. The following statement made by a Bosnian refugee summarizes Germany's unclear and restrictive policies so well that further elaboration is hardly necessary: "I haven't been in Germany for seven years, but rather twenty-eight times for three months each. That is something different".[2]

This quotation seems to me to demonstrate three things. First, it shows how refugees are handled at the administrative and political level in Germany.[3] It also presents a different picture of refugee life than the one commonly presented in public here: the prejudice that refugees "are doing just fine". Refugees experience this "perception through the other" in both their host and their home countries. They see themselves not as refugees but as exiles. I, too, prefer and will use the terms "forced migration" or "expulsion". Refugees do not want to live as official minorities at home, because then they would not really be at home at all, insofar as being a minority would determine their status, rights and future opportunities.

There is little understanding for this sentiment in either their host or their home countries. The third thing the quotation conveys is an internal view of the world that refugees experience. Internal and external conditions diverge for them in extremes that are hardly bearable.

This is what I would like to discuss here, namely, the internal views of a special group of people who have fled, and who have become members of the category "single mothers" as a result of the war. Women, who represent a majority of the population but nonetheless a minority in society, suffered in many different ways during the war. Everything they experienced and suffered is still so present that it is taboo to discuss inner feelings, particularly at a time when they are still struggling to satisfy their most basic needs, such as getting enough to eat and finding work and a place to live. For this reason it was and is my intention to encourage discussion between different groups about their subjective viewpoints and personal experiences.

In what follows I will introduce, with an anthropologist's perspective and methods, a group of women whose lives have been in limbo since the war began. They themselves describe this state of limbo as a life neither in "heaven nor on the earth, neither in paradise nor in hell, neither at home nor in a foreign place, neither love nor hate, neither rage nor mourning and neither mother nor wife".[4] But it is all of these at once. This article is based on life stories that were told and recorded in the context of the empirical research I conducted with these women, using the methods of "empathetic observation".[5] I would like to emphasize, however, that empathetic observation should be understood here more as accompanying one another during the day than as friendship that developed through years of cooperative work. The process of developing mutual understanding allowed both partners (each woman and myself) to learn new things about and from one other.[6] Hope was the word used most often in our conversations, when we talked about the future. As became evident, hope is a resource from which one can draw strength. In the ambiguous, unclear and invisible space called the future, hope defines the horizon between the present and a future extending indefinitely. But this horizon has still to be placed on solid ground.

I view the lives of these women as a being in a state of transition leading from one spatial, temporal and social situation to another, or, as I would like to put it for this article, "from a frozen past to an imagined future".[7] Theirs was a past that was cut off from an imagined future by the sudden incursion of a catastrophe boding chaos. Their future must first be recovered under new conditions and through extreme experiences, which could be called traumatic. The contradictions between an abruptly foreclosed past and an uncertain future cannot simply be smoothed over, for they relate to one another like the components of a collage, in which the ruptures are not concealed and the parts cannot simply be replaced. But it is precisely these visible ruptures that provide the creative and innovative space in which the power of the available resource, *hope,* can develop. Through the opposition of the individual parts, a clear structure comes into view. These "open spaces" point beyond the past and the present to a model of the future that makes it possible live in the space-in-between.[8] In order to view these women in their unstable situation (from their marginalized perspective and their position of weakness) and in this way finally to approach the positive aspect of "liminality," the progressive unfolding of their lives, one needs a model that is capable of grasping the dynamic elements of their lives, particularly the spatial, temporal and social transgression of boundaries.

Methodological Consideration: Liminality as Innovation

It was the British anthropologist Victor W. Turner[9] who appropriated the structural scheme of the rites of passage from Arnold van Gennep and developed it further. Van Gennep was concerned with the spatial, temporal and social passages such as birth, initiation, marriage and death. He described society as "a house with different rooms and floors,"[10] composed of many social groups that are clearly differentiated from one another. Each of the passages, which in a way represent ruptures and crises in the process of social development, are presented in the form of a three-phase structure. The first phase, in which one is separated from an earlier place, time or situation, is followed by a border or transformative phase, in which the person or group is located in two worlds at once. The process comes to an end with the integration phase, in which the person or group integrates into their new surroundings or is reintegrated into the order they inherited.[11]

According to Turner, the second of the three phases—"liminality," during which the transformation takes place—is the most important. It is the "turning point of the transformation". Using the example of an initiation ritual that places much emphasis on the transformation phase while also retaining a certain amount of independence, he analyzes the defining characteristics of this phase: unstructured, ambiguous and paradoxical. The neophytes experience a crisis of identity during this phase. They are neither male nor female, neither dead nor alive, neither human nor animal, neither the old nor the new. On the other hand, they are all of these things at the same time. They can be compared to passengers and travelers.

This condition of liminality has both positive and negative aspects. The negative aspects are represented by death: decomposition and complete dissolution. Those engaged in the transgression of boundaries become structurally invisible, ritually impure, spatially set apart, naked and without possessions. They demonstrate no status, property, or insignia that would differentiate them from their group. They have no names; their familial relations have dissolved. They are reduced and leveled. They are bound to one another by "*communitas*," a feeling of equality, solidarity and spontaneity. This community brings with it other positive aspects as well, such as the state of becoming or of not yet being classified, which also suggests an analogy to pregnancy, birth and growth. Liminality characterizes the sphere of pure possibilities. Those transcending boundaries [*Grenzgänger*] are betwixt and between. Because of this condition, their marginality, their social distance and their isolation, they develop a consciousness that is interpretive, reflexive and critical. Those transcending boundaries, like outsiders, view the traditional order from a different perspective, which makes them potential agents and protagonists of innovation and change.[12]

"I'm living neither in heaven nor on the earth. Do you know what that's like?" The Stages of Spatial, Temporal and Social Passages

The following analytical treatment of these women's life stories draws upon the model outlined above, particularly with respect to spatial, temporal and social passages. The slow process of extricating oneself from a situation of undifferentiated chaos and developing a new model for one's own life, under a given set of external conditions and using one's own individual abilities, will be depicted in the foreground. To this end I will divide the relevant segment of these women's lives—from the beginning of the war up to the present—into seven different parts. This should clarify the process of gradual separation and change that takes place during this time.

But first let me offer a brief description of the women and a few statistics about them, in order to provide at least some superficial characterization and orientation. They arrived in Germany in 1994 as a contingent under the auspices of the *Frauen, Opfer des Krieges* (Women, the Victims of War) project. They are all Muslim women from the territory that is today the Republika Srpska. They came from small towns or village communities. They were either housewives or worked part-time. When the war began, they were between 25 and 30 years old. They had either just married or had been married for only a few years. They had children, usually between one and three in number. They were occupied above all with establishing their own homes, which they were building at the time or had already begun to furnish. Some were still living in their in-laws' homes, or nearby.[13] Thus, they were already going through a passage at the time; they were entering a new phase in their lives.

First Step: Outbreak of the Catastrophe

> One knew about it already, but I didn't think about it.

The outbreak of war, or, as I call it, the "catastrophe," broke into everyday life suddenly and without any forewarning. This is where separation from the men first took place: they were either transported to camps or attempting to flee—without, however, ever coming back. This was the beginning of a ghetto-like life: people lost their jobs, were isolated in their villages or were transported to Serbian camps. No one knew for certain what would happen next. It seemed unbelievable and everyone hoped that by tomorrow everything would return to normal.

> When he said that I should take care of the children, I realized that the end had come. I told myself that we would probably never see each other again.

Second Step: The Expulsion

> We spent the night sitting under a cliff and watched as the village burned down.

At this point the women had to leave behind their houses, villages, cities, camps, the region and the country. Like a large wave, or a surging river, they began their voyage accompanied by all the other deportees and by those relatives and children who had remained. They were either transported by bus or they had to reach the Croatian border by foot, where they were housed in temporary camps in or nearby Zagreb.

> I took my children and went to this camp. There we had something to eat.

Third Step: The Category Single Mother

> It was absolute chaos, chaos in the barracks...it was a madhouse.

The "Women, Victims of War" project made it possible for single women with children, whose husbands were dead or missing, to seek refuge in Germany. For the women this meant an additional separation from their relatives by marriage (usually their parents-in-law) and other family members as well as an abandonment of their "familiar old home" (the former Yugoslavia). Together with unfamiliar women in the same situation, they were taken by bus to various relocation sites. They were traveling to a strange new place which held the hope of something better, or at least allowed them to escape from chaos.

> When the first group of women went to Germany, they included me in this group as well.

Fourth Step: Arrival in the Federal Republic of Germany

> I saw that I had a room, peace, a refrigerator and water in my room and everything that we didn't have there. In Croatia all you did was wander around.

The new life in communal quarters that was made available to these women led to further ghettoization and serious personal crises. They lived in a compound that offered peace and protection, but they were cut off from the rest of the world and stigmatized as refugees. They had managed to escape from the greater mass of those fleeing, but they were now reduced to a small, specific group who were damned to doing nothing. They were waiting for something, but they did not know what. Their inactivity led to a condition of torpor. There was no present and no future, only the immediate past, which repeated itself and continued to exist through the daily exchange of stories about the events. Their days and nights passed, filled with the images of what they had just experienced, the uncertainty about the further course of their lives and the despair of being unable to help themselves or their friends and family.

> I can't reconcile myself, not in the least, with having to live here, for who knows how many more years, in this compound, in a single room.

Fifth Step: The Decentralization

> We are in a situation in which we have to start from the beginning, to the extent that it is possible.

After a certain period of orientation in their new socio-cultural environment, an extensive network of relations developed (with the locals, other refugees, and the translators who were employed there along with the social workers), which provided the women access to a wealth of information, including that concerning the legal options of refugees. The need for a "normal life" led to frustration and depression over their current living situation. They were also confronted with an administrative apparatus that was against their moving into apartments of their own, and did what it could to prevent this. After a self-initiated survey among the women, they decided (despite a minority who were opposed to the plan) to seek a way to move into their own apartments. After lengthy discussion with the responsible administrators, they were finally "given permission" to move into private apartments.

> I am satisfied. After the war, flight, Croatia and communal living, things are better now.

Sixth Step: Dispersal

> If I could find a job, lead a normal life, feed my children and pay for my apartment and my living costs, I would be satisfied.

The women quickly dispersed from the compound into their own apartments. Suddenly they had a life once again: taking care of their apartments, personalizing their furnishings, and taking their children to school or kindergarten. Their lives attained a certain "normality" that corresponded to that of their fellow citizens. But the community of single mothers that had come into being through force did not fall apart, either. With the dissolution of the necessity for communal living, the relations between the women became less strained. The women were able to help one another, and important information was immediately shared and passed along. The fact that the women had now divided up into smaller, more intimate friendships did not detract from the ties binding the larger group of single mothers together. The distance that they had gained from one another actually stabilized the group as a whole.

> We hear from and see each other on a regular basis. We help each other.

Seventh Step: Still Undecided

> You can't think about the next two years, five years, about the future right now.

The women still have the special, protected status of traumatized persons, which, for the time being, prevents them from being deported from Germany. But the duration of their stay is limited, as is their freedom of movement, and their right to work has not been defined in exact legal terms either. Those who have decided to stay in Germany have at present only a limited right to work. The women perceive their dependence upon the state as a limitation of their right to the self-determination of their personal lives. The independence they have gained offers new prospects for the future, but they still do not know what the next year will bring.

> If there was no hope, I really don't know how one could live, you understand?

Hope as Resource

The seventh step is not the last in this process of changes, which has now already lasted eight years. Three of my interview partners have found ways out of this state of limbo. They could no longer cope with the existing uncertainties in Germany, such as their residence rights and other important conditions that directly affected their lives. One opted to emigrate further, although this also meant reintegration with her family (brother and mother) who had already emigrated to the United States. Another of my interview partners married a German man, which signified an important step toward integration into her new socio-cultural surroundings. The third interview partner chose to return to her sister and her family in Bosnia and Herzegovina. Further emigration, marriage and return all represent the third passage, or integration phase, in van Genneps' construction. Old or new social ties are (re)established, either in the old or in the new surroundings, even though the social ties and the new cultural spaces may be old and new at the same time.

Those among my interview partners who decided to stay in Germany opted to continue their state of limbo. Their future will remain uncertain for an unknown period of time. I believe that the women entered the transformation phase, or liminality, as defined by Victor Turner, with the incursion of the catastrophe—when the war began. The first three steps that I outlined signify their departure from the old world: separation from their husbands, their relatives, and finally the gradual separation from their familiar socio-geographic and cultural surroundings. The fourth, fifth and sixth steps are characterized by the gradual growth of *"communitas"* in a new space, which the women experience in the form of solidarity and spontaneity. The seventh step already points in the direction of further restructuring.

Each of the seven steps is unstructured and paradoxical; everything occurs unexpectedly and spontaneously. The occurrence of the next event cannot be predicted, either with respect to its form or its timing, for life can be planned only a few months in advance. Nevertheless, they remain in the state of limbo, which is also a realm of pure possibilities within liminality, and which still contains an expectation of becoming and change. The women in the seventh step are still marginalized and isolated, and distant socially from their surroundings, both in their home and host countries. For them, staying in Germany despite the uncertain living situation also means remaining near to their former homeland. Even if they are not living there now, they have the possibility to return one day. "Returning to Bosnia simply appeals to me. That's where my people are; they speak my language and have my mentality". They would like to buy a house or an apartment, but they do not know where, since for the time being they cannot return to the areas where they used to live.

The myth of return[14] is placed in both a spatially and temporally indeterminate future. Since the old order collapsed and a condition of chaos arose, the present remains unordered and uncertain: the women exist in the margins of both their old (home country) and their new (host country) worlds. They have not anchored themselves in yet. But liminality, being betwixt and between, is precisely the condition in which creation of the new occurs. In this process imagination is a constant that expresses alienation but also symbolizes the power of creation. Hope, the human source of inspiration, lies in the imagination. The open structure of liminality provides the imagination with the necessary space for pure possibility, where the potential protagonists of change and innovation can act.[15]

Notes

* Translated from the German by John Abromeit.
1 Ernst Bloch, *Das Prinzip Hoffnung*, Vol. 5 (Frankfurt: Suhrkamp, 1998), p. 1618.
2 FATRA e.v. (*Frankfurter Arbeitskreis für Trauma und Exil*–Frankfurt Working Group for Trauma and Exile): "Appel für die Anwendung der Genfer Flüchtlingskonvention und ein Bleiberecht für traumatisierte Flüchtlinge aus Bosnien und Herzegowina," published in *Frankfurter Rundschau*, November 9, 1999.
3 Marie Rössel-Cunovic, "Kurz-Therapien für Flüchtlinge mit befristeter Duldung? Die Auswirkungen des Ausländerrechts auf die psychotherapeutische Behandlung traumatisierter Flüchtlinge," in *Jahrbuch Menschenrechte 2000* (Frankfurt: Suhrkamp, 1999).
4 This quote and those that follow are excerpts from these women's biographies. To maintain the anonymity of the women, I will not include any of their names.
5 Bronislaw Malinowski, *Argonauten des Westlichen Pazifik* (Frankfurt: Syndikat 1994).
6 See Edith Wolber, "Du hältst mir die Schlüssel hin, die Türen zu öffnen..," in *Eine Begegnung zwischen einer Ethnologin und Frauen mit einer Körperbehinderung* (Berlin: Verlag für Wissenschaft und Bildung, 1996).
7 Compare with the following statement by Dabag Mihran: "The concept of catastrophe approximates only imperfectly that which the Armenian term *Aghet* describes: not the situation of catastrophe, but a catastrophic situation. This is a situation that is not past and that forecloses the future. This is a situation in which going back and overcoming both seem impossible". See "Katastrophe und Identität," in *Erlebnis – Gedächtnis – Sinn: Authentische und konstruierte Erinnerung,* Hanno Loewy and Bernhard Moltmann (ed.), (Frankfurt and New York: Campus Verlag, 1996), p. 177 - 235.
8 Enida Delalić, *Der Spielraum des Mythos*, unpublished M.A. Thesis (Frankfurt: 1994).
9 Victor Turner, *Das Ritual: Struktur und Anti-Struktur* (Frankfurt and New York: Campus Verlag, 1989).
10 Arnold van Gennep, *Übergangsriten* (Frankfurt and New York: Campus Verlag, 1986).
11 See Sylvia M. Schomburg-Scherff, *Die Spinne im Herrenhaus: Karibische Romane als Identitätserzählungen. Eine Anthropologische Perspektive* (Berlin: Dietrich Reimer, 1999), pp. 47–55.
12 See Sylvia M. Schomburg-Scherff; Victor Turner, "Betwixt and Between: The Liminal Period in Rites de Passage," in *Symposium on New Approaches to the Study of Religion,* Proceedings of the American Ethnological Society, June Helm (ed.), (New York : AMS Press, 1994), pp. 4–20.
13 Tone Bringa, *Being a Muslim the Bosnian Way. Identity and Community in a Central Bosnian Village* (Princeton: Princeton University Press, 1995).

14 See Beate Steinhilber, *Grenzüberschreitungen: Remigration und Biographie – Frauen kehren zurück in die Türkei* (Tübingen: Verlag für Interkulturelle Kommunikation, 1994).
15 See Vera Saller, "Die Bedeutung des Kulturbegriffs für psychoanalytische Therapien," in *Kultur, Migration, Psychoanalyse,* Fernanda Pedrina (ed.) (Tübingen: Edition Diskord, 1999), pp. 105–7; Cornelius Castoriadis, *Gesellschaft als imaginäre Institution* (Frankfurt: Suhrkamp, 1984); Zygmunt Baumann, *Moderne und Ambivalenz: Das Ende der Eindeutigkeit* (Frankfurt: Fischer, 1991).

12 Restructuring Regions: The Case of Croatia

SLOBODAN BJELAJAC

This paper has two main starting assumptions. The first one is a known tenet of regional theory. It states that the region is a dependent as well as an independent variable of the central city.[1] The second one states that regionalism in practice can be defined by scientific as well as by non-scientific criteria. Regionalism is very important part of the overall system, since, just as relations between the central city and the region are frequent and complementary, so too are those between the region and the central government. Therefore, creating regions is not just a question of free will, but demands scientific research.

Although the first approach is more complicated, it is also less expensive and more functional for the needs of regions and of society as a whole. The second approach is much easier, but it could cause functional problems for regions and for society as a whole.

Societies with democratic traditions tend to use the first approach, and therefore they are more flexible and open to form international regional relationships. By contrast, societies with non-democratic traditions, since they have unified attitudes in their parliaments, mostly use the second approach, and therefore remain less flexible and closed toward international regionalism. The centralized political decision making of the previous societies has no scientific criteria, but relies on the political will of the governing party as its main criterion.

The term "region" originates from the Latin *regio, regionis* and means a certain territory with numerous specific and particular characteristics. It can be defined as a certain administrative as well as economic and natural physical unit, settled by certain social group of people.[2] Since regions have their central cities that organize certain functions for the whole region, the central city must be the biggest settlement with the widest range of functions. However, the rest of the region also offers natural and population resources to the central city. Therefore, the relations between the central city and the region are highly frequent and their relationship is complementary.

The "regiopolis" is a constellation of moderate-sized communities with large open areas linked by roads.[3] It integrates a number of cities, towns, villages and industrial complexes and connects them with the central city. Important changes in economy, employment and population will directly or indirectly produce changes in all other parts of the system.[4]

Alden and Morgan see the region as a homogeneous area polarized through functional interactions around one or more foci of strong social or economic activity. They define the region as a part of the societal planning process that determines the future of the society. The nodal-functional definition describes the region as an open system with flexible borders.[5]

The region is an open area receiving different nodal and functional influences from the city that depend on the intensity of their functional gravitation. Since the region consists of rural as well as urban settlements with their own influential areas, we can consider the region as a relative and hierarchical system with different levels of influence. Therefore, the term "surroundings," meaning a complex of natural and social aspects, together with the active relationships among them, has been very frequently used in place of the term "region." The quality and quantity of communications between a population and its surroundings crucially determine its quality and its relative influential frontiers. Differing from the term "environment," a social and physical radius of interacting biological factors, the term "surroundings" implies everything around it. It is important that humans determine the area by evaluating the surroundings as well as its adequacy for sustaining life. From the anthropological point of view, human needs and human control in eliminating dangers from environment define the surroundings.[6]

"Surroundings" also implies a very active center. A huge number of elements flows to the center and effects its structural changes. Populations commute to the center for jobs, higher levels of trade, education, cultural needs, health care, and even amusements. The center is, therefore, the most attractive area. If the traffic between center and the rest of region is bad, the population of the surroundings tends to immigrate to the center. That effects the center, and also the region. To reduce the pressure, centers must develop systems of smaller centers in order to minimize unwanted changes and to satisfy the human and social needs within the system.

We can divide the notion of region into the macro-, sub- and micro-levels. The macro-regional center is the *nodus* with the widest influence, since it organizes the highest level of functions for the whole macro-region (such as clinics, operas, universities, etc.). The sub-regional center is the *nodus* of a smaller area, and organizes lower level functions (such as hospitals, theaters, faculties, etc.) for smaller parts, or sub-regions, of the macro-region. The micro-regional center is the *nodus* of the smallest area, and organizes local, everyday functions of work, consumption, and cultural, political and administrative character in the so called micro-region.

If the regional system did not consider these basic structural conditions, there would be problems for society and its development as a whole. However, this does not mean that practical political decision making always takes them into consideration. It uses political instead of scientific criteria. The party, or the bureaucracy, of course, can make decision without scientists, especially if two-thirds of parliament consists of a single party. It always has different results than it intends, and it follows the line of social power instead of the line of social functions. It may also seek to satisfy particular interests instead of that of society.

The scientific approach also implies a flexibility of regional size according to social and natural needs. Furthermore, it permits the members of local communities to choose the region to which they want to belong.

At this time, it is especially important for Croatia to implement a scientific rather than a voluntary approach to regional issues, because the ruling power of one man and one party in Croatia has so recently changed to a multi-party parliament with a promise from the winning coalition to transform the semi-presidential system into a parliamentary one.[7] But it is also important for Bosnia and Herzegovina. Most of all, it is highly important for both countries together, because the realization of their natural cross-border regions has been dampened by Croatia's current regional organization. While there are seven regions in Bosnia and Herzegovina (Banja Luka, Bihać, Doboj, Mostar, Sarajevo, Tuzla and Zenica), grouped in ten cantons in the Bosniak-Croat Federation and the highly centralized Republika Srpska,[8] Croatia's twenty-one regions are generally centralized and transmit central governmental power through high local authority.

The main purpose of this paper is to compare two regionalisms in Croatia: the one that fell in 1992, at the beginning of transition (the "old one"), with the "new one," which was introduced subsequently. Considering the lack of available data, it is very difficult to judge which one is better. However, one can begin by saying that the new one's problems are bigger than those of the old one. These problems start with the method of deciding about the number and the borders of regions and extend to the way they function as transmitters of the power of the central government. To test them, we could pose the following three main hypotheses:

1. The new system of regions in Croatia, although established within a pluralistic system, was created by the will of a single party. The ruling party wanted to decrease the power of cities and transmit it to the regions in order to compensate for lost political control. On the other hand, the old system, which had been established by a single-party system, was nonetheless created by associated communes based on their free will and taking functional and historical criteria into consideration.
2. Compared to the old, the new system has increased the number of regions on all levels, and, consequently, their bureaucracy and costs. The new system also increases the tensions among regions and between regions and their central cities.
3. Compared to the old, the new system has amplified the differences between regions and discourages equality among them—one of the most important goals for stabilizing the society.

A qualitative analysis of the regulation documents and the way the laws were made can prove the first hypothesis. The number of regions and other differences caused by the change in systems can prove the second hypothesis. Finally, the third hypothesis can be proven by the coefficients of variation for the old and new regional systems.[9]

The Republic of Croatia as an independent country was established with the split of former Yugoslavia. 4,700,000 inhabitants live in an area of about 57,000 km^2 (82.5 citizens per km^2). The capital of Croatia is Zagreb, which is almost four times larger than the second-largest city (Split).[10] The traditionally centralized organization of the state suggests a high level of inequality among regions in Croatia.

Presently, Croatia is administratively divided into regions (županije) whose size, population, and level of urbanization and development differ very much. There are 21 regions and more than 400 cities and communes in Croatia. Before the transition, the number of regions and communes was much smaller.

Since regionalism is connected with political power, regions are not assigned according to developmental criteria in centralized systems, but rather, according to political will. Given the political structure of the Croatian Parliament, it happened this way in Croatia, too, since the ruling party's 66 percent of votes enabled the Croatian Democratic Union (HDZ) to decide what ever it wanted.

Relative to the previous regional system, the number of regions and communes doubled. Considering the changed relationship between regions and local communities, one can assume that the possible preferences of the dominating party had taken priority over the interests of the society as a whole. Following the 1992 legislative regulation, the new regional administrations were assigned more functions than the previous ones had been, and in some functions, they received more competence than local communal or city municipalities.

Before 1992, Croatia's regional system consisted of only 11 regions and 115 associated communes, and respected the principle of function and the free will of inhabitants. Each region was an association of communes, with an average of 11 communes and 460,000 people per region. However, if we compare the associations, we can see that their sizes varied.

Table 12.1 The Old Croatian Regions

Associations of communes	Population (1981)	Area in Km^2	Number of associated communes	Population per commune
Bjelovar	370916	5803	10	37092
Croatian Highlands	126792	1015	5	25358
Dalmatia	882050	11758	24	36752
Karlovac	172144	2962	6	28691
Lika	90336	5563	5	18067
Osijek	867646	11090	14	61975
Rijeka	540485	8442	19	28447
Sisak	175260	2855	5	35052
Varaždin	303590	1950	5	60718
Zagreb area	338474	4410	13	26036
Zagreb City	855568	1705	14	61112
TOTAL	4596469	56538	115	
Average	417861	5140	10	39969

The number of regions doubled after 1992. There are 21 regions in Croatia today, established on sub-regional criteria. Their average population is at least half what it had been before, and their average area has been similarly halved. The number of communes also increased, but much more (four times) than the number of regions did. Consequently, the average population of the communes decreased.

Before the transition, the Croatian regions were "Associations of Communes" that held very little power. Finally, the decision about regional divisions had been made after huge public discussion. In 1992, however, the central governmental created the 21 new regions without public discussion, and transferred strong power, money and bureaucracy to them.

Table 12.2 The New Croatian Regions

Regions (Županije) after 1992	Population (1991)	Area (in km²)	Number of communes	Population per commune
Bjelovarsko-Bilogorska	144042	2638	18	8002
Brodsko-Posavska	174998	2027	26	6731
Dubrovačko-Neretvanska	126329	1782	17	7431
Istarska	204346	2813	29	7046
Karlovačka	184577	3622	16	11536
Koprivničko-Križevačka	129397	1734	20	6470
Krapinsko-Zagorska	148779	1230	25	5951
Ličko-Senjska	86992	5350	8	10874
Međimurska	119866	730	21	5708
Osječko-Baranjska	367193	4149	33	11127
Primorsko-Goranska	323130	3590	21	15387
Požeško-Slavonska	99334	1821	6	16556
Šibensko-Kninska	152477	2994	12	12706
Sisačko-Moslovačka	251023	4448	13	19309
Splitsko-Dalmatinska	474019	4524	40	11850
Varaždinska	187853	1260	22	8539
Virovitičko-Podravska	104625	2021	13	8048
Vukovarsko-Srijemska	231241	2448	24	9635
Zadarska	212920	3643	26	8189
Zagreb City	777826	640	0	777826
Zagrebačka	283298	3078	26	10896
TOTAL	4784265	56542	416	
Average	227822	2692	20	11500

The regional transition also increased costs by increasing bureaucracy relatively. 1998 data indicates that before the transition 64,660 people were employed in central and local government, foundations, associations and organizations. Alongside a 1997 claim that socialist-style bureaucracy had decreased, we found 47,270 people employed in these activities—which, though numerically lower, is a relatively higher amount than before the transition. In essence, the number of employees decreased much more than the amount of bureaucracy.

In 1988 the government employed 1.6 million individuals, while in 1997, only one million. But 4.6 percent of all employees in 1997 could be claimed by bureaucracy, compared to only 4.1 percent in 1988. Considering the increased wages of the bureaucracy, one can conclude that the cost of the new bureaucratic system is higher than before. In 1988, the wages of the bureaucracy were only 13 percent higher than average wages, but in 1995, they were 20 percent higher. In 1988, bureaucratic wages were 17 percent lower than the wages of scientists, but in 1995, they were 4 percent higher.

One can conclude from the above that along with the increase in the number of regions, the number of communes and the average population density per region also increased. Consequently, the average area and population of the regions, and, in particular, the average population per commune decreased, as follows:

Table 12.3 Old and new Regional Comparison

Indicators	Old Regions	New Regions	Index
Number of regions	11	21	191
Number of communes	115	416	362
Average physical size of regions	5140	2692	52
Average number of population per region	417861	227822	55
Average number of communes per region	10	20	200
Average population number per commune	39969	11500	29
Average population density per region	81	85	105

It was the political will of the ruling party that created the new regionalism in Croatia, not scientific criteria. The main goals were to avoid, as much as possible, tendencies towards federalization among the larger regions, and to regain the lost power over cities by redistributing competence to the regions. The majority of the ruling party's support comes from rural voters with little education. The opposition, on the other hand, tends to attract more educated urban voters. The fact is, HDZ has the majority in very few cities, while the opposition has been able to take power in very few regions. For example, in the city of Zagreb, the Croatian Democratic Union (HDZ) has only one-third of the mandates of the municipal Assembly. Similarly, in the city of Split, only 30 percent of Assembly members belong to this party. In the city of Rijeka, the Social Democrats have the majority; in the city of Osijek, the Social Liberals, etc. By comparison, there is only one regional assembly in which the opposition has been able to take more than 50 percent of the mandates.

At the beginning, there was very strong regionalist enthusiasm among Istrians, Dalmatians and Slavonians, which in certain parts decreased after the administrative transformations. Before 1992 regional parties were represented in the Croatian parliament, but after the 1995 elections the Istrian Democratic Association was the only regional party that still held seats in parliament.

The second statement is clearer upon the knowledge that, since the HDZ's appearance on the political scene, which caused a lot of general enthusiasm, it has continued to lose urban votes. It is for this reason that the ruling party decreased the power of urban populations in favor of rural populations through the 1992 regional transformation. The result is also both very expensive and very confusing, since the transformation reduced the powers of decision making in big cities, despite the large-scale problems that big cities face.

To illustrate this, statement 23 of the Legislation on the Governmental Administration covers the regional inspecting activities and tax system, the two most important functions of the regional system. Statement 15 of the Legislation on Local Self-Management and Management obligates the regions to direct activities concerning treatment and protection of the environment.[11]

It is obvious that this legislation makes it very easy for the central government to control the local communities. If a local government is not obedient, the central government can send inspections through the regional administration at any time. Through regional institutions, they can control the lost power in cities.

Transforming the regional system also increased regional inequalities. The coefficient of variation shows that all measured indicators are higher in the new regional system than in the old one.[12]

The greater the differences are, the higher the tension that will exist among regions, which is quite contrary to the original idea of transforming the regional system.

National per capita income, relative employment, number of inhabitants per physician, activity sector employment and gross fixed capital per capita, each show bigger differences in the new than in the old regional system, as follows:

Table 12.4 The Coefficient of Variation in Old and New Regions

Indicators	Old Regions	New Regions	Index
National Per Capita Income	30	44	147
Proportion of Employed and Other Population	29	35	121
Number of Inhabitants per Physician	46	72	156
Gross Fixed Capital Per Capita	41	46	112
Percentage of Employed in Primary Sector	90	123	137
Percentage of Employed in Secondary Sector	21	26	124
Percentage of Employed in Tertiary Sector	20	21	105

The organization of regions in Croatia neglected to take into consideration some very important existing scientific achievements having to do with regional organization. The political elite made the decision about the new regional organization exclusively. It did not take in the account the functional criteria, and it did not respect the free will of the regional population. From the previous discussion, we can deduct that the main criterion for the regional changes was the will and the interest of the party with the great majority in parliament.

It is partially proven that one single party established the new system of regions in Croatia. It is also partially proven that the central government wanted to transmit the power to regions to compensate for their lost political control in the cities. The new system of regional organization is therefore a question of the political power of the ruling party, but not of the agreement of all subjects in political life.

It is also completely proven that the new system of regions in Croatia has increased the number of regions with respect to the old system, and consequently, the bureaucracy and costs have increased. However, the second part of the second hypothesis has been proven with less strength: one can conclude that the new system has increased tensions both among regions and between regions and their central cities. By proving the third hypothesis, we see that the new system of regions in Croatia has increased the differences among regions. It discourages equality, which is, however, one of the most important steps toward stabilizing a society. The transformation also changed the relationship between the regions and local communities, causing rising conflicts. Only one regional government is free from conflicts with the local government, since the opposition holds the majority in both regional and local governments.

The conflicts and costs produced by politics, but not by societal and developmental interests, could bring new problems in the future, and could have an influence opposite to what was intended. For example, they can negatively influence opportunities to connect Croatian regions with regions outside the Croatian borders with which they traditionally had relationships, such as Zagreb, Bihać and Banja Luka, Dalmatia with all of Herzegovina, Croatian and Bosnian areas around the Sava river, and others. The regional and communal system in Croatia needs further scientific, critical evaluation, but the now-former ruling party was not interested in it.

Notes

1. Philip M. Hauser, "Urbanization: An Overview," in *The Study of Urbanization* (1965), p. 41 and Brian J. L. Berry, "Research Frontiers in Urban Geography," in *The Study of Urbanization* (1965), p. 423.
2. Igor Vrišer, *Regionalno planiranje* (Ljubljana: Mladinska knjiga 1978), p. 132.
3. Clarence S. Stein, "A Regional Pattern for Dispersal," in *Architectural Record* No.136 (1964), pp. 205–206.
4. Yehuda Gradus and Eliahu Stern, "Changing Strategies of Development: Toward a Regiopolis in the Negev Desert," in *Journal of the American Planners Association (JAPA)*, No. 4 (1980).
5. Jeremy Alden and Robert Morgan, *Regional Planning: A Comprehensive View* (Leonard Hill Books, 1974), p. 3; and Milan Vresk, *Osnove urbane geografije* (Zagreb: Školska knjiga, 1980).
6. Ivan Cifrić, *Socijalna ekologija* (Zagreb: Globus, 1989), p. 41.
7. This is the first time after the transition that Croatian parliament has consisted of parties which cannot overvote each other by wielding a majority. Thanks to the January 3, 2000 parliamentary elections, there are two main parties in Croatian parliament plus some smaller parties (the Coalition of Social Democrats and Social Liberals has 47 percent of the mandates, the Croatian Democratic Union (HDZ) has 30.5 percent, the Coalition of Liberals, Peasant Party, Istrian Democratic Union and Croatian Folk Party together have 15.9 percent, the coalition of the Croatian Law Party and the Christian Democrats has 3.3 percent, and national minorities parties hold 3.3 percent). Therefore, parties must now discuss every topic in detail, and no one party will have the opportunity to overvote.
8. Steven, L. Burg, "Bosnia Herzegovina: a Case of Failed Democratization," in *Politics, Power, and the Struggle for Democracy in South-East Europe* (1997), pp. 122–145.
9. The Coefficient of Variation (V) is the relative Standard Deviation of arithmetic average calculated in this paper by Excel 7.0.
10. According to the rank-sized-rule, the second city in the system should be half the

size of the first city. The difference, by a factor of four, in the populations of Zagreb and Split, indicates centralization. See Brian J.L. Berry, "Research Frontiers in Urban Geography, in *The Study of Urbanization* (1965), p. 415.

11 "*Zakon o lokalnoj samoupravi i upravi*," in *Lokalna samouprava i uprava u Republici Hrvatskoj* (1993), pp. 457–458.

12 The Coefficient of Variation (V) is a percentage of the Standard Deviation and Arithmetic Average multiplied by 100 ($V = 100 \times \sigma / \bar{X}$). Therefore, It is not dependent on the unit of measure, permitting the comparisons of deviations of two completely different scales. See Ljubica Škara-Vidojević, *Osnovi statistike* (Beograd: Savremena administracija, 1963), pp. 134–136.

Bibliography

Agreement for Self-Government in Kosmet. Proposal by the Yugoslav Government. Paris, March 18, 1999.

Akehurst, Michael: *A Modern Introduction to International Law.* 6th edition. London: Routledge, 1995.

Albert, Sophie: "The Return of Refugees to Bosnia and Herzegovina: Peacebuilding with People." *International Peacekeeping* 4, no. 3 (1997), pp. 1-23.

Alden, Jeremy, and Robert Morgan: *Regional Planning: A Comprehensive View.* Leighton Buzzard: Leonard Hill Books, 1974.

Alsop, Ruth, and John Farrington: "Nest, Nodes and Niches: A System for Process Monitoring, Information Exchange and Decision Making for Multiple Stakeholders." *World Development* 26, no. 2 (1998), pp. 249–260.

American Bar Association: *Central and East European Law Initiative Annual Report* (1995).

Amnesty International: *Annual Report 1999.* Available at: http://www.amnesty.org/ailib/Aireport/ar99/eur63.htm.

———: "Bosnia-Herzegovina. All the Way Home: Safe 'Minority Returns' as a Just Remedy and for a Secure Future." Available at: http://www.amnesty.org/ailib/aipub/1998/EUR/46300298.htm.

Amy, Douglas J: "Improving Representation for Women and Minorities: Is Proportional Representation the Key?" Paper delivered at the Annual Meeting of the American Political Science Association, Washington DC, September 1991.

Arcel, Libby Tata et al., eds.: *Psycho-Social Help to War Victims: Women Refugees and Their Families from Bosnia and Herzegovina and Croatia.* Zagreb and Copenhagen: IRCT, 1995.

Arthur, John, ed.: *Democracy, Theory and Practice.* Belmont, California: Wadsworth Publishing Company, 1992.

Bakić-Hayden, Milica: "Nesting Orientalisms: The Case of Former Yugoslavia." *Slavic Review* 54, no. 4 (1995), pp. 917–931.

Bakić-Hayden, Milica, and Robert Hayden: "Orientalist Variations on the Theme 'Balkans': Symbolic Geography in Recent Yugoslav Cultural Politics." *Slavic Review* 51, no. 1 (1992), pp. 1–15.

Barnett, Michael N.: "The Politics of Indifference at the United Nations and Genocide in Rwanda and Bosnia." In *This Time We Knew: Western Responses to Genocide in Bosnia*, ed. Thomas Cushman and Stjepan Mestrovic. New York: New York University Press, 1996, pp. 128–162.

Barry, Brian: "Is Democracy Special?" In *Philosophy, Politics and Society*, ed. P. Laslett and J. Fishkin. New Haven: Yale University Press, 1979, pp. 403–430.

Bartolini, Stefano: "Exit Options, Boundary Building, Political Structuring: Sketches of a Theory of Large-Scale Territorial and Membership 'Retrenchment/Differentiation' versus 'Expansion/Integration' (With Reference to the European Union)." *EUI Working Paper SPS* No. 98/1 (1998).

Bassiouni Cherif, et al.: Guiding Principles for Combating Impunity for International Crimes (Draft).

Battiata, Mary: "A Town's Bloody 'Cleansing'," The Washington Post, November 2, 1992.

Baumann, Zygmunt: *Moderne und Ambivalenz: Das Ende der Eindeutigkeit.* Frankfurt: Fischer, 1991.

BBC Summary of World Broadcasts, September 20, 1997, EE/D3 029/A.

Beitz, Charles R: *Political Equality.* Princeton: Princeton University Press, 1989.

Benda, Julien: *Le Trahison des Clercs (The Treason of the Intellectuals).* New York: W.W. Norton & Company, 1969.

Beran, Harry: "A Liberal Theory of Secession." *Political Studies* 32 (1984), pp. 21–31.

———: *The Consent Theory of Political Obligation.* Beckenham: Croom Helm, 1987.

Berry, Brian J.L.: "Research Frontiers in Urban Geography." *The Study of Urbanization* (1965), pp. 403–430.

Bieber, Florian: "Consociationalism – Prerequisite or Hurdle for Democratization in Bosnia?" *South-East Europe Review* 2, no. 3 (1999), pp. 79–94.

Billig, Michael: *Banal Nationalism.* London: Sage, 1995.

Blessington, Daniel J.: "From Dayton to Sarajevo: Enforcing Election Laws in Post War Bosnia and Herzegovina." *American University International Law Review* 13, no.3 (1998).

Bloch, Ernst: *Das Prinzip Hoffnung,* Vol. 5. Frankfurt: Suhrkamp, 1998.

Bosco, David L.: "Reintegrating Bosnia: A Progress Report." *The Washington Quarterly* 21 (1998), pp. 65–81.

Boutros-Ghali, Boutros: *An Agenda for Peace – Preventative Diplomacy, Peacemaking and Peace-Keeping Report of the Secretary-General.* U.N. GAOR/SCOR, 47th Sess., Preliminary List Item 10, United Nations Documents A/47/277 & S/24111 (1992).

Bowering, Bill: "Russia's Accession to the Council of Europe and Human Rights: Compliance or Cross-Purposes," *European Human Rights Law Review* 6 (1997).

Bowles, Samuel, and Herbert Gintis: *Democracy and Capitalism*. New York: Basic Books, 1986.

Boyle, Francis A.: "Negating Human Rights in Peace Negotiations," *Human Rights Quarterly* 18, no. 3 (1996), pp. 515–516.

Brassinne, Jacques: *Belgique Fédérale*. Brussels: CRISP, 1994.

Bretherton, Charlotte, and John Vogler: *The European Union as a Global Actor*. London and New York: Routledge, 1999.

Brierly, J.L.: *The Law of Nations. An Introduction to the International Law of Peace*. Edited by Sir Humphrey Waldock. 6th edition. Oxford: Oxford University Press, 1963.

Brilmayer, Lea: "Secession and Self-Determination: A Territorialist Reinterpretation." *Yale Journal of International Law* 16, no. 1 (January 1991), pp. 177–202.

Bringa, Tone: *Being a Muslim the Bosnian Way: Identity and Community in a Central Bosnian Village*. Princeton: Princeton University Press, 1995.

Brownlie, Ian: *Principles of Public International Law*. 4th edition. Oxford: Clarendon Press, 1996.

Buchanan, Allen: "Democracy and Secession." In *National Self-Determination and Secession*, ed. Margaret Moore. Oxford: Oxford University Press, 1998, pp. 14–33.

Buchheit, Lee C.: *Secession: The Legitimacy of Self-Determination*. New Haven and London: Yale University Press, 1978.

Burg, Steven, L.: "Bosnia Herzegovina: a Case of Failed Democratization." In *Politics, Power, and the Struggle for Democracy in South-East Europe*, ed. Karen Dawisha and Bruce Parrott. Cambridge: Cambridge University Press, 1997, pp. 122–145.

Burnheim, John: *Is Democracy Possible?* Berkeley: University of California Press, 1985.

Busch, Ronald J.: "Proportional Representation and Religious and Ethnic Minorities." Paper delivered at the Annual Meeting of the American Political Science Association, Washington DC, September 1991.

Carothers, Thomas: "Democracy Assistance: The Question of Strategy," *Democratization* 4, no. 3 (1997).

Castoriadis, Cornelius: *Gesellschaft als imaginäre Institution*. Frankfurt: Suhrkamp, 1984.

CEELI Update 4 (1997).

Chandler, David: "Democratization in Bosnia: The Limits of Civil Society Building Strategies." *Democratization* 5, no. 4 (1998), pp. 78–102.

———: "The Bosnia Protectorate and the Implications for Kosovo." *New Left Review*, no. 235 (May/June 1999), pp. 124–134.

Cifrić, Ivan: *Socijalna ekologija*. Zagreb: Globus, 1989.

Cigar, Norman: *Genocide in Bosnia: The Policy of "Ethnic Cleansing."* College Station, TX: A&M University Press, 1995.

Clark, John: "The State, Popular Participation, and the Voluntary Sector." *World Development* 23, no. 4 (1995), pp. 593–601.

Clarke, Jonathan: "Don't Encourage Separatist Aims of Kosovo Albanians." *International Herald Tribune*, January 12, 1998.

Cohen, Jean L., and Andrew Arato: *Civil Society and Political Theory*. Cambridge, Mass.: MIT Press, 1992.

Cohen, Lenard J.: *Broken Bonds. The Disintegration of Yugoslavia*. Boulder, CO: Westview, 1993.

Constitution of Bosnia and Herzegovina (1995).

Constitution, Interim Agreement for Peace and Self-Government in Kosovo (February 23, 1999).

Constitutional Guidelines for a Democratic South Africa (1989), reprinted in *Columbia Human Rights Law Review* 21, no. 1 (Fall 1989), pp. 235–246.

Convention for the Protection of Human Rights and Fundamental Freedoms, Nov. 4, 1950, 213 U.N.T.S. 221, Europ. T.S. No. 5.

Cousens, Elizabeth M.: "Making Peace in Bosnia Work." *Cornell International Law Journal* 30, no. 3 (1997), pp. 789–818.

Cox, Marcus: "The Right to Return Home: International Intervention and Ethnic Cleansing in Bosnia and Herzegovina." *International and Comparative Law Quarterly* 47 (1998), pp. 599–631.

"Croatian Leader Warns of Crisis." *International Herald Tribune*, May 15, 1991.

Crocker, Chester A., and Fen Osler Hampson: "Making Peace Settlements Work." *Foreign Policy* 104 (Fall 1996), pp. 54–71.

Cutler, Lloyd, and Herman Schwartz: "Constitutional Reform in Czechoslovakia: E Duobus Unum?" *The University of Chicago Law Review* 58 (1991).

Dabag, Mihran: "*Katastrophe und Identität*." In *Erlebnis – Gedächtnis – Sinn: Authentische und konstruierte Erinnerung*, ed. Hanno Loewy and Bernhard Moltmann. Frankfurt and New York: Campus Verlag, 1996, pp. 177–235.

Dahl, Robert A.: *Democracy and Its Critics*. New Haven: Yale University Press, 1989.

Dani, April 26, 1996.

Dani, April 14, 2000.

Danner, Mark: "Endgame in Kosovo." *New York Review of Books*, May 6, 1999.

Dawson, John P.: *Oracles of the Law*. Ann Arbour: Institute of Continuing Legal Education, 1968.

Deacon, Bob, and Paul Stubbs: "International Actors and Social Policy Development in Bosnia-Herzegovina: Globalism and the 'New Feudalism'." *Journal of European Social Policy* 8, no. 2 (1998), pp. 99–115.

Delalić, Enida: "*Der Spielraum des Mythos*," Master's Thesis, University of Frankfurt, 1994.

"Democratic Symmetry." *The Economist*, March 4, 2000.

Denitch, Bogdan: *Ethnic Nationalism*. Minneapolis and London: University of Minnesota Press, 1994.

Dimitrijević, Vojin: "The Yugoslav Precedent: Keep What You Have." In *Breakdown: War and Reconstruction in Yugoslavia*, ed. Anthony Borden et al. London: Institute for War and Peace Reporting, 1992.

———: "The Post-Communist Apotheosis of the Nation-State." In *Religion & War*, ed. Dušan Janjić. Belgrade: European Movement in Serbia, 1994, pp. 18–36.

Dixon, Martin: *Textbook on International Law*. 3rd edition. London: Blackstone Press, 1996.

Dolgopol, Ustinia: "A Feminist Appraisal of the Dayton Peace Accords." *Adelaide Law Review* 19 (1997), pp. 59–71.

Donia, Robert J., and John V.A. Fine, Jr.: *Bosnia and Hercegovina: A Tradition Betrayed*. New York: Columbia University Press, 1994.

Dummett, Michael: *Principles of Electoral Reform*. Oxford: Oxford University Press, 1997.

Dumont, Georges Henri: *Histoire de la Belgique*. Paris: Hachette, 1977.

Edwards, Michael, and David Hulme: "Too Close for Comfort? The Impact of Official Aid on Nongovernmental Organizations." *World Development* 24, no. 6 (1996), pp. 961–973.

Elkins, David J.: *Beyond Sovereignty: Territory and Political Economy in the Twenty-First Century*. Toronto: University of Toronto Press, 1995.

Emerson, P J: *Beyond the Tyranny of the Majority*. Belfast: The de Borda Institute, 1998.

Emery, Fred: *Toward Real Democracy*. Toronto: Ontario Ministry of Labour Occasional Paper, 1989.

Engstrom, Richard L., and Charles J. Barrilleaux: "Native Americans and Cumulative Voting: The Sisseton-Wahpeton Sioux." *Social Science Quarterly* 72 (June 1991), pp. 388–393.

Evaluation of the PHARE Partnership Programme, produced by Local and Regional Development Planning. Commissioned by the European Commission, DG 1A, November 1998.

Evans, Malcolm D., ed.: *Blackstone's International Law Documents*. 3rd edition. London: Blackstone Press Limited, 1991.

"Excerpts from Address by de Klerk on Change." *New York Times*, February 3, 1990.

Eyal, Jonathan: *Europe and Yugoslavia: A Lesson From A Failure*. Royal United Services Institute for Defence Studies, 1993.

Fagin, Adam: "Environment and Transition in the Czech Republic." *Environmental Politics* 3, no. 3 (1994), pp. 479–494.

Farrand, M.: *Framing of the Constitution of the United States*. New Haven: Yale University Press, 1913.

Finkelkraut, Alain: *Comment peut-on être Croate?* Gallimard: Paris, 1992.

Fishkin, James S.: *Democracy and Deliberation: New Directions for Democratic Reform*. New Haven: Yale University Press, 1991.

Frankfurter Rundschau, November 9, 1999.

Freji, Hanna Y., and Leonard C. Robinson: "Liberalization, the Islamists, and the Stability of the Arab State: Jordan as a Case Study." *The Muslim World* 86, no. 1 (1996), pp. 1–33.

Gaeta, Paolo: "The Dayton Agreements and International Law." *European Journal of International Law* 7, no. 2 (1996), pp. 147–163.

Gauthier, David: "Breaking Up: An Essay on Secession." *Canadian Journal of Philosophy* 24, no. 3 (September 1994), pp. 353–371.

Gearty, Conor: "The European Court of Human Rights and the Protection of Civil Liberties." *Cambridge Law Journal* 52 (1993), pp. 89–127.

Gennep, Arnold van: *Übergangsriten*. Frankfurt and New York: Campus Verlag, 1986.

Giddens, Antony: *The Nation-State and Violence*. Cambridge: Polity Press, 1985.

Glenny, Misha: *The Fall of Yugoslavia: The Third Balkan War*. New edition. London: Penguin, 1993.

Gradus, Yehuda, and Eliahu Stern: "Changing Strategies of Development: Toward a Regiopolis in the Negev Desert." *Journal of the American Planners Association*, no. 4 (1980).

Green, Andrew T., and Carol Skalnik Leff: "The Quality of Democracy: Mass-Elite Linkages in the Czech Republic." *Democratization* 4, no. 4 (1997), pp. 63–87.

Green, Philip: *Retrieving Democracy*. Totowa, NJ: Rowman and Littlefield, 1985.

Greenfeld, Liah: "War and Ethnic Identity in Eastern Europe: Does the Post-Yugoslav Crisis Portend Wider Chaos?" In *This Time We Knew: Western Responses to Genocide in Bosnia*, ed. Thomas Cushman and Stjepan Mestrovic. New York: New York University Press, 1996, pp. 304–312.

Gross, Oren: "'Once More unto the Breach': The Systemic Failure of Applying the European Convention on Human Rights to Entrenched Emergencies." *Yale Journal of International Law* 23, no. 2 (1998), pp. 500–508.

de la Guérivière, J.: *Belgique: La Revanche des Langues*. Paris: Editions du Seuil, 1994.

Gunter, Dolores: "Women Reconcilers in Bosnia." *Fellowship* 64, no. 11/12 (November/December 1998), pp. 27–28.

Guttman, Roy: *A Witness to Genocide*. New York: Macmillan Publishing Company, 1993.

Habermas, Jürgen: *Die Einbeziehungen des Anderen: Studien zur politischen Theorie*. Frankfurt: Fischer, 1996.

Hackworth, G.H.: *Digest of International Law*, vol. 1. Washington: Government Printing Office, 1940.

Hadenius, Axel, and Fredrik Uggla: "Making Civil Society Work, Promoting Democratic Development: What can States and Donors Do?" *World Development* 24, no. 10 (1996), pp. 1621–1639.

Hansen, Annika S.: "Political Legitimacy, Confidence-building and the Dayton Peace Agreement." *International Peacekeeping* 4, no. 2 (1997), pp. 74–90.

Harden, Blaine: "The Yugoslav Gulag: Days in the Life of Bosnian Inmates." *The Washington Post*, August 7, 1992.

"Hard-Liners Tie Up Bosnian Serb Entity." *International Herald Tribune*, December 29, 1997.

Hauser, Philip M., and Leo F. Schnore: *The Study of Urbanization*. New York: John Wiley & Sons, 1965.

Hayden, Robert M.: "Schindler's Fate: Genocide, Ethnic Cleansing and Population Transfers." *Slavic Review* 55, no. 4 (1996), pp. 727–748.

———: "Bosnia's Internal War and the International Criminal Tribunal." *The Fletcher Forum of World Affairs* 22 (Winter/Spring 1998), pp. 45–64.

———: "The State as Legal Fiction: American Proposals for the Constitutional and Political Status of Kosovo." *East European Constitutional Review* 7, no. 4 (Fall 1998), pp. 45–50.

———: "Humanitarian Hypocrisy." *Pittsburgh Post-Gazette*, March 28, 1999. Available at: http://commondreams.org/kosovo/views/hayden.htm.

———: *Blueprints for a House Divided: The Constitutional Logic of the Yugoslav Conflicts*. Ann Arbour: University of Michigan Press, 1999.

de la Haye, Jos: "Les élections municipales peuvent-elles rompre le pouvoir informel des partis nationalistes?" Rapport 1/2000, University of Leuven, Belgium. Center for Peace Research, Department of Political Sciences.

Hedges, Chris: "Fearful Serbs Fleeing Last Enclave in Croatia." *International Herald Tribune*, December 18, 1997.

Herman, Edward S., and Frank Brodhead: *Demonstration Elections*. Boston: South End Press, 1984.

Hirschman, Albert O.: *Exit, Voice, and Loyalty*. Cambridge, Mass.: Harvard University Press, 1970.

Holbrooke, Richard: *To End a War*. New York: Random House, 1998.
Horowitz, Donald L.: *Ethnic Groups in Conflict*. Berkeley: University of California Press, 1985.
———: "Democracy in Divided Societies." *Journal of Democracy* 4, no. 4 (October 1993), pp. 18-38.
———: "Self-Determination: Politics, Philosophy, and Law." In *National Self-Determination and Secession*, ed. Margaret Moore. Oxford University Press, 1998, pp. 181-214.
Hostetter, Doug: "Ethnic Cleansing Cleansed." *Fellowship* 64, no. 9/10 (September/October 1998), p. 27.
Hrženjak, Juraj: *Društvena struktura naselja u SR Hrvatskoj*. Zagreb: Sveučilišna naklada Liber, 1983.
———: *Lokalna samouprava i uprava u Republici Hrvatskoj*. Zagreb: Informator, 1993.
Hukanovic, Rezak: *The Tenth Circle of Hell: A Memoir of Life in the Death Camps of Bosnia*. New York: Basic Books, 1996.
Human Rights Watch: *Bosnia-Hercegovina: The Fall of Srebrenica and the Failure of U.N. Peacekeeping* (October 1995).
———: *Human Rights in Bosnia and Hercegovina Post Dayton: Challenges for the Field* (1996).
———: *No Justice No Peace: The United Nations International Police Task Force's Role in Screening Local Law Enforcement* (1996).
———: *Politics of Revenge: The Misuse of Authority in Bihac, Cazin, and Velika Kladusa* (1997).
———: *Human Rights Watch World Report 1999: Bosnia and Hercegovina* (1999). Available at: www.hrw.org/Worldreport99/europe/bosnia.html.
Ibrahimbegić, Omer: *Supremacy of Bosnia and Herzegovina over its Entities*. 2nd revised edition. Sarajevo: Vijeće Kongresa bošnjačkih intelekualaca, 1999.
International Crisis Group: "Aid and Accountability: Dayton Implementation" (November 24, 1996). Available at: www.crisisweb.org/projects/bosnia/reports/bh17exec.htm.
———: "Beyond the Ballot Boxes: Municipal Elections in Bosnia and Herzegovina" (September 10, 1997). Available at: www.crisisweb.org/projects/bosnia/reports/bh26rep.htm.
———: "The Balkan Refugee Crisis: Regional and Long-term Perspectives" (June 1, 1999). Available at: www.crisisweb.org/projects/sbalkans/reports/ba02rep.htm.
———: "Preventing Minority Return in Bosnia and Herzegovina: The Anatomy of Hate and Fear" (August 10, 1999). Available at: www.crisisweb.org/projects/bosnia/reports/bh50main.htm.

———: "Is Dayton Failing? Bosnia Four Years After the Peace Agreement" (October 28, 1999). Available at: www.crisisweb.org/projects/bosnia/reports/bh51main.htm.

———: "Denied Justice: Individuals Lost in a Legal Maze" (February 23, 2000). Available at: www.crisisweb.org/projects/bosnia/reports/bh53main.htm.

Janckar-Webster, Barbara: "Environmental Movement and Social Change in the Transition Countries." *Environmental Politics* 7, no. 1 (1998), pp. 69–90.

Jefferson, Thomas: *The Portable Thomas Jefferson*. Edited and with an introduction by Merrill D. Peterson. New York: Viking Press, 1975.

Jenkins, Bonnie: "The Enhancement of Political and Military Stability in the Former Yugoslavia through the use of International Law: Annex 1-B of the General Framework Agreement." *Fordham International Law Journal* 19 (1996).

Johnston, Alexander: "Introduction: South Africa Since February 1990." In *Constitution Making in the New South Africa*, ed. Alexander Johnston, Sipho Shezi, and Gavin Bradshaw. London and New York: Leicester University Press, 1993.

Kamminga, Meno T.: "Is the European Convention on Human Rights Sufficiently Equipped to Cope with Gross and Systematic Violations?" *Netherlands Quarterly of Human Rights* 12, no. 2 (1994), pp. 153–164.

Kelman, Herbert C.: "Violence without Moral Restraint: Reflections on the Dehumanization of Victims and Victimizers." *Journal of Social Issues* 29 (1973), pp. 25–61.

Kesteloot, Chantal: "Mouvement Wallon et Identité nationale." *Courrier Hebdomadaire*. Brussels: CRISP, 1993.

Kjafija, Hasan: "*Temelji mudrosti o uredjenju svijeta*," *Behar* 3, no. 13 (1994), p. 20.

Klinke, Andreas, and Ortwin Renn: "Ethnic Cooperation and Coexistence: International Mediation, International Governance, and Civil Society for Ethnically Plural States." In *Ethnic Conflicts and Civil Society: Proposals for a New Era in Eastern Europe*, ed. Andreas Klinke, Ortwin Renn and Jean-Paul Lehners. Aldershot: Ashgate, 1997, pp. 251–279.

Kofman, Daniel: "Rights of Secession." *Society* 35, no. 5 (July/August 1998), pp. 30–37.

———: "Secession, Rights, Law: The Case of the Former Yugoslavia." *Human Rights Review* 1:2 (2000), pp. 9–26.

Kymlicka, Will: *Multicultural Citizenship*. Oxford: Oxford University Press, 1995.

"Legal Ethnic Cleansing Keeps Sarajevo Muslim." *International Herald Tribune*, February 3, 1998.

Leurdijk, Dick A.: "The Dayton Agreement: A Tremendous Gamble." *International Peacekeeping* (Dec. 1995–Jan. 1996).

Lijphart, Arend: "Consociational Democracy." *World Politics* 21, no. 2 (1969), pp. 207–225.

———: *Democracy in Plural Societies: A Comparative Exploration*. New Haven: Yale University Press, 1977.

———: "Democratic Political Systems Types, Cases, Causes, and Consequences." *Journal of Theoretical Politics* 1 (1989).

Lippman, Peter: "On the Record: Your Independent Link to the Refugees of Bosnia." *The Advocacy Project* (1999). Available at: www.advocacynet.org.

Lukács, Georg: *Povijest i klasna svijest*. Zagreb: Naprijed, 1970.

Lukic, Reneo, and Allen Lynch: *Europe from the Balkans to the Urals: The Disintegration of Yugoslavia and the Soviet Union*. Oxford: Oxford University Press, 1996.

Maass, Peter: *Love Thy Neighbor: A Story of War*. New York: Alfred A. Knopf, 1996.

Malcolm, Noel: *Bosnia: A Short History*. New York: New York University Press, 1994.

Malinowski, Bronislaw: *Argonauten des westlichen Pazifik*. Frankfurt: Syndikat, 1994.

Marks, Stephen P.: "Preventing Humanitarian Crises Through Peace-Building and Democratic Empowerment: Lessons From Cambodia." *Medicine and Global Survival* 1, no. 4 (1994). Available at: www2.healthnet.org/MGS/MarksMGS1-4.html.

McRae, Kenneth D.: *Conflict and Compromise in Multilingual Societies: Belgium*. Waterloo, Ontario: Wilfrid Laurier University Press, 1986.

Mearsheimer, John: "Shrink Bosnia to Save it," *New York Times*, March 31, 1993.

———: "Partition in Bosnia is unavoidable," *New York Times*, September 24, 1996.

———: "The Only Exit From Bosnia," *New York Times*, October 7, 1997.

Mearsheimer, John, and Stephen Van Evera, "Redraw the Map, Stop the Killing," *New York Times*, April 19, 1999.

Mertus, Julie: "The Liberal State vs. the Nation Soul: Mapping Civil Society Transplants." *Social & Legal Studies* 8, no. 1 (1999), pp. 121–146.

Mihailović, Srećko: "The War started on May 13, 1990." In *The War started on Maksimir: Hate Speech in Yugoslav Media*, ed. Svetlana Slapašak et al. Belgrade: Media Center, 1997, pp. 97–156.

Mill, John Stuart: *Three Essays*. Oxford: Oxford University Press, 1975.

Morgan, Edmund S.: *Inventing the People*. New York: Norton, 1988.

Murphy, Alexander: "The Sovereign State as Political-Territorial Ideal." In *State Sovereignty as Social Construct*, ed. Cynthia Weber and Thomas Biersteker. Cambridge: Cambridge University Press, 1996, pp. 81–120.

Musgrave, Thomas: *Self-Determination and National Minorities.* Oxford: Clarendon Press, 1997.

Nelson, William: *On Justifying Democracy.* New York: Routledge, 1980.

New York Times, March 29, 1989.

New York Times, June 25, 1991.

Ni Aolain, Fionnuala: "The Emergence of Diversity: Differences in Human Rights Jurisprudence." *Fordham International Law Journal* 19 (1995).

ONASA, December 18, 1997.

Oppenheim, L.[assa]: *International Law.* Ed. H. Lauterpacht. 8th edition. London, New York, Longmans, Green and Co., 1995.

OSCE Mission to Bosnia and Herzegovina Democratization Department: *Semi-Annual Report.* July–December 1998.

Owen, David: *Balkan Odyssey.* London: Victor Gollancz, 1995.

Pajic, Zoran: "A Critical Appraisal of Human Rights Provisions of the Dayton Constitution of Bosnia and Herzegovina." *Human Rights Quarterly* 20, no. 1 (1998), pp. 125–138.

Pellet, Alan: "The Opinions of the Badinter Arbitration Committee: A Second Breath for Self-Determination of Peoples." *European Journal of International Law* 3, no. 1 (1992), pp. 178–185.

Petritsch, Wolfgang: "The Future of Bosnia Lies with its People." *Wall Street Journal (Europe)*, September 17, 1999.

Phillips, Anne: *Engendering Democracy.* University Park, Penn.: The Pennsylvania State University Press, 1991.

Phillips, Ann L.: "Exporting Democracy: German Political Foundations in Central-East Europe." *Democratization* 6, no. 2 (1999), pp. 70–98.

Phillips, David L.: "Comprehensive Peace in the Balkans: The Kosovo Question." *Human Rights Quarterly* 18, no. 4 (1996), pp. 821–832.

Pinson, Mark, ed.: *The Muslims of Bosnia-Herzegovina: Their Historic Development from the Middle Ages to the Dissolution of Yugoslavia.* Cambridge, Mass.: Harvard University Press, 1993.

Plato: *State*, book IV, XVI.

Prica, Ines, and Maja Povrzanović: "Narratives of Refugee Children as the Ethnography of Maturing." In *War, Exile, Everyday Life*, ed. Renata Jambresic Kirin and Maja Povrzanovic. Zagreb: Institute of Ethnology and Folklore Research, 1996, pp. 83–113.

Reidy, Aisling, et al.: "Gross Violations of Human Rights: Invoking the European Convention on Human Rights in the Case of Turkey." *Netherlands Quarterly of Human Rights* 15, no. 2 (1997), pp. 161–173.

Reljić, Dušan: *Killing Screens – Media in Times of Conflict.* Düsseldorf: Droste Verlag, 1999.

Rich, Roland: "Recognition of States: The Collapse of Yugoslavia and the Soviet Union." *European Journal of International Law* 4, no. 1 (1993), pp. 36–65.

Rieff, David: *Slaughterhouse: Bosnia and the Failure of the West.* New York: Simon & Schuster, 1995.

Rizvić, Muhsin: *Panorama Bošnjačke Književnosti.* Sarajevo: Ljiljan, 1994.

Rokkan, Stein, and Derek W. Urwin: *Economy, Territory, Identity: Politics of West European Peripheries.* London: Sage, 1983.

Rössel-Cunović, Marie: "Kurz-Therapien für Flüchtlinge mit befristeter Duldung? Die Auswirkungen des Ausländerrechts auf die psychotherapeutische Behandlung traumatisierter Flüchtlinge." In *Jahrbuch Menschenrechte 2000.* Frankfurt: Suhrkamp, 1999.

Ruys, Manu: *De Vlamingen, Een Volk in Beweging, Een Natie in Wording.* Tielt: Lannoo, 1981.

Sack, Robert David: *Human Territoriality: Its Theory and History.* Cambridge: Cambridge University Press, 1986.

Saller, Vera: "Die Bedeutung des Kulturbegriffs für psychoanalytische Therapien." In *Kultur, Migration, Psychoanalyse,* ed. Fernanda Pedrina. Tübingen: Edition Diskord, 1999, pp. 99–144.

Saradamov, Ivelin: "Ethnic Warriors: Ethnicity and Genocide in the Balkan." Paper presented at the 4th Annual Convention of the Association for the Study of Nationalities, New York, April 1999.

Sartori, Giovanni: *The Theory of Democracy Revisited.* Chatham, NJ: Chatham House Publishers, 1987.

Scharf, Michael P.: *Balkan Justice: The Story Behind the First International War Crimes Tribunal since Nuremberg.* Durham, NC: Carolina Academic Press, 1997.

Schmitter, Phillippe C.: "The Consolidation of Democracy and Representation of Social Groups." *American Behavioral Scientist* 35, no.4/5 (1992), pp. 422–449.

Schneider, Heinrich: "Friede für Bosnien-Herzegowina? Das Vertragswerk von Dayton als Herausforderung für Europa." *Integration* 19, no. 1 (1996), pp. 1–13.

Schomburg-Scherff, Sylvia M.: *Die Spinne im Herrenhaus: Karibische Romane als Identitätserzählungen. Eine Anthropologische Perspektive.* Berlin: Dietrich Reimer, 1999.

Sedelmeier, Ulrich, and Helen Wallace: "Politics towards Central and Eastern Europe." In *Policy-Making in the European Union,* ed. Helen Wallace and William Wallace. 3rd edition. Oxford: Oxford University Press, 1996, pp. 353–385.

Selle, Per, and Kristin Strømsnes: "Medlemskap og demokrati: Må vi ta passivt medlemskap på alvor?" *Politica* 29, no. 1 (1997), pp. 31–48.

Sells, Michael: *The Bridge Betrayed: Religion and Genocide in Bosnia.* Berkeley: University of California Press, 1996.
"Serbian Mob Stones Muslim Women's Bus." *Los Angeles Times,* May 28, 1996.
Shelton, Dinah L.: "The Inter-American System for the Protection of Human Rights: Emergent Norms." In *International Human Rights Law Theory and Practice,* ed. Irwin Cotler and F. Pearl Eliadis. Montreal, The Canadian Human Rights Foundation, 1992.
Shirer, William: *The Rise and Fall of the Third Reich.* New York: Fawcett, 1988.
Shoup, Paul: "The Elections in Bosnia and Herzegovina. The End of an Illusion." *Problems of Post-Communism* 44, no. 1 (January/February 1997), pp. 3–15.
Silber, Laura, and Allan Little: *The Death of Yugoslavia.* London: Penguin, 1995.
Simon, Robert L.: "Pluralism and Equality: The Status of Minority Values in a Democracy." In *Majorities and Minorities,* ed. John W. Chapman and Alan Wertheimer. New York and London: New York University Press, 1990, pp. 207–225.
Simor, Jessica: "Tackling Human Rights Abuses in Bosnia." *European Human Rights Law Review* 6 (1997).
"Sins of the Secular Missionaries." *The Economist,* January 29, 2000.
Škara-Vidojević, Ljubica: *Osnovi statistike.* Belgrade: Savremena administracija, 1963.
Slone, James: "The Dayton Peace Agreement: Human Rights Guarantees and Their Implementation." *European Journal of International Law* 7, no.2 (1996), pp. 207–225.
Smith, R. Jeffrey: "Legal Ethnic Cleansing Keeps Sarajevo Muslim." *International Herald Tribune,* February 3, 1998.
Snyder Jack, and Karen Ballentine: "Nationalism in the Marketplace of Ideas." In *Nationalism and Ethnic Conflict,* ed. Michael E. Brown. Cambridge, Mass. and London: MIT Press, 1997, pp. 61–96.
Spitz, Elaine: *Majority Rule.* Chatham, NJ: Chatham House, 1984.
St. Louis Post-Dispatch, April 19, 1993.
Stanovčić, Vojislav: "Problems and Options in Institutionalizing Ethnic Relations." *International Political Science Review* 13, no. 4 (1992), pp. 359–379.
Statistički godišnjak SR Hrvatske. Zagreb: Republički zavod za statistiku, 1989.
Statistički ljetopis Republike Hrvatske. Zagreb: Državni zavod za statistiku, 1996.
Stein, Clarence S.: "A Regional Pattern for Dispersal." *Architectural Record,* no.136 (1964), pp. 205–206.
Stein, Eric: "International Law in Internal Law: Towards Internationalization of Central-European Constitutions?" *American Journal of International Law* 88, no. 3 (July 1994), pp. 427–450.

Steinhilber, Beate: *Grenzüberschreitungen: Remigration und Biographie – Frauen kehren zurück in die Türkei.* Tübingen: Verlag für Interkulturelle Kommunikation, 1994.

Sunnstein, Cass: "Approaching Democracy: a new legal order for Eastern Europe – Constitutionalism and secession." In *Political Restructuring in Europe: Ethical Perspectives,* ed. Chris Brown. London and New York: Routledge, 1994, pp. 11–49.

Tabaković, E.: *"Bosanci Su Odlični Studenti." Unsko Novine Sanske,* August 7, 1998.

The Independent, August 11, 1992.

Thompson, Mark: *Forging War.* London: Article 19, 1994.

Tomuschat, Christian: "*Quo Vadis, Argentoratum*? The Success Story of the European Convention on Human Rights and a Few Dark Stains." *Human Rights Law Journal* 13.

Traynor, Ian: "How They Wiped out Kozarac." *The Guardian,* October 17, 1992.

Trifunovska, Snežana, ed.: *Yugoslavia Through Documents: From its Creation to its Dissolution.* Dordrecht: Martinus Nijhoff Publishers, 1994.

Turner, Victor: "Betwixt and Between: The Liminal Period in *Rites de Passage.*" In *Symposium on New Approaches to the Study of Religion,* proceedings of the American Ethnological Society, ed. June Helm. New York: AMS Press, 1994, pp. 4–20.

———: *Das Ritual: Struktur und Anti-Struktur.* Frankfurt and New York: Campus Verlag, 1989.

UN Chronicle 33, no. 3 (1996).

United Nations General Assembly Resolution 146 (December 13, 1985).

United Nations: *Yearbook of the United Nations 1960.* Lake Success, N.Y: Department of Public Information, United Nations, 1960.

———: Report of the Secretary-General Pursuant to the Security Council Resolution 1026, UN Documents S/1995/1031 (1995).

———: Report of the High Representative Carl Bildt to the Secretary- General. UN Documents S/1996/542 (1996).

———: Report of the High Commissioner to the Secretary-General. UN Documents S/1996/814 (1996).

United Nations High Commissioner for Refugees: *Bosnia and Herzegovina: Repatriation and Return, Operation 1998.* Geneva: UNHCR (December 17, 1997).

United Nations Security Council Resolution 1021 (November 22, 1995)

United Nations Security Council Resolution 1022 (November 22, 1995).

United Nations Security Council Resolution 1026 (November 30, 1995).

United Nations Security Council Resolution 1244 (June 10, 1999).

United States Department of State Bureau of European Affairs: "Understanding the Rambouillet Accords" (March 1, 1999).

Uyttendaele, Marc, and Jérôme Sohier: *La Belgique Fédérale – Fondements Constitutionnels et Légaux.* Brussels: Quorum, 1994.

Vakil, Anna C.: "Confronting the Classification Problem: Toward a Taxonomy of NGOs." *World Development* 25, no. 12 (1997), pp. 2057–2070.

Várady, Tibor. "Minorities, Majorities, Law and Ethnicity: Reflections of the Yugoslav Case." *Human Rights Quarterly* 19 (1997), pp. 12–54.

———: "On the Chances of Ethnocultural Justice in Central-Eastern Europe – with Comments on the Dayton Agreement." Unpublished manuscript.

Volf, Miroslav: *Exclusion and Embrace: A Theological Exploration of Identity, Otherness, and Reconciliation.* Nashville: Abington Press, 1996.

Vresk, Milan: *Osnove urbane geografije.* Zagreb: Školska knjiga, 1980.

Vrišer, Igor: *Regionalno planiranje.* Ljubljana: Mladinska knjiga, 1978.

Waller, Michael: "Geopolitics and the Environment in Eastern Europe." *Environmental Politics* 7, no. 1 (1998), pp. 29–52.

Watt, Donald Cameron: "You are a liar and an outcast." *The Observer,* July 30, 1995.

Weber, Max: "Politics as a Vocation." In *From Max Weber,* ed. H.H. Gerth and C.W. Mills. London: Routledge and Kegan Paul, 1970, 1991.

"We have been negotiating mini 'Daytons' all over the place." *International Herald Tribune,* Dec 11, 1997.

Weine, Stevan M.: *When History is a Nightmare.* Rutgers: Rutgers University Press, 1999.

Weller, Marc: "Current Developments: The International Response to the Dissolution of the Socialist Federal Republic of Yugoslavia." *The American Journal of International Law* 86 (1992), pp. 569–607.

———: "Peace-Keeping and Peace-Enforcement in the Republic of Bosnia and Herzegovina." *Zeitschrift für ausländisches öffentliches Recht und Völkerrecht* 56, nos. 1–2 (1996), pp. 70–177.

Williams, David, and Tom Young: "Governance, the World Bank and Liberal Theory." *Political Studies* 42, no. 1 (March 1994), pp. 84–100.

Wolber, Edith: *"Du hältst mir die Schlüssel hin, die Türen zu öffnen..."* In *Eine Begegnung zwischen einer Ethnologin und Frauen mit einer Körperbehinderung.* Berlin: Verlag für Wissenschaft und Bildung, 1996.

Wolin, Sheldon S.: "Fugitive Democracy." In *Democracy and Difference: Contesting the Boundaries of the Political,* ed. Seyla Benhabib. Princeton, Princeton University Press 1996, pp. 31–45.

Woodward, Susan L.: *Balkan Tragedy: Chaos and Dissolution after the Cold War.* Washington DC: Brookings, 1995.

World Bank: *Governance: The World Bank's Experience.* Washington DC: The World Bank, 1994.

Wyte, Nicholas: "Bosnian Municipal Election 2000: No Need for Despondency." *CEPS Europa South-East Monitor* 10 (April 2000).

"*Zakon o lokalnoj samoupravi i upravi.*" In *Lokalna samouprava i uprava u Republici Hrvatskoj* (1993), pp. 452–516.

Zimmermann, Warren: *Origins of a Catastrophe.* New York: Times Books, 1996.

Zolo, Danilo: *Democracy and Complexity: A Realist Approach.* Cambridge: Polity Press, 1992.